Analysing Underachievement in Schools

Empirical Studies in Education

ANALYSING UNDERACHIEVEMENT IN SCHOOLS

Emma Smith

continuum

Continuum International Publishing Group

The Tower Building	80 Maiden Lane
11 York Road	Suite 704
London	New York
SE1 7NX	NY 10038

British Library Cataloguing-in-Publication Data
A catalogue record for this book is available from the British Library.

ISBN 08264 9487 0
    978 08264 9487 0

Typeset by Servis Filmsetting Ltd, Manchester
Printed and bound in Great Britain by MPG Books Ltd, Bodmin

Contents

List of tables		vi
List of figures		viii
Preface		ix
1	Introducing underachievement	1
2	Underachievement and national educational crisis accounts	8
3	Reconsidering the 'failing nation' debates	30
4	Failing boys and 'moral panics'	60
5	Reconsidering underachieving students	82
6	What is underachievement?	105
7	Measuring underachievement	117
8	Measuring low achievement	135
9	Understanding underachievement	142
10	So, what works? Strategies to close the achievement gap	155
	Appendix 1 Further details of research methods	174
	Appendix 2 Multiple regression model for identifying underachieving students	179
	Appendix 3 Profiles of students who were identified as underachieving	182
	Glossary of terms and acronyms	186
	References	187
	Index	209

List of Tables

3.1 Response rates for UK schools sampled in PISA   33
3.2 Mean reading score, according to PISA indicator of
     family wealth   37
3.3 Average scores and proficiency levels on NAEP Grade 8
     reading tests   44
3.4 Proportional increases in Grade 8 reading scores,
     according to ethnic group   45
4.1 GCSE achievements according to gender, England
     (1996–2003)   63
4.2 Percentage of students achieving Key Stage 3 Level 5 or
     above in the core subjects according to ethnicity in 2002   70
4.3 Permanent exclusions by ethnic group in England
     (1998–2002)   73
4.4 Proportion of students awarded Key Stage 2 Level 4 or
     above, according to FSM status   77
4.5 Proportion of students awarded Key Stage 3 Level 5 or
     above, according to FSM status   78
4.6 Achievements at GCSE/GNVQ, according to FSM
     status   78
5.1 Likelihood of achieving good GCSE passes in the core
     subjects, according to gender   88
5.2 Proportional increase in number of students achieving
     5+ good GCSE/GNVQ results, 1995–2003   89
5.3 Changes in the proportion of pupils achieving 5+ A★–C
     GCSE passes   93
5.4 Achievement of 5+ A★–C GCSE passes, according to
     ethnic group   94
5.5 Trends in the proportion of pupils gaining 5+ A★–C
     GCSE passes by ethnic group, 1992–95   95

5.6	Students achieving 5+ A*–C GCSE grades, by ethnic group and gender, Birmingham 1998–2001	96
5.7	GCSE achievement, according to occupational group	99
5.8	Percentage of boys who achieve Key Stage 3 Level 5 or above in England	100
7.1	Predicting outcomes at Key Stage 3	118
7.2	The distribution of pupils in each social class	120
7.3	Social class of boys in the overachieving and underachieving groups	120
7.4	Social class of girls in the overachieving and underachieving groups	121
8.1	Key Stage 3 results according to gender	137
8.2	Key Stage 3 results according to receipt of free school meals	138
8.3	Percentage of pupils who achieved Key Stage benchmark levels, according to receipt of free school meals	138
10.1	Texas Assessment of Academic Skills: trends in achievement of Grade 8 students (all subjects)	159
A.1	Percentage of pupils achieving at least benchmark Level 5 at Key Stage 3	177
A.2	Correlations between CAT and Key Stage 3 Level (sample)	178
A.3	R^2 values for all variables – stepwise entry	179
A.4	R^2 values for predictive model – stepwise entry	180

List of Figures

3.1   Distribution of reading scores according to parental
      occupation in selected countries   36
3.2   Variations in SAT-verbal and SAT-mathematics scores
      1972–2002   43
3.3   Reading performance of Grade 8 students according to
      ethnic group   45
4.1   Students achieving 5+ A★–C GCSE passes according to
      ethnic group (1992–2002)   71
5.1   Achievement gaps in English language examinations   86
5.2   Achievement gaps in favour of girls attaining 5+ GCSE
      grades A★–C or equivalent   87
5.3   Attainment inequalities by race, class and gender, GCSE
      results for England and Wales 1988–1997   102
10.1 Texas Assessment of Academic Skills: trends in
      achievement of Grade 8 students (reading)   159

Preface

If you were to make a list of the issues that concern those who teach, research or seek to change education, it would not be long before you came to 'underachievement'. Today, underachievement is a synonym for much that is perceived to be wrong in today's society, from low scores on international children's reading tests to the social consequences of underachievement, such as criminal behaviour, social exclusion, unsuccessful relationships and marriages (Bentley 1998). But how do you define underachievement and how do you measure it? Simply labelling one group of students, such as boys, as underachieving compared to another group, such as girls, tells us nothing about either which boys may be in need of additional support in school or what the nature of this support might be. Frequently the terms 'underachievement' and 'low achievement' are conflated (especially in media accounts of the phenomenon), and the subject becomes even more complex if you ask what any underachievement might be relative to: is it related to some kind of innate ability on the part of the individual, or is it achievement relative to that of a larger group? In addition, the underachievement label is not only confined to describing the relative achievement of groups of students, or indeed individual students, but is frequently offered as an explanation for the relatively poorer academic performance of schools and of nations.

Questions and confusions like these have prompted the studies that form the basis of this book. Seeking to further understand what it is that we actually mean by 'underachievement' has prompted the following questions, which this book attempts to answer:

- What is the evidence to substantiate claims of underachievement on an international, national, school and individual level?
- How can underachievement be defined?
- How can underachievement be measured?

- What is the difference between underachievement and low achievement?
- Which pupils are underachieving in school?

This book has two aims. The first is to describe some of the confusion and complexity that underline the underachievement discourse. The term 'underachievement' has been used to describe the relatively poorer academic performance of schools and individual groups of students, as well as national school systems. Each of these claims is reconsidered, and the results leave us with a very different picture of success and failure in school. The second aim of this book is simply to understand what it is that we actually mean by the term 'underachievement'. Several models are suggested that should help us understand which groups of students – if any – are underachieving in school.

Fundamental to any discussion of school standards is the extent to which raising achievement ensures that all children are educated equitably. Indeed, this book begins by considering some of the implications of the underachievement discourse for preserving the equity of school systems. Chapters 2 and 3 consider two aspects of the underachievement debate, as it is applied to the underachievement of nations and schools. The first perspective gives us the 'crisis account' of falling standards and failing students that characterizes the school reform debate in the UK and USA. The second raises concerns about the equity of high-stakes testing and school accountability systems, which although seeking to raise the standards of all students might just leave otherwise successful schools labelled as failing or underachieving.

Chapters 4 and 5 describe the underachievement debate from the starting-point of the attainment of students in secondary schools in England and Wales. Once again, different perspectives emerge. The first is the 'traditional' account of underachievement among boys, students from ethnic minority backgrounds and those from less economically advantaged homes. In the second, by carrying out a proportionate analysis of school performance data, existing inaccuracies in the way this data has been interpreted are revealed. The results again present us with a very different perspective of success and failure in school.

The second half of the book focuses on understanding what it is that we actually mean by the term underachievement, and on finding a suitable definition that might allow the phenomenon to be empirically measured and described. Different models are suggested, which aim to differentiate between the concepts of 'low' and 'under' achievement as well as to identify students who may be underachieving or even overachieving in school. One important outcome from this study has been the realization that underachievement may not be a particularly useful concept to help us understand who 'succeeds' and who 'fails' in school. However, achievement gaps between different groups of students do exist. The concluding chapter provides a critique of recent high-profile research that purports to close the gaps between the highest and lowest achievers. On the one hand, the findings from such research projects offer much to be optimistic about and show that well-conceived research in partnership with policy makers and practitioners may make a real difference to raising the achievement of all students. On the other, it seems that we still do not really know what works in attempting to close the achievement gaps in our school. The book concludes by offering some tentative suggestions about how we might wish to rethink the way we carry out research in education.

I would like to thank Professor Stephen Gorard for his continued guidance throughout the researching and writing of this book, and in particular for agreeing to read the final version twice. I also thank Patrick White for his patience and encouragement during the final stages of putting the book together. Thanks also to John Fitz, Tony Edwards, Neil Selwyn, Emma Renold, Jane Salisbury, Pete Nash, Nigel Clifton and James Keedwell. I would also like to acknowledge the teachers and students who participated in the study and thank them for their interest and willingness to take part; I am especially grateful to the staff in each school who helped track down and compile the data. Finally, I would like to thank my parents, Tom and Christine Smith, to whom this book is dedicated.

CHAPTER 1

Introducing underachievement

> The GCSE scrapheap: more leave without any exam passes.
>
> *(Daily Mail,* 21 August 2003, 6)

> Today's underachieving boy is tomorrow's unemployed youth. He is public burden number one, needing benefit in the world of global competition where governments want to get taxes down.
>
> (Mahony, cited in Dean 1998)

> To overcome economic and social disadvantage and to make equality of opportunity a reality, we must strive to eliminate and never excuse underachievement in the most deprived parts of our country. (DfEE, 1997, 3)

> West Indian children as a group are underachieving in our education system . . . (DES 1985, 2)

Here are four statements used to describe four different groups of 'underachievers': a sex, a social group, an ethnic group and a national school system. 'Underachievement' is a familiar word to those in education. Indeed, it has been described as probably the 'predominant discourse' in education in recent times (Weiner *et al.* 1997, 620). Hardly a week passes without an article in *The Times Educational Supplement* describing the attempts of schools up and down the country to eliminate the 'underachievement' of a certain group of pupils. The list of related initiatives is considerable: homework clubs, black gospel choirs, school trips, ICT programmes to get fathers more involved with their sons' education, mentoring schemes and so on (for example, Wallace 2000; Learner 2001; Evans 2004; Wallace 2004). However, there are two fundamental questions the underachievement debate has yet to answer: first, what is meant by the term 'underachievement'? and second, how can we identify the 'underachievers'? These two questions form the backbone of this study and should surely be addressed before any attempts are made to remedy the underachievement of any particular groups.

In this introductory chapter, the arguments for and against the existence of underachievement in our schools are outlined. Because it is such a widely referenced phenomenon, it is perhaps unsurprising that different views of the nature and importance of the concept exist. The need to balance both sides of the underachievement debate in the context of ensuring that our schools provide a fair and equitable experience for all students is a key focus of this first chapter.

For and against underachievement

The increased scrutiny of examination performance as the most tangible outcome of schooling has led to sections of the school population being labelled as failing or underachieving. In this book, we look closely at what we mean by the term 'underachievement' and describe its manifestation at three different levels – of a nation, its schools and its students. Education systems can often involve considerable inequalities for certain individuals, for example, some pupils achieve better examination results than others, attend more 'effective' schools and have longer school careers (Meuret 2002). But are these inequalities all unfair? Certain inequalities in the examination system seem to be acceptable: for example, some students achieve higher examination results than others – that is the nature of examinations. On the other hand, inequalities in the achievement of specific groups of students, for example boys and girls, are considered to be unjust. The interrogation of examination data, alongside the assumption that students should not underachieve in school because they are male, black or from the working class, presents something of a paradox: what are examinations for if not to differentiate between groups of students? Examinations are arbitrary allocators of success; that boys do less well than girls in some examinations should tell us more about the nature of the exams than it does about boys. Even if it were found to be true that boys underachieve, we cannot adjust their sex in order to improve their attainment. We could, however, change the examinations. Nevertheless, the continued scrutiny of examination results has identified particular groups of students who appear to be doing less well. We perceive this to be inequitable and consequently identify large and diverse groups of students, schools and nations as underachieving. The usefulness of this underachievement label is the central theme of this book.

The notion of equity as it applies to our education system is important for several reasons. As the link between earnings and academic qualifications grows, so does an individual's stake in their education. The view is increasingly held that education is something the state owes to its citizens, and that it is the state's responsibility to ensure that the school system is fair (Meuret 2002). As a result, ensuring a fair and equitable education system has political as well as social implications. This to some extent has manifested itself in the school accountability and high stakes testing policies that we see today. Coupled with the desire to ensure a fair national school system is the need for a nation to remain economically competitive, and underlying this is the assumption that better schools equate to a better economy.

This desire for international competitiveness and success in economic as well as educational terms brings us to the first aspect of the underachievement debate – that of the underachievement of nations. The emergence of sophisticated international comparative tests such as the Programme for International Student Assessment (PISA) and the earlier Third International Maths and Science Study (TIMSS) has enabled nations to look critically at the achievement of their students in the international arena. This has led to many nations re-examining their education systems in light of perceived failings in these comparative assessments. In some countries, this has been used to further justify dissatisfaction with the domestic school system and has led to accusations of underachievement and a 'crisis account' of falling academic standards and failing pupils.

In the United States, a long tradition of what has been perceived as mediocre performance on international tests such as TIMSS has contributed to a re-focusing of educational priorities. A move has been made away from policies that have attempted to resolve the inequities faced by poorer children – for example, by increasing access to education, desegregating schools and reducing achievement gaps – towards those concerned with more testing, more accountability and market-driven systems of school choice (Orfield 2000). Systems of high stakes testing, epitomized by the recent 'No Child Left Behind' (NCLB) legislation, have been put in place in order to raise standards in schools and to help propel the United States up the international school league tables. Much of what is set out in NCLB is praiseworthy: the Act is essentially equitable for it ensures that schools pay due regard to the progress of those sections of the school population who have traditionally done less well in the educational environment (students from economically disadvantaged homes, from ethnic minority backgrounds, those who have special educational needs and those who have limited proficiency to speak English (Department of Education 2002)).

However, as we shall see with almost every aspect of the underachievement debate, there is another perspective on this seemingly equitable piece of legislation, which suggests that unproven systems of testing, coupled with punitive accountability measures, can do much to reinforce inequities and label many otherwise good schools as failing. In the United Kingdom, unfavourable international comparisons have contributed to the assertion that the performance of certain groups of students is characterized by a 'long tail' of underachievement. As in the United States, recent UK government policy has its focus firmly on raising standards and eliminating all forms of underachievement. As a result, we have a system of national testing and target setting on an unprecedented scale.

One consequence of international comparative tests has been for nations who generally occupy a mid-table position in the international rankings, such as the UK and USA, to look to other, apparently more successful, countries for lessons in education reform that may be replicated back at home. In particular, recent achievements on international tests, coupled with impressive economic track records, have established Pacific Rim nations such as Korea and Japan as academic success stories. Japan's place in the international underachievement discourse is interesting. Its unassailable success in international tests places it as an academic overachiever – an 'academic paradise' with a centralized educational control and standardized curriculum worthy of replication. However, as we shall see again and again throughout this book, an alternative account also exists. This labels Japan as an academic underachiever, where high scores on international tests have come at a high price, and explores the 'dark underside' of Japanese schools, where students are subjected to intense pressures within the confines of a restrictive curriculum. The consequences can be deadly, with schools characterized by high levels of teenage suicide, bullying and violence, as well as increasing numbers of students who simply refuse to attend. This leaves us with an interesting paradox in the achievement debate, a country whose school system is said to be both underachieving and overachieving.

Given the high stakes of drawing comparisons between different nations, schools and students that can leave one side labelled as an academic success and the other as an academic underachiever, it is perhaps unsurprising to find that such alternative accounts occur throughout the underachievement discourse. Sometimes these accounts are used to oppose reforms either that are seen as unjust or unnecessary (as is the case maybe with some US accounts of Japanese underachievement), or which perhaps have been founded upon no empirical basis, or (as is often the case in this book) which have occurred as a reaction to the use of 'evidence' for underachievement that is based on incorrect readings of examination data. Often a middle ground is called for, but this must also be one that explicitly seeks to uncover what it is we actually mean by the term 'underachievement'.

The place of the school within the wider context of ensuring equity for its pupils is also important: education is not a final good. Schools have a responsibility to society for producing at least minimally qualified individuals. It is clear that a fair and equitable education system is important for many reasons – social, political and economic, and closely linked to this is the desire to raise academic standards in schools. However, in the UK, according to some researchers, rather than widening their access, schools have become more stratified in terms of the attendance and achievement of different groups of students – for example, boys and students from ethnic minority homes – and so have become less equitable. This dissatisfaction with schooling has contributed much to the domestic 'crisis account' that gives us our second level of underachievement – that of different schools.

The notion that schools matter and should be held accountable for the performance of their students is an important reaction to suggestions that schools are failing their pupils. In both Britain and America, it has resulted in high stakes testing and punitive school accountability measures that make the assessment results of individual schools publicly available – even those of small primary schools which may have fewer than 30 students in an examination cohort – and which are designed to coerce schools into raising their standards. Many of these reforms are certainly equitable in their intent, such as the National Literacy and Numeracy Strategies and programmes like Excellence in Cities in the UK and the No Child Left Behind legislation in the USA. However, the evidence for their success is often tenuous at best, and can lose sight of the tremendous increases in school achievement that have already been made by all students in recent years. This is not to say that there are no concerns over the relative attainment of students in school. On the contrary, examining the assessment data in both Britain and the USA, reveals considerable inequalities in the relative attainment of different groups of students, and this brings us to our third level of underachievement – that of different student groups.

In the UK, the underachievement of boys has occupied a prime place in the educational discourse for many years. Theories have evolved to explain the phenomenon and costly programmes have been put in place to try and remedy it. More recently, the discourse has expanded to include the underachievement of certain ethnic minority students and, to a lesser extent, students from poorer homes. Once again, strategies and programmes have been developed, including those that instruct teachers on best practice for raising the attainment of students from

Bangladeshi or African–Caribbean communities (two groups perceived to be at greatest risk of failure in the school system). Strategies aimed at poor children have been less apparent, although in the UK programmes such as Excellence in Cities have been targeted to include the urban – although not the rural – poor. The differential attainment of groups of students according to their sex, ethnic group or socioeconomic status is a key facet of the underachievement debate, and one that is considered and evaluated in some detail in this book. Our specific focus here is on students from the UK. In the USA, similar disparities between the achievements of different groups exist – most especially the achievement gap between the black–white and the Hispanic–white communities. The presence of a national assessment system in England and Wales (not available in the USA) provides plenty of evidence both for the differential achievement of students and, all too often, for their purported underachievement.

That boys perform consistently worse than girls in the GCSE examinations is taken as evidence for their underachievement. Here we reevaluate this evidence and suggest that boys have always achieved lower results than girls on these measures. Rather than this being a problem that is inherent with boys, it is conceivable that it might rather be a consequence of our assessment system. For example, should we continue to assume that the examination system, itself an artificial allocator of success and failure, is gender neutral? Of course, it could become so by ensuring equal success for boys and girls, in much the same way that places in the former grammar schools were allocated 40 years ago – but is that really what we want from our school assessment system?

Underachievement is a concept over which there is much confusion and little consensus. Understanding what it is that we actually mean by the term underachievement is an important aim of this book and forms the basis of the second section.

Understanding underachievement

The complexities surrounding the underachievement debate are outlined in the first half of the book. In the second, the focus is on understanding what underachievement actually means. That 'underachievement' is one of the most widely used terms in education is well established, alongside the evidence both for and against the existence of the phenomenon at an international, school and individual level. However, underachievement is a concept over which there is little agreement on either its definition or its measurement.

In this second section, we explore ways of defining and measuring underachievement. We describe a strategy for predicting student achievement in the Key Stage 3[1] national tests that takes into account a range of student background and contextual variables, and allows us to identify students who may be underachieving. By looking at school outcomes, we also consider which groups of students perform less well in school, and so at the notion of low achievement. Often the terms 'underachievement' and 'low achievement' are confused and conflated. As we demonstrate, students who are underachievers do not necessarily belong to the same group as students who are low achievers – underachievement and low achievement are not the same thing. For example, an individual who achieves three Level 6s at Key Stage 3 instead of their predicted Level 7s may well be considered to be underachieving, but it is unlikely that they can reasonably be considered a low achiever. With this in mind, we argue for a rethinking of how we use the term 'underachievement', particularly as it applies to the differential performance of students in school. We argue that underachievement is more easily understood as being an individual phenomenon, where high and low ability students may, at certain times in their school careers, not perform as well as expected. While important, this is a difficult issue to address and one that might be better dealt with by schools on an individual basis, rather than by national policy reform. Low achievement, on the other hand, can be shown to apply to a large and distinct section of the school population – students who come from poorest homes. Perhaps it is here that educational reform programmes ought first to be targeted.

Summary

'Underachievement' is one of the most widely used, and perhaps overused, terms in education today. Because it is such an important concept, it is perhaps unsurprising that different perspectives on its impact and relevance exist. This chapter has provided an overview of both sides of the underachievement debate as it applies to the three areas most frequently associated with the underachievement label – national school systems, the schools themselves and different groups of students. However, 'underachievement' is also a term over which there is little consensus over either its definition or its measurement. Resolving this uncertainty and gaining a clearer understanding of what is it that we actually mean by underachievement is a key theme of this book.

[1] National tests at the end of lower secondary school (13–14 years).

CHAPTER 2

Underachievement and national educational crisis accounts

> For years education was a social cause. Today it is an economic
> imperative. A nation is only as good as its education.
>
> (Blair, 2004)

The link between a nation's economic competitiveness and the standard
of its schools reveals an important facet of the underachievement debate.
This chapter considers the role that international comparisons of educational standards has had both in contributing to national educational
'crisis accounts' and in shaping education policy reform. We will focus
on three different school systems: the UK (specifically England and
Wales), the USA and Japan. In both England and Wales and in America,
the underachievement discourse has followed a similar trajectory: falling
scores on domestic and international assessments, coupled with economic insecurity, have resulted in programmes of standards-driven
reform that are linked heavily to school accountability. In Japan, the
underachievement account is very different. Japan is a country that has
been praised as an educational success story and whose policies have
been 'borrowed' by countries seeking to emulate its success. However,
Japan has developed its own 'crisis account' – one that accuses the school
system of failing in its duty to care for its students and that places it very
much as a victim of its own success. Before presenting one perspective
of the underachievement debate in each of these three countries, we
begin by considering the role of international comparisons of academic
achievement in setting the agenda for national education reform, and
the contribution these tests have made to the domestic underachievement discourse.

International comparative tests

Since the 1960s, large-scale international comparative tests have given nations the opportunity to compare the progress of their students with those in other countries. The importance of international comparisons in focusing a nation's education policy cannot be underestimated, and reflects the changing role of education in many industrialized countries. While still very much in the 'service' of the nation state, changes to global political and economic geographies have resulted in the education policies of many European, Asian and North American countries losing some of their 'preoccupation with localism and regionalism' (Husen and Tujinman 1994, 13) and becoming both much more concerned with accountability and efficiency measures and a lot more sensitive to educational trends in other countries. For this reason in particular, policy makers turn to large-scale international comparative tests to answer many of their questions about the impact of education reform in both their own country and those of their neighbours or economic competitors (Schleicher 1994). However, international comparative tests are expensive, they are complex to design and administer, and much care needs to be taken with their interpretation. Education systems are evolving all the time, policy focus shifts in its priorities, and the different contexts in which education systems operate can also change. These and many other factors have to be taken into account when lessons are being learnt about the relative performance of students in the national and especially the international context.

Perhaps it is unsurprising therefore that the stakes for 'failure' in these comparative tests are high. As a consequence, and despite the reservations of the test designers, these test outcomes are frequently reduced to a form of international Olympiad, in which success is praised and low rankings can equate to a national 'crisis account' of falling standards and failing students. A good example of this is Germany, a country whose education system was once considered 'world class'. Relatively poor performance in the 2000 Programme for International Student Assessment (or PISA) firmly established Germany's own 'crisis account' of school underachievement. National reform of the school system was called for, and educational inspectors were sent north to Finland – the PISA success story – to look for remedies (Sharma 2002; Slater 2001). One of the tangible outcomes of international comparative tests has been this tendency for nations to 'policy-borrow' from academically more 'successful' countries. However, as we shall see in Chapter 3, this desire to cherry-pick from the best a nation has to offer presents its own difficulties. As has happened with Japan, another educational success story, differences in the historical and social cultures of nations can be magnified when attempts are made to draw direct comparisons on the basis of the results from international tests (LeTendre 1999).

So why are these tests so important? One key reason is the presumed link between better schools and a better economy. The consequences of economic globalization, such as the movement of semi-skilled work out of western countries, have identified the need for industrialized countries to refocus their economic priorities and in doing so develop a highly qualified and a technically competent workforce: and that, it seems, is the job of the schools (see, for example, Lieberman 1993; Istance and Rees 1994). Perhaps then it is not surprising that the intensity of scrutiny given to nations' relative performance in these tests has contributed to the 'crisis account' of falling standards and failing schools apparent in many western nations (Sharma 2002a). This is a key facet of the underachievement debate. Although work on underachievement has mainly focused on individual attainment, such as differential performance between girls and boys, it is the perception of a crisis at the national level that can often drive policy reform forward.

International underachievement: the perspective from the UK

This section considers the underachievement debate as it applies to the differential success of British schools (more specifically those in England and Wales). It begins by describing some of the evidence that has led to accusations that schools are failing their students. The discussion then moves on to consider government strategies to address the issue and the school improvement policies that these have entailed.

An increased scrutiny of national and international examination and test results has resulted in an ever-closer interrogation of the education system in Britain and – from some quarters – accusations of the underachievement of a nation (see, for example, Barber 1996; Phillips 1996a; Prais 1990). According to some commentators standards in schools have reached unacceptable levels, with a 'yawning gap' (Phillips 1996, 3) in maths performance between the UK and other European countries, undergraduates being ill-prepared for their courses, and modern language teachers having to resort to teaching grammar in secret. Official statistics tell us that students from Black Caribbean backgrounds are nearly three times more likely to be excluded from school than their white peers (DfES 2002a) and that half of all students leave school without achieving five or more 'good' GCSE passes (Tate and Clarke 2002). According to one teachers' union, English and Welsh students are the most tested in the world, and the increased workload for teachers has resulted in unfair examination practices and 'teaching to the test' (NUT 2003). Despite this, pupils in school in the UK are less likely to remain in education after the age of 16 than many of their European counterparts (Nuthall 2001).

Poor performance is not just restricted to Britain's schools. According to the International Adult Literacy survey, 22 per cent of Britons could not read and understand information from a newspaper article, compared with 19 per cent of German-speaking Swiss and 17 per cent of Canadians. It also found that 23 per cent of Britons could not calculate the potential savings offered by a sale advertisement in a newspaper, compared with 14 per cent of the Swiss and 17 per cent of Canadians (Abrams 2000).

A great deal of the criticism over the relatively poor examination performance of the home nations has its foundation in the interpretation of international standardized test scores and the evidence they present of a 'two-track' education and training system in Britain, where the top 10 per cent of the population perform relatively well but the less able underachieve (Reynolds and Farrell 1996). This contention has continued with the publication of results from more recent comparative tests that suggest that, despite improvement in the performance of the more able students, Britain's performance in these international tests is dogged by a 'long tail of underachievement' (Johnson 2002). The British government's recognition of polarized achievement between the least and most able students, as well as the importance of international comparative tests, has long been apparent. For example, in his speech to the Lord Mayor's Banquet in London in November 1993, John Major criticized the underachievement of British students in international tests:

> The best of our schools produce pupils educated as well as any in the world – we can be proud of them – but too many do not and as a result standards have slipped below those of our competitors. Let me give you just one example. In arithmetic, 13-year-olds were asked to multiply 9.2 by 2.5. In Korea and Taiwan, 70 per cent got it right, in Western Europe 55 per cent and in England 13 per cent, and against that background . . . I cannot understand opposition to simple tests in maths.
>
> (cited in Istance and Rees 1994, 8)

Speeches like this demonstrate governments' desires to raise educational standards and hence global competitiveness, and as a result, by the start of the new millennium pupils in England were being tested at ages 7, 11, 14, 16, 17 and 18.

John Major's speech was given in response to the findings of international tests in mathematics. Further consideration of the results of such tests is given below and focuses specifically on three relatively recent large-scale analyses of educational achievement: the Third International Maths and Science Study (TIMSS 1996), the Programme for International Student Achievement (PISA) (OECD 2003) and the Progress in International Literacy Survey (PIRLS) (NFER 2003), and examines the contribution these, and other forms of international comparisons, have made to the national 'underachievement' debate.

British performance in international comparative tests

Concern over the academic performance of Britain's school children relative to those in other countries received a great deal of attention in 1996 with the publication of the 'Worlds Apart?' document (Reynolds and Farrell 1996). This was an Ofsted-commissioned review of international comparative studies of achievement, with a specific focus on mathematics and science, two subjects generally considered to be most free of cultural bias, and to represent an assessment of the key skills required for a modern society. The document concluded that levels of performance had deteriorated, particularly in mathematics, and that relative to its economic peers schools in England contained a large proportion of low-achieving pupils. The solution, according to the authors, would involve a shift in pedagogical thinking, with teachers embracing whole class teaching methodologies. This call for 'policy-borrowing' from more 'successful' countries (Gorard 2000, 75) argues against 'progressive' teaching methods, where children are encouraged to be independent learners, and instead calls for a return to 'traditional' methods of chalk and talk (Phillips 1996a; Reynolds 1997). The problem, it would seem, lies within the schools.

Surprisingly, the media attention that had surrounded 'Worlds Apart?' was more muted in 1997 with the publication of a major post-National Curriculum evaluation of international achievement in maths and science. TIMSS was the result of a large-scale assessment of standards in over 40 countries. The main findings of this report indicated that in England, pupils achieved relatively high mean scores in science and relatively low mean scores in mathematics. However, it was the poor performance in mathematics, which placed English 13-year-olds nineteenth out of 27 countries, that appears to have filled the most newspaper column inches. A glance at the headlines in *The Times Educational Supplement* at the time provides evidence of this (for example Budge 1997; Pyke 1996; Reynolds 1997; *The Times Educational Supplement* 1996 and 1997).

With the publication of findings from more recent international tests such as PISA in 2000 and PIRLS in 2002, these headlines have continued and, despite the relative success of English performance in these tests, the story has varied only slightly. For example, in PIRLS, English 10-year-olds were ranked third in the world in terms of reading achievement, a success which has been attributed variously to a return to traditional teaching methods in primary schools (*Daily Mail*, 7 April 2003), the National Literacy Strategy (DfES Press Release, 8 April 2003, *Guardian*, 9 April 2003), and Harry Potter (*Daily Express*, 9 April 2003). In PISA, where English 15-year-olds were placed seventh out of 32 countries on reading achievement, the headlines were similarly upbeat: 'Shocking news – we are doing OK' (*The Times Educational Supplement*, 7 December 2001) and 'English pupils among world's top' (*Guardian,* 20 May 2002). However, these headlines were typically tempered by accounts of underachievement. In PIRLS, while at aggregate level our students appeared to be performing at world-class levels, their profile was masking a 'long tail' of underachievement in which England had one of the highest proportions of students in the bottom 25 per cent, so giving it a wider spread of ability than countries like Belize, Morocco and Argentina (*Daily Telegraph*, 9 April 2003). In PISA, it is again the discrepancy between the high achievers and the low achievers that gave cause for concern (*Guardian*, 30 January 2003).

Thus, this 'long tail of underachievement' has emerged as the legacy of recent, relatively successful English performance in international comparative tests. For the British government it provides evidence for the need to reform a system that has a tradition of success only for a minority at the top (Blair 2004), as well as presenting challenges to raise the 'quality and equality' of our entire school system (Miliband 2004). How the current Labour government has addressed this aspect of the underachievement discourse is considered next.

The UK government and the underachievement debate

> Education remains the Government's top priority . . . A generation ago, Britain tolerated an education system with a long tail of poor achievement because there was a plentiful supply of unskilled and semi-skilled jobs. This is no longer the case. By breaking the cycle of underachievement in education we can extend opportunity across society.
>
> (DfES 2001a, 5)

When New Labour won the 1997 British general election, its priorities of 'Education, education and education' brought with them a focus on standards and accountability that were intended to create an education system to match the best in the world (Blair 1996). According to Michael Barber, then employed as head of the new Standards and Effectiveness Unit in the Department for Education and Employment, despite the reform of the 1980s, around two-fifths of all young people in secondary schools in Britain were disappointed with the education they received (to say nothing of the disaffected and the disappeared). In April 1996, 296 schools (2 per cent of all schools) were found to have been failing, a figure Barber projects to almost one state school in eight 'providing its pupils with an inadequate education' (Barber 1996, 123). In short, he claimed that standards had slipped, grades had become diluted and the public examination system had been 'corrupted by a deadly combination of educational ideology and crude market forces' (1996, 21). The Blair government's commitment to reform and to raising standards soon became evident: Stephen Byers, then standards minister, was charged with addressing the 281 schools identified by Ofsted as failing, and it became clear that the hard line taken by the previous Conservative administration would remain:

> For those schools which are unable to improve, we will close them and order a fresh start. Good schools, which co-exist with the bad, will be brought in to support them and set the underperforming school on a new path. We will not shrink back from tough decisions.
>
> (Stephen Byers, cited in Rafferty *et al.* 1997)

Key to the British government's plans for raising standards has been the 'vision of a school system which values opportunity for all, and embraces diversity and autonomy as the means to achieve it' (DfES 2001a, 6). The creation of diverse and autonomous schools would allow freedom to innovate, to engage with business and enterprise and for schools to develop their own ethos and specialisms. In short, a new type of school has been emerging, one much less like the 'bog-standard' comprehensives of old and much more likely to define its own identities of excellence and diversity.

Specialist schools are one example of this new era of schools. The Specialist Schools Programme in England encourages maintained secondary schools to form partnerships with private-sector sponsors and to establish 'distinctive identities through their chosen specialisms and achieve their targets to raise standards' (DfES 2004b). Schools can be designated as specialist in one of ten areas, including humanities, engineering and sport. In September 2004, there were 1,686 specialist schools in England, teaching more than 1.5 million children – over half the secondary school population (DfES 2004b). The driving force behind much of this reform is the Excellence in Cities (EiC) Programme. This is a major initiative which aims to raise the aspirations and achievement of pupils who live in the country's urban areas. The programme is implemented through local partnerships, each of which includes the Local Education Authority and all its secondary schools. There are, at present, seven strands to the EiC programme: Learning Mentors, Learning Support Units, City Learning Centres, Beacon and Specialist schools, EiC Action Zones and extended opportunities for gifted and talented pupils (DfES 2004a)

However, these reforms have not been without their critics. The development of schools which specialize or are allowed to select a greater proportion of pupils on the basis of their faith are seen by many as being in danger of creating both further inequalities and a two-tier system where 'discerning' parents consider specialist schools as 'better' than the 'bog-standard' ones. This can sit uneasily with Labour's traditional commitment to comprehensive education and equal opportunities for all: 'a government believing in collective responsibility is surely obliged to be much less cavalier about the right of one school to take a decision directly affecting the fortunes of others' (Edwards *et al.* 1999, 42). The Labour government's supposed commitment to a quasi-market system along the Conservative ideals of encouraging parental choice and competition between schools has also been criticized, although attempts to mitigate some of the market's inequitable effects through emphasis on social exclusion policies have also been evident (West and Pennell 2002). Nevertheless, the plans for increased numbers of specialist schools and enhanced mechanisms for parental choice revealed in the government's recent five-year strategy for education suggest that – at least in England – the trend is here to stay (DfES 2004).

If increased funding, investment in capital building programmes, concessions over teacher workloads and greater autonomy for schools constitute the carrot behind new Labour's policies to improve standards, the accountability measures that accompany the reform would be the stick. Within the first four years of Labour coming into office, 138 failing schools had been closed (DfES 2001a); by autumn 2003, the number of schools on special measures had risen to 311 (Smithers 2004) and all secondary schools where fewer than 25 per cent of students achieved 5 or more A*–C grades at GCSE were subjected to 'additional scrutiny'. Many of these accountability measures aim to encourage 'zero tolerance of underperformance' and a close scrutiny of standards through the publication of performance data, baseline assessments, value added test results, target-setting and, of course, performance-related pay. They place the impetus to improve squarely on the shoulders of the schools themselves: 'all the evidence indicates that standards rise fastest where schools themselves take responsibility for their own improvement' (DfEE 1997, 24).

In their submission to the House of Commons Education and Skills Committee inquiry into secondary school achievement, the Department for Education and Skills (DfES) tabled a two-pronged approach to delivering change in schools both by targeting the mainstream of education and by programmes that address specific groups of students, in particular those from ethnic minority backgrounds (House of Commons 2003). The contention driving forward such initiatives as the Key Stage 3 Strategy, the National Literacy and Numeracy Strategies, Excellence in Cities and reforms to the 14–19 curriculum is that it is the school that matters: or, more specifically, that school reform can be driven by models of school collaboration, specialization and innovation, coupled with effective leadership, and a well-qualified and competent profession. This contention embraces what is known as the School Effectiveness Research (SER) movement, which has been well established in Britain since the late 1980s and has become one of the 'biggest growth areas in education research in recent years' (Coe and Fitz-Gibbon 1998, 421). Indeed, this area of educational research has had perhaps the greatest influence on the efforts of politicians and government officials to prioritize school reform (Wrigley 2003). The development of SER over the last twenty years can be seen as a reaction to work in the USA by Jencks (1972) and Coleman et al. (1966), who argued that the social class/prior achievement mix of schools was the only school variable that seemed to have any impact on academic outcomes. Their 'deterministic interpretation' (Sammons et al. 1995, 2) of the factors related to academic achievement has become superseded by the school effectiveness researchers and their thesis that, although background factors are important, it is schools that have the most significant effect on student achievement. More than any other research area, the findings from research into school effectiveness have contended that by failing to provide the best education for their pupils, many British schools are underachieving.

For example, Mortimore (1991) defines an effective school as one in which 'students progress further than might be expected from a consideration of its intake' (14) and where pupils will exceed any expectations made on the basis of the school's characteristics. In formulating the methodology for assessing the effectiveness of a school, researchers have 'sought to find ways to distinguish the impact of the school from the dowry brought by the pupil' (Mortimore and Sammons 1997, 177). This has involved the use of increasingly complex statistical tools (such as multi-level modelling) to allow researchers to give a better account of differences between schools. According to many of the proponents of SER, these differences can be significant, 'as much as four times more important than background factors for reading progress and ten times more for progress in mathematics' (Sammons *et al.* 1995, 6). A list of the features of successful schools as reported by the research of school effectiveness researchers would read very much like the strategies for reform submitted by the DfES in evidence to the House of Commons Select Committee: that is professional leadership, a focus on teaching and learning, high expectations, shared visions and goals, and so on (Reynolds 1994). Thus, the parallels between school effectiveness research and government policies to raise standards in schools have become quite apparent. Indeed, school effectiveness research which has been accused of divorcing the school from its 'social and political context' (Gibson and Asthana 1998, 196) is considered by Elliot (1996, 199) to be 'music in the ears of politicians and government officials', who have used its results to justify a refusal to respond to concerns about issues such as school financing and instead to blame teachers and LEAs for failing or underachieving schools. It is perhaps not surprising, therefore, that a research paradigm which contends that it is the school that matters and whose results are 'naturally attractive' to those politicians who wish to 'prioritise a particular set of outcomes' (Wrigley 2003, 93) should attract criticism from both inside and outside academic circles. The place of this criticism in the context of the underachievement of schools and government strategies to raise standards will be discussed in the next chapter.

This first look at the case for the existence of an underachievement crisis in British schools has presented us with a scenario in which a tradition of poor performance on international comparative tests has resulted in an achievement profile that is defined by relatively high performance scores for a minority of the most able students, but where the achievement of the majority is characterized by a 'long tail of underachievement'. This pattern of underachievement is reflected in domestic examination scores. Here, once again, the achievement of some students is consistently world class, but around 50 per cent of the population leave school without reaching what are perceived by some to be minimum competency levels. That the British government is keen to address the issue is apparent from their commitment to high-profile and high-cost initiatives like the Excellence in Cities programme and the National Literacy and Numeracy strategies. However, the research basis on which many of these initiatives are founded is contentious and, as we shall see in the next chapter, the cost benefit return on the government's investment – in terms of academic success – has yet to become apparent. However, for now, we consider how the underachievement debate has manifested itself in the American context and describe recent US government initiatives to raise the academic standards in its schools.

International underachievement: Perspectives from the USA

> There have been two basic policy eras in US education policy since mid-century: a struggle for access and equity that dominated the period from 1960 to 1980 and a focus on competition and standards that prevailed in the 1980s and 1990s.
>
> (Orfield 2000, 406)

This refocusing of US educational policy was perhaps no better demonstrated than on 8 January 2002, when President George W. Bush signed into law what is arguably the most important piece of US educational legislation for the past 35 years. For the first time, Public Law 107–110 linked high-stakes testing with strict accountability measures designed to ensure that, at least in schools receiving government funding, 'No Child is Left Behind'. This section examines how strict accountability measures became so entwined with government policy. We begin by outlining the key tenants of the No Child Left Behind Act, before describing the emergence of the 'crisis account' of underachieving American schools that has made so great a contribution to the Act's conception and manifestation into law.

No Child Left Behind? America's underachieving schools

The No Child Left Behind (NCLB) Act is a reauthorization of the Elementary and Secondary Education Act which provides federal (i.e. government) funding for America's public schools. Much of what is set out in NCLB is praiseworthy: the Act is essentially equitable in that it ensures that schools pay due regard to the progress of those sections of the school population which have traditionally done less well – students from economically disadvantaged homes, from ethnic minority backgrounds, who have special educational needs and who have limited proficiency in speaking English (Popham 2004; West and Peterson 2003). Under NCLB, all schools and school districts which receive Title-1 federal funding must put into place a set of standards, together with detailed plans outlining how these standards with be monitored and met.

Title-1 is the part of the Elementary and Secondary Schools Act that distributes federal funds to disadvantaged areas. About 90 per cent of America's 15,000 school districts receive this type of funding (Ravitch 1995). A major consequence of this legislation is that schools will be required to set targets and monitor the progress of students, and of subgroups of students, in order to ensure that 100 per cent of students reach certain minimum proficiency levels by 2014. Failure to achieve proficiency targets would lead to 'corrective action', which in its most extreme manifestation would result in school closure.

Unlike the UK and many other industrialized countries, the United States has a very de-centralized system of education, with much of the control over the day-to-day running of schools left in the hands of school districts acting on behalf of the individual states. There is neither a national assessment system nor a national curriculum, and the responsibility for ascertaining standards, assessment tools and curriculum coverage lies with each state. However, just like in the UK, a 'crisis account' exists over the apparent underachievement of American schools, particularly with regard to their relative performance in international comparative tests. Legislation like NCLB is designed, through complex systems of school accountability and sanctions, to remedy this.

America's crisis account

The NCLB legislation rose from a 'primeval soup' (Kingdon, quoted in Rudalevige 2003, 27) of education policy intended to raise standards in public schools that has spanned several decades. Many of the components of the Act contain little that is completely new – the majority of America's states already have testing and accountability measures in place. What is unusual, however, is how the Act managed to achieve widespread bipartisan support from Congress. Traditionally, Republican administrations have distanced themselves from involvement in education issues, particularly as the federal government only contributes 7–8 per cent of education revenues. Therefore, for George W. Bush – a Republican president – to get involved in the machinations of America's public school system was always going to be risky. However, Bush had previously been Governor of Texas, where education was, and (as we shall see later), still is, an important issue.

In order to understand this unprecedented level of federal interest in the consequences of educational achievement, it is important to recognize that standards in America's public schools have long been under scrutiny. The launch of Sputnik in 1957 by the USSR had far-reaching repercussions for the school system in America, and created pressure for schools to raise academic standards. Although much of this emphasis was directed at identifying talent and improving training for the elite, high school graduation rates and test scores for all students did show some improvement (Ravitch 1995). However, the first major indication of a potential crisis came in the 1960s and 1970s, when falling scores on the Scholastic Aptitude Test (SAT) began to raise widespread concern. The SAT is traditionally a curriculum-free verbal and mathematical reasoning test, taken by students who are applying for entrance to college. Between 1967 and 1982 students' scores on this test fell by 0.3 of a standard deviation. In addition, the gap between the achievement of black and white students amounted to one whole standard deviation. This corresponds to a substantial difference: a gap of one standard deviation would equate to the performance difference between students in the fourth[2] and eighth grade (West and Peterson 2003). Between 1972 and 1983 there was also a reduction in the proportion of students achieving the highest scores on the test. Some commentators account for these fluctuations in SAT scores by describing the changing demographics of college entrants (Berliner and Biddle 1995), although others counter that the composition of the SAT pool did not change as dramatically as some believe (Ravitch 1995).

The National Assessment of Educational Progress (NAEP) is another large-scale national test that is used to monitor achievement trends in the United States. Also known as 'the Nation's Report Card', NAEP has been administered annually to a randomly selected sample of students aged 9, 11 and 17 since 1969. In 2003, around 10 per cent of 9 and 11-year-old students took part in the tests. Subjects assessed include reading, mathematics, science, US history, geography and the arts. The results are disaggregated for different sub-groups of students, and have been available at state level since 2000 (NCES 2003). According to West and Peterson (2003), between 1970 and 1982 the progress of 17-year-old participants in the NAEP science assessments fell by 0.4 of a standard deviation, while mathematics fell by 0.2. Trends for 9 and 13-year-olds 'revealed more stagnation than progress'. Achievement gaps between the performance of students from African-American and white backgrounds were also apparent in some states, ranging from 0.6 standard deviations in West Virginia to over 1.2 in Michigan (Kane and Staiger 2003).

Dissatisfaction with American performance in both domestic and international assessments was crystallized in 1983, when the Regan administration published the document 'A Nation at Risk' (NCEE 1983). This searing indictment of educational standards in the US signalled a shift in focus towards accountability and testing. The invective used is

---

[2] US Grade 4 is equivalent to National Curriculum Year 5

strong, and condemns the 'rising tide of mediocrity' that was eroding the American public school system:

> If an unfriendly foreign power had attempted to impose on America the mediocre educational performance that exists today, we might well have viewed it as an act of war.
>
> (NCEE 1983, 3)

The rhetoric is little different today. American students still occupy a mid-table position in the international achievement rankings, and commentators still despair over the apparent underachievement of American schools:

> Today, nearly 70 percent of inner city fourth graders are unable to read at a basic level on national reading tests. Our high school seniors trail students in Cyprus and South Africa on international math tests. And nearly a third of our college freshmen find they must take a remedial course before they are able to even begin regular college level courses.
>
> (Department of Education 2002)

The United States has been participating in large-scale international comparative assessments since the 1960s. The general pattern has been one of underachievement: 'US students have performed poorly in international assessments, seldom rising above the median, often scoring near the bottom' (Ravitch 1995, 84). More recently, US performance on TIMSS (and the later TIMSS-Repeat) has attracted significant attention in academic, policy and media circles. The preoccupation with analysing US performance in these tests has continued into the new millennium with an intensity that appears to surpass that given to more recent international tests such as PISA and PIRLS. So great is the level of interrogation that not only is the TIMSS data disaggregated at the state level, comparisons are even made between individual schools (Hoff, 2001).

America's achievement in international tests

Criticism of US students' performance in TIMSS has focused mainly on achievement in Grade 8 mathematics, where US students scored 27 points below the international median; 143 points separated the US from top-scoring Singapore, and 105 points from third-placed Japan (Stedman 1997; Schmidt *et al.* 1999). Grade 8 students' performance in science was slightly better, with scores just above the international median (534 points, compared with the median score of 531), but was still 73 points behind top-scoring Singapore and 37 points behind third-placed Japan (Stedman

1997; Schmidt *et al.* 1999). As an estimate, one year's growth corresponds to about 30 scale points in mathematics and about 37 in science (Stedman 1997). This means that American students were approximately 3 years behind their Japanese counterparts in mathematics and about one year behind in science; the gaps between the US and Singapore were, of course, even greater. Performance in TIMSS among American Grade 4 students was more encouraging. In science they were among the highest scorers, and were placed just above the international mean in mathematics (Schmidt *et al.* 1999). However, American scrutiny, and the media headlines, remain firmly fixed on the scores of Grade 8 students.

The reasons given for America's relatively poor standing, not only on TIMSS, but also on other international comparative tests, vary. Some commentators concern themselves with the sampling and technical aspects of the surveys, which appear to place American students at a disadvantage compared to those from other countries (Bracey 1996, 1997). Others (and perhaps this is the dominant view) consider the very structure of education in the USA to be at fault. A lack of a broad, intellectually coherent, commonly accepted guiding vision; a fragmented curriculum which is a 'mile wide and inch deep'; a lack of high-stake external school exit examinations; textbooks which are too broad; the differential exposure to the curriculum through academic tracking, and lessons that lack focus are all oft-cited reasons for the systemic problems faced by the country's school system (Schmidt *et al.* 1999; Stedman 1997; Wössmann 2003; Department of Education 2002). In sum:

> US variability for 9- and 13-year olds in maths was not so much *natural* as *created*. It appears to have been influenced by the structure of our educational systems, especially our characteristic decentralized decision-making and by our practice of tracking.
> (Schmidt *et al.* 1999, 177).

These criticisms of the decentralized nature of America's school system have played a fundamental role in determining the focus of policy-borrowing strategies from other academically 'successful' nations, and in particular from school systems in the Far East. For example, the 'Nation at Risk' report (NCEE 1983) recommended that students be presented with more 'challenging' tasks, extensions to the length of the school day and year, a raising of the standards for high school graduation and college entrance and higher quality and better pay for school teachers (Ravitch 1995; West and Peterson 2003).

Thus, falling scores in the SAT and NAEP, coupled with dubious performance in international comparative tests, have contributed much to the failing schools debate in the United States. That the federal government has taken it upon itself to direct educational standards reform, in this instance through the No Child Left Behind legislation, is a surprising, although a not entirely new, development. What is new, however, is the extent of the federally-mandated sanctions and their potential impact on schools. The concern among many commentators is that by forcing school improvement through sanctions linked to testing, many otherwise successful schools, in particular those that serve students in disadvantaged communities, may be unfairly labelled as underachieving. These schools, which may serve communities with very transient populations, as well as large proportions of students with limited proficiency in English, are perhaps more likely to fail to reach the rigorous minimum-competency levels demanded by the NCLB tests. As a consequence, they are likely to face sanctions such as the transfer of pupils from the school, reductions in school finance and, ultimately, school closure. This is an important consequence of the NCLB legislation, but is also perhaps an obvious result of labelling schools as underachieving on the basis of test scores that have little or no value-added basis. This presents us with an alternative perspective on the consequences of the underachievement debate, which is considered in more detail in Chapter 3.

International overachievers? Perspectives from Japan

The document 'A Nation at Risk', which so comprehensively denounced America's public schools, viewed the Japanese education system in an altogether different light:

> America's position in the world may once have been reasonably secure with only a few exceptionally well-trained men and women. It is no longer . . . The risk is not only that the Japanese make automobiles more efficiently than Americans and have government subsidies for development and export . . . It is also that these developments signify a redistribution of trained capacity throughout the globe.
>
> (NCEE 1983, 6–7)

The success of Japan and other Asian Tiger economies during the 1970s and 1980s led American commentators to draw parallels between this and the effectiveness of Japanese schools. High-profile visits to Japan by education reformers and policy makers in the 1980s and onwards found much to admire in the uniformity and efficiency of the Japanese school curriculum. Gradually, however, their calls for 'policy borrowing' strategies such as national standards and centralized control over the curriculum have had to compete with a very different perspective of Japan's education system. This account is far less positive and describes the 'examination hell' (LeTendre 1999, 23) faced by young students and the prescriptive control that schools have over their lives, frequently with tragic consequences. In short, it portrays a system that rather than being world class is failing its youth. Thus, the underachievement story in Japan is very different from the 'crisis accounts' of falling educational standards that characterize the discourse in the United Kingdom and America. Before considering both the perceived overachievement and under-achievement of Japanese education, we will begin with a very brief overview of the Japanese public school system.

Schooling in Japan

The Japanese school system is modelled on a 6–3–3–4 structure. For the majority of students, that means 6 years of primary education (including kindergarten), 3 years of junior high school, 3 years of senior high school, and, for about 50 per cent of students, 4 years of university (DeCocker 2002). Compulsory education ends with junior high school at the age of 15, although around 98 per cent of students remain in education and proceed to senior high school. There are no national examinations *per se*: high-stakes testing occurs at the end of junior high school, when students sit entrance exams for senior high school, and again at the end of senior high school, when students sit college or university entrance exams. These entrance exams are taken extremely seriously. Competition to secure a place in a highly regarded senior school is intense because it is seen as the gateway to an elite university, which in turn can lead to high-status employment. The quality of senior high schools is estimated not by their examination results, but by the number of students they place in the top tier of Japan's universities, and in elite universities, such as those of Tokyo or Kyoto, in particular (Roesgaard 1998). According to Lynn (1988), the achievements of these leading schools receive wide media coverage in Japan and are of great interest to the population in general, who follow their progress avidly 'somewhat as they do of sports teams in the West'.

One aspect of the Japanese school system that has received much attention from overseas is the *juku* or 'cram school'. Many Japanese students begin to attend the *juku* during junior high school. They are often commercially run enterprises, although they might equally consist of small groups run in the home by students' mothers, who provide coaching lessons for high school entrance exams. It is estimated that at any one time 6.5 million of Japan's 15 million school children attend *juku* or equivalent (Manzo 2002). Students would normally attend twice a week after school, often for up to 2 hours (Yang 1999).

Japan as 'academic paradise'

To the casual observer, Japan has a highly centralized education system, where top-down reforms under the control of the Ministry of Education are adopted seamlessly by schools, which in turn produce students who are capable of world class performance on international comparative tests (LeTendre 2002). Every decade or so the Ministry of Education produces the 'Course of Study', a document that acts as a guideline for what must be taught in schools. Although prescriptive in nature, the Course of Study does leave the teacher much flexibility to be creative over the mode of delivery, if not over the actual content, of their lessons (DeCocker 2002). In contrast to the US system, where the control over what is taught in school is largely determined at the state level, Japan's highly centralized structure is often given as the reason for the country's superior performance in international tests (DeCocker 2002). In the United States, where it is the commercial textbook companies who are said to have more control over shaping the nation's curriculum than elected officials, the stability of the Japanese system holds many attractions as a remedy for the American Department of Education's 'hodge-podge of congressionally mandated and largely peripheral programmes' (Rohlen 2002, 184). The success of Japan in international comparative tests is unassailable, and a key reason why many US educational officials have visited Japan in attempts to find out what works and whether it can be transported to US schools (policy borrowing). In the years following the publication of 'Nation at Risk', cohorts of US educationalists and politicians have visited Japan to try and discover what makes their particular system of education so successful. The visitors praised the shared routines, co-operative learning, and coherent and focused lessons of Japanese schools (see, for example, Ravitch 1995). One educational researcher, upon returning from a visit to Japan, was said to have exclaimed: 'I think it is portable. Gumption and will-power, that's the key' (quoted in Berliner and Biddle 1995, 3).

As a consequence of this perceived success, demands for more challenging curriculum content, extensions to the hours students spend in schools, increased levels of support and training for teachers, and the use of incentives to motivate the most able students have found their way into American policy reforms (DeCocker 2002). For example, even recently an article in *Education Week* (the US equivalent of *The Times*

Educational Supplement) describes the adoption of a Japanese mathematics teaching model by schools in the state of Georgia (Galley 2004). However, these examples of strategies cherry-picked from the best of a country's education system have also received much criticism. Their lack of regard for contextual factors, coupled with the assumption that a strategy can simply be transplanted at will into a very different school system without any regard to empirical evidence, have been raised as concerns by several experts on Japanese education (Lewis 1999; LeTendre 1999, 2002; Rohlen 2002). There is, however, another side to the American perspective on education in Japan, one that, rather than praising the high achievement of Japanese students, reflects upon what it sees as the true cost of examination success.

Japan as 'examination hell'

In the introduction to their book *The Manufactured Crisis*, Berliner and Biddle (1995) lead with eight news reports which portray a frightening picture of occurrences we might at first believe to have taken place in American schools. But the authors quickly reveal that the descriptions of criminality, murder, extortion and suicide are rather shocking portrayals of the failings of the *Japanese* school system, and allude to what some commentators call 'the dark underside' of Japanese education.

Thus we have a polarized debate: on the one hand Japanese schools are viewed as world class or epitomes of 'academic paradise', while on the other they are viewed as 'hell' where creativity is stifled and students are treated as automatons (Bracey 1997). Consider, for example, this description of Japanese schools by Yoneyama (1999, 244):

> The Japanese high school to which students are bound is a stifling place. Its organizational structure is extremely formal, rigid and autocratic. Not only student–teacher relationships, but relationships between teachers and between students are hierarchical. Student–teacher communication is typically teacher-centered, one-way and top-down, and the student–teacher relationship is bureaucratic, distant and impersonal. In this milieu, students largely do not expect things like understanding, respect and personal care from teachers. Paternalistic care is nothing but a myth. Students are assigned a subordinate role and expected to remain silent.

Without doubt, Japanese students devote considerable time to preparing for entrance examinations, both for high school and at university level. Two books, *Shogun's Ghosts* (Schoolland 1990) and *The Japanese High School: Silence and Resistance* (Yoneyama 1999), deal explicitly with shocking accounts of suicide, murder, bullying and drop-out, which, they claim, characterize the intense pressure that the Japanese school system exerts on many of its students. According to Yoneyama, between 1995 and 1996 violence in junior high schools increased by 37 per cent, and violence against teachers by 48 per cent. Both of these books present account after account of students who are beaten to death by their teachers for minor infractions of school rules, of students committing suicide in the face of both mounting examination pressure and humiliation by bullying, in which teachers are frequently cited as willing participants. Even Keng and LeTendre's (1999) more moderate account of some of the problems facing Japanese schools acknowledges that between 1985 and 1990 'only five students died nationwide as a result of beatings by teachers' (emphasis added). Although corporal punishment is illegal in Japan, this is not widely known among students (Okan and Tsuchiya 1999); also, when incidents where the school has failed in its duty of care to students do come to light (usually through media coverage), any penalties that are enforced can be relatively minor: for example, limited suspensions of staff and temporary reduction in salaries (Schoolland 1990).

One consequence of these perceived failings of the Japanese school system is the increasing numbers of students who simply refuse to attend school. The Ministry of Education, which began collecting data on this during the 1980s, estimates that the proportion of 'school refusers' in junior high schools has risen from 0.47 per cent of the school population in 1985 to 1.42 per cent in 1995 (Okan and Tsuchiya 1999). Tsuneyoshi (2000) reports that the number of dropouts from both junior and senior high schools reached an all-time high in 1998 of 2.6 per cent of the high school population. Issues such as bullying and the intense pressure to succeed in school and to conform to group norms can be traced, according to some, directly back to the schools themselves: 'the life of Japanese students is affected most not by drug problems, family breakdowns or delinquency but by school related problems' (Yoneyama 1999, 10). The rigid control of the Japanese classroom, the intense pressure of preparing for entrance examinations, the use of physical violence by teachers, the reluctance of parents to complain for fear that unfavourable school reports would jepordize their son or daughter's chances of entering their chosen high school or university, and the Course of Study, which according to Yoneyama (1999) invades every aspect of a student's life, are all cited as contributing to the 'self destruction' of the school system and the failure of Japanese education, despite its plaudits among the international community for producing world class achievers.

However, tragic cases of extreme violence, bullying and suicide do receive considerable media attention in Japan, and have contributed to pressure for reform. Criticism of the system from the Ministry of Education has stated that 'the Japanese system of schooling lacked individuality, that the students were pressured into conformity and lacked creativity' (Roesgaard 1998, 238). Suggested reforms of Japanese education include restructuring the levels of schooling; revising higher education; improving teacher training; introducing concepts of internationalism, moral training and Japanese traditions; an emphasis on life-long learning, and introducing aspects of school choice and privatization. But reform in Japanese schools is measured in decades, not in 'quick fixes', and some commentators see the changes as favouring only students who excel in schools and thereby providing 'useful talent' for business and industry, rather than as addressing fundamental concerns with the school system (Roesgaard 1998; Okan and Tsuchiya 1999). Thus, we have another very different account of underachievement at the international level. As we shall see in the next chapter, however, the underachievement debate is anything but straightforward.

Summary

This chapter has revealed the importance of international comparative tests in contributing to how nations view the success of their education systems. It has pointed out some of the problems that simple rankings of performance scores have presented, as well as their influence in formulating national school policy reform. By considering the 'crisis accounts' surrounding school performance in three countries, the discussion has sought to place the underachievement discourse in its international context. In both the USA and in the UK, the national underachievement account has focused on falling achievement scores on both domestic and international forms of assessment. In Britain, this has become crystalized in the 'long tail' of underachievement that is said to characterize the achievement of our least able students, and of those from certain social groups in particular. In America, mediocre test scores have prompted school reform on an unprecedented scale. The governments of both countries have sought similar strategies to remedy the issue: high stakes testing, coupled with punitive school accountability measures for schools that fail to make adequate progress. In Japan, however, the underachievement discourse is different. The country's undoubted success in international comparative tests has attracted those who wish to replicate Japanese education strategies in their own systems. But Japanese schooling also has its critics, who point to high levels of violence and bullying in a school system that, despite its obvious successes, is accused of failing its young people.

However, given the contentious nature of the underachievement discourse, perhaps it is unsurprising that an alternative perspective of each nation's particular educational 'crisis accounts' also exists. These alternative accounts challenge this 'failing nation' discourse and will be evaluated in Chapter 3.

CHAPTER 3

Reconsidering the 'failing nation' debates

We have a genuine national crisis. More and more, we are divided into two nations. One that reads, and one that doesn't. One that dreams, and one that doesn't.

(George W. Bush, Department of Education 2002)

The importance of cross-national comparisons of school achievement in focusing initiatives to raise standards in schools was described in the previous chapter. Under-pinning these comparisons is the assumption that better schools equate to a better economy. However, this 'spurious' causal link between education and economics remains unproven by current research in comparative education (LeTendre 1999, 2002; Bracey 1996). According to Stedman (1997, 4), 'international standing is affected more by government trade policies and corporate flight to low wage countries than by weak school achievement'. Why countries want to compare the academic achievement of their school children with those in other countries is one issue. Another is what, if anything, the results of these comparisons can tell us about the relative 'health' of our school systems, as well as about strategies that might be adopted to improve any shortcomings. Unfortunately, the answer to these questions cannot be gleaned only from studying the rankings of international league tables, but rather ought to involve a close contextual study of a nation's school system and the structures and ethos that are at its very foundation. A good example of this is Japan. The fervour to emulate Japan's high ranking in the international league table has produced a polarized account in which the 'awe' of high academic standards has been tempered by the 'yes . . . but at what cost?' perspective we saw in Chapter 2. As LeTendre and other experts on the Japanese education system contend, cross-national comparisons, as demonstrated by US interest in Japan, are anything but straightforward: 'the debate over international tests scores has acerbated the tendency to use educational data from Japan, divorced from its cultural context, to make arguments about schooling practise in the US' (LeTendre 1999, 22).

This chapter reconsiders the underachievement debate as it applies to the relative performance of national school systems and the 'crisis account' of falling standards that often emerges from the publication of international league tables. The aim here is not to deny that there are problems to be solved, that all is well, and that educators should just be left to get on with teaching – although there are many who share that perspective. Rather, this chapter endeavours to provide a balanced account of the real comparative value of international tests, especially as they are used in the current context of a type of academic Olympics. We move on to re-evaluate some of the evidence for underachievement at the national level. We reconsider the 'long tail of underachievement' that now characterizes the debate in the UK, and look once more at the implications of the No Child Left Behind Act in the USA and its 'crisis account' of school failure. In the final section, an alternative account of the underachievement discourse in Japanese schools is presented.

Re-considering international comparative tests

> Modern nations are believed to be engaged in relentless economic competition in the international markets and education is regarded as a country's basic form of defence.
>
> (LeTendre 1999, 3)

Cross-cultural studies of academic achievement have been of interest to educators, politicians and the public since the post-Sputnik days of 1950s America, when anxiety over Russian superiority in the fields of science and engineering led to a re-think of education policy in the USA. It is not surprising, therefore, that the theories, hypotheses and conjectures arrived at by these international studies have traditionally excited much media interest. However, there are other factors that may affect intellectual development and academic achievement – including the cultural bias of tests, student motivation and attitudes towards test-taking, socio-economic differences and cognitive and social stimulation – which cannot be assessed by standardized testing alone (Fletcher and Sabers 1995).

The complexities of achieving cross-nation comparability on the tests are also worthy of attention. Indeed, if comparability between different domestic examination boards, different subjects and different cohorts is problematic, then the difficulties faced at the international level must surely be even greater (Gorard and Smith 2004; Nuttall 1979). These can be compounded by a lack of proportionate analysis of test data, as well as methodological shortcomings in the very design and administration of the tests (Gorard 2000; Brown 1998). It is these methodological difficulties, in particular concerning the sampling and validity of the tests, that are considered here. Although the focus is on performance in the UK context, many of the issues raised are of relevance to all countries that participate in international comparative tests.

Brown (1998) describes several problems with the sampling, reporting and curriculum coverage of TIMSS and similar international studies. One of the major sampling issues in TIMSS involved the selection of the test cohort. Here, the test designers opted to sample whole classes of pupils, for example those in Year 9. However, it is the practice in many countries to hold children back a school year until they have reached certain minimum competency levels. This meant that in TIMSS, 25 per cent of pupils in these particular countries were not in their age appropriate year group, and also that the groups who did participate in the study now comprised the more able pupils, who were of sufficiently high ability to progress academically. The problem of age-related sampling was so acute in 16 out of the 42 participating countries (including Germany, Denmark and the Netherlands) that their results were not thought to allow for fair comparison. The generally linear relationship between age and attainment also meant that countries with older cohorts of students were likely to achieve higher mean scores. This is important, as nearly 30 per cent of the variance in the test's outcome could be explained by differences in mean age (Gorard 2000).

Where TIMSS had sampled whole classes of pupils, PISA defined their cohort as those pupils born in a particular calendar year (1984 in PISA 2000). Given the practice in many countries of holding some students back a school year, this strategy ought to have countered some of the criticisms of the TIMSS sampling strategies: all students would now participate in the test, whether they were in their age appropriate year group or not. Prais (2003), however, disputes the validity of this arrangement. He argues that the PISA sample of 15-year-old students would now include the less able students who had previously been excluded from international tests such as TIMSS. Consequently, these countries would have seen their scores in PISA fall compared with previous tests. This would not have happened in the UK, where the practice of holding less able students back a year is uncommon, and so here scores ought to remain largely unaffected by the change. On the other hand, sampling older students could also mean that in some countries, where the end of compulsory education is around age 15, large groups of students, conceivably the least able, might have already left school and would be excluded from the analysis, resulting in possible grade inflation for some countries.

Other concerns have been raised over the different response rates from schools. While there is no consensus regarding a minimum rate sufficient for the conduct of particular statistical tests, few experts would deny that the closer a response rate is to 100 per cent the less chance there is of introducing errors into the analysis (White and Smith 2005). However, non-response had been anticipated by the architects of PISA, and two replacement schools were identified for every sampled school: this meant that response rates were bolstered by approaching the replacement institutions after the initial rejections. The response rates for the countries that make up the UK were not high. In England, almost half the schools originally approached were not willing to take part in the study (Table 3.1).

Table 3.1   **Response rates for UK schools sampled in PISA**

	Weighted school participation before replacement (%)	Weighted school participation after replacement (%)
UK	61.72	82.14
England	58.83	82.32
N. Ireland	70.90	79.37
Scotland	79.88	81.70

Source: OECD 2001

According to Brown (1998), another important methodological shortfall with TIMSS, and indeed with many other international comparative tests, came in the reporting of the results. In TIMSS, the final test scores showed that many countries had small differences in their mean score: but when these scores were ranked this closeness was not reflected, with countries ranked as high or low performing being separated by only a few percentage points. For example, in the TIMSS science test, fourth-ranked Korea had only 8 per cent more correct answers than seventeenth-ranked USA. In fact, in this test, 24 nations scored within 5 percentage points of each other (Bracey 1997; Schmidt *et al.* 1999).

American researchers have also criticized the use of average scores (Hitz 1996; Forgione 1998; Bracey 1998), particularly for a country with such a diverse population as the USA, where average scores can mask important differences in the distribution of marks, particularly where there is a relatively large group of low-scoring students. Differentiating the impact of variables that tend to be specific to a particular school year (such as classroom instruction or curriculum) from the effect of cumulative achievement that has been acquired over many years gives us yet another shortcoming of international comparative tests (Nelson 2003).

Another problem with the validity of these tests became apparent when the actual material being tested was examined. This, of course, is a fundamental problem with any type of assessment that is not based around an agreed core curriculum. In the case of TIMSS, the American-sponsored test ensured that each of its 162 test items were familiar to US children but such curriculum coverage for English Year 8 pupils was not so great, with only 93 out of the 162 items previously being covered in class. The Year 9 pupils fared slightly better but had covered more items than only two of the eleven comparison countries (Brown 1998). Although the American pupils were expected to have had the advantage of previously studying all the test items, their mean average scores ranked them near the bottom of the eleven comparison countries.

Differing test design and coverage have also made comparing different tests problematic: for example, comparing trends in PISA and PIRLS. This is perhaps not surprising, as TIMSS and PISA set out to measure different things. In TIMSS, the emphasis was on mastery of subjects, while in PISA the focus was students' application of knowledge: direct comparison between the two tests is therefore meaningless (Prais 2003). For example, the correlation between Reading Achievement scores on PIRLS and PISA was only 0.15, (DfES 2003c).

Avoiding ecological fallacies when generalizing the results of student level data to national policy is also relevant to international comparative studies. The 'virtual absence' of cross-national *educational* variables that predict student achievement suggest that it is difficult to separate the effect of educational policies and instructional practices from the contexts in which they are developed and implemented (Nelson 2003, 6). Even so, links between achievement on these tests and education reform are frequently made. For example, in the UK the recent high performance of students in PIRLS was attributed to the success of the National Literacy Strategy (Milliband 2004). In the USA, relatively poor achievement in the tests during the 1980s was used as a lever to re-focus reform towards the high-stakes accountability system we have today (NCES 1983). The impact of context may also affect the relationship between what students know and how well they actually perform on these tests. For example, Boe *et al.* (2002) estimate that over half the variance in national mean achievement scores in the TIMSS can be accounted for by 'student task persistence'. One popular account of the

1995 TIMSS assessments appears to support this. American students were reportedly kept back from their games lesson to complete the tests, which they were assured would not count towards their grades. In South Korea, on the other hand, students were marched into the hall to the sound of their school band and urged to do their best for their country (Brown 1998).

A substantial amount of resources and expertise goes into getting these tests right, but no matter how careful the test designers are over the issues of validity and reliability, international comparisons of performance are such a political issue that it is questionable whether a true picture of one nation's performance against another can ever be ascertained. A point of reflection must surely be over the need for these massive, expensive and complex tests. What purpose do they serve in the wider field? Does superior performance really lead to economic prosperity? The World Economic forum think it does not: it found no relationship between international competitiveness and performance in TIMSS (Bracey 1998).

Re-evaluating underachieving schools in the UK

In the United Kingdom, the most recent focus of the underachievement debate has been on the perceived 'long tail' of underachievement (DfES 2003; Johnson 2002). This section reconsiders the evidence for this perspective. By reviewing the relative achievement in PISA of students from low-income homes, we present an alternative account that challenges some of these perceived inequities in the British school system. That is not to say that there are no concerns about the relative performance of students from poorer homes: indeed their relatively lower achievement in national examinations is amply demonstrated in the following two chapters. Instead, this section re-evaluates the evidence that the education system in the UK is more inequitable than that in other countries, in particular our European Union partners.

The two examples given below are derived from the PISA 2000 database. By avoiding simple comparisons of students based on mean achievement scores, we have tried to avoid some of the methodological shortcomings which characterize the PISA survey and were described in the previous section.

Figure 3.1 shows the average differences in reading scores according to students' parental occupation. The bottom of each bar represents the mean reading score for the 25 per cent of students in each country with the lowest-ranking parental occupations. The top of each bar shows the mean reading score for those 25 per cent of students whose parents have the highest-ranking occupations. The length of each bar gives an indication of the mean difference in reading scores between the most and least advantaged students in terms of their parents' occupation. In Korea the bar is short, thus suggesting that there is little difference between the reading scores of the most and least advantaged students. The bar for the UK is long: in fact it represents a difference of 97 points between the top and bottom 25 per cent. The average score on the reading test is 500, with around two-third of students achieving scores of between 400 and 600: this 97-point gap between the least and most advantaged students is therefore of concern. It is this that has contributed to the claims of a 'long tail' of underachievement which is said to dog our lower performing students, and in particular, as this graph has illustrated, students from relatively poorer homes.

However, if you look again at Figure 3.1, you can see that the band for the UK is skewed towards the high scoring end. In fact, the reading scores for the students in the lowest 25 per cent occupational group are higher than those for similar students in Spain, Austria, France, Germany, Belgium, Italy, Denmark and the USA. Of the 27 OECD countries who participated in PISA, only 7 had scores that were close to or higher than the scores of the lowest performing UK students, while the scores for the top 25 per cent of UK students were the highest of all the participating countries (OECD 2001).

Figure 3.1 **Distribution of reading scores according to parental occupation in selected countries**

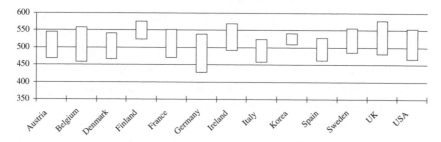

Source: OECD 2001

To sum up: although there is a wide distribution in the reading scores of UK students from the top and bottom occupational groups, this distribution is skewed towards the higher performing end, with little evidence that we have a 'long tail' of underachievement relative to other countries. The issue here is rather that 'the gap between our top and bottom pupils is not because the bottom are doing badly. It is because our most academic pupils are doing extremely well' (Sammons, quoted in Abrams 2003, 22).

The second example uses the PISA index of family wealth and focuses on the relative achievement of students from the richest and poorest homes. Table 3.2 presents the results for reading performance according to the students' score on the PISA indicator of wealth (Smith and Gorard 2002). Students who fall into the lowest 10 per cent according to wealth generally perform less well on the reading tests. In general, countries with the smallest gap in reading performance between richest and poorest are also those in which even the poorest have relatively high scores. Finland and Ireland have high scores for both groups, while France, Germany and Luxembourg have both very low scores for the poorest 10 per cent and only average scores for the richer 90 per cent. The UK has the fourth highest score for the poorest 10 per cent and the third highest score for the richer 90 per cent. In fact, the scores in the UK are so far from polarized that the reading score for the lowest 10 per cent is higher than the overall score for most countries (Gorard and Smith 2004a). Once again, there is little to suggest here that there is a purported crisis of underachievement in UK education, or that when compared with our economic peers our profile in these tests is characterized by a long tail of underachievement.

Table 3.2 **Mean reading score, according to PISA indicator of family wealth**

Country	Poorest 10%	Richest 90%	Proportionate gap
Luxembourg	385	452	0.08
Portugal	422	483	0.07
Germany	454	504	0.05
Greece	456	475	0.02
France	465	509	0.05
Spain	469	499	0.03
Italy	472	492	0.02
Austria	477	502	0.03
Denmark	479	502	0.02
Belgium	489	519	0.03
Sweden	495	519	0.02
UK	502	529	0.03
Ireland	512	530	0.02
Finland	540	550	0.01

Note: the gap is estimated as the difference divided by the sum, or $(a-b)/(a+b)$
Source: Gorard and Smith (2004a)

Alongside claims of underachievement have come accusations that the school system in the UK is one of the least equitable and most segregated in the world (Johnson 2002; *The Times Educational Supplement* 2002). Analysis of the PISA data has shown the inaccuracy of these claims. For example, considering the distribution of students in schools who fell into the lowest performing 10 per cent showed that segregation by test outcome was largely explicable by the use of academic (and other forms of) selection (Gorard and Smith 2004a). Countries who retained mainly comprehensive systems, such as Finland, Denmark and Sweden, showed less segregation. The UK had below average levels of segregation on all indicators, giving little support to the claim that schools are now more 'socially stratified that the old grammar schools they replaced' (*The Times Educational Supplement* 2002).

Reconsidering the impact of policies to reduce underachievement

This section briefly reviews the impact of some recent government initiatives to eliminate underachievement in schools. These initiatives are school-wide and are generally aimed at raising the performance of all students, regardless of their social group (the underachievement of students according to sex, ethnic group and social class is considered later in Chapters 4 and 5).

The key point here is not to suggest that the government is wrong to want to raise standards in school, but rather to question the evidence base on which many of these initiatives have been premised, and in particular the area of school effectiveness research (SER). Whether school effectiveness work has ever in fact generated a sufficient evidence base to support its claims about the extent to which schools matter is clearly a matter of concern – more so because its findings form the basis for very expensive and time intensive strategies that schools and teachers are expected to adopt, without anyone really knowing whether or not they actually work (the role that the SER evidence base has had in helping shape school standards reform was described in Chapter 2). Some of the most contentious criticisms come from those who, although not denying that schools do make a difference to the individuals who attend them, challenge the notion that the school is central to a child's success and that background factors such as socio–economic status are to be dismissed as mere 'noise'. In fact, the level of criticism directed at SER is surprising. SER has been described variously as something akin to a 'cult' where 'one either buys the approach or one doesn't' (Vaill 1991, 64, quoted in Ouston 1999, 1); as having a 'social Darwinist eugenic rationale'

(Hamilton 1997, 129), and as being an 'ethnocentric pseudo-science' (Hamilton 1997, 125).

School effectiveness work has estimated that national systems, school sectors, schools, departments and teachers combined have been found to explain approximately 20 per cent of the total variance in school outcomes (Gorard and Smith 2004). This effect is relatively small, and the remaining 80 per cent or so of the variance in outcomes can be attributed to student background, prior attainment and 'error components' in the model. The process whereby 'family background, social class and any notion of context are typically regarded as "noise", or "outside" background factors which must be controlled for and then stripped away' (Angus 1993, 341) is one of the key areas of criticism of school effectiveness work. By underplaying the role of contextual factors in influencing attainment and 'explicitly avoiding engaging with the socio-economic dimensions of variations in academic performance' (Gibson and Asthana 1998, 204), school effectiveness research has been accused of taking a narrow range of easily measurable rather than important outcomes and assuming that a single outcome is appropriate for all (Coe and Fitz-Gibbon 1998, 423). This sidelining of the other goals of education (such as citizenship, self-esteem, political awareness and social responsibility) in favour of measuring only academic outcomes seems to assume that the 'main task of the educational institution is to lever as many pupils as possible through a given targeted and often narrow assessment system' (Rea and Weiner 1998, 30; see also Davies 1997). This begs the question: what do we mean by an 'effective' school? A good school might be an effective one but an effective school with a high level of 'technical efficiency' might not necessarily be a good one if it neglects social outcomes (Elliot 1996). Where claims have been made regarding the superiority of one school over another, it is usually the case that these more successful schools are situated in more affluent areas or are able to select a portion of their intake, either by taking on specialist school status or via the admissions system, as in faith-based or foundation schools. Indeed, once background factors have been taken into account, there is no evidence that any type of school performs any better than any other (Gorard *et al.* 2003).

That the government has gone some way to recognizing the link between poverty and relatively low academic achievement is to be welcomed. Through initiatives such as Excellence in Cities (EiC), they have invested large sums of money and expertise in raising the attainment of pupils in the poorest urban communities. However, the results of this programme, which embraces many of the characteristics of school effectiveness work, have so far been relatively modest, especially when one considers the large sums of money – around £3.6 billion – that have been invested in the scheme (House of Commons 2003, Ev. 35). In 2002, secondary schools within the Excellence in Cities programme improved their GCSE results by 2.3 percentage points, whereas schools not in the programme improved by 1.3 percentage points: not a large difference (House of Commons 2003, Ev. 34). The early reports from the programme's external evaluators also point to limited impact at this stage. In their evaluation of pupils' performance at Key Stage 3 and 4, Kendall and Schagen (2004) found the evidence for the impact of Excellence in Cities (EiC) on pupil achievement to be limited. For students in the Phase 1 schools (where EiC was first implemented in 1999) there was no clear pattern of improved performance in the 2002 Key Stage 3 examinations. For example, while the EiC cohort had made about two months additional progress in English, no improvement over students in non-EiC schools was found in mathematics. At Key Stage 4, similar pupils in EiC and non-EiC schools made similar progress.

The evaluation of the gifted and talented strand of EiC does suggest that the programme has had a 'significant positive impact' (Morris *et al.* 2004, 28) on the performance of all gifted and talented pupils at Key Stages 3 and 4, as well as raising the attainment of gifted and talented students whose levels of attainment were previously below those of their gifted and talented cohort peers. The attitudes of this group of students towards school were also reported as being more positive.

However, these improvements are relatively modest: for example, the gifted and talented cohort in Year 9 achieved 0.45 of a level higher than their peers with similar prior attainment scores. At GCSE, the performance of the gifted and talented cohort was 0.46 points per GCSE higher. While it may be that achievement at the highest grades will be bound by a ceiling effect, the outcomes of these evaluations appear to fall short of the claims that in many areas the EiC programme has worked 'stupendously well' (House of Commons 2003, Ev. 36). In addition, evaluations of the gifted and talented part of the EiC programme do not appear able to establish whether the positive attitudes displayed by the students in this group were a consequence of their membership of the group or predated the EiC intervention. It is also unclear how the gifted and talented cohorts were identified. Although it is clear that students were assigned to the group by their school, this designation could vary between schools – a child identified as being gifted and talented in one school would not necessarily be so by another.

While few would dispute the need for programmes like Excellence in Cities which focus on raising the achievement of students in the most disadvantaged communities, there is concern about their reliance on a research base (such as school effectiveness research) that many critics see as being essentially flawed. It is of course true that some schools in challenging communities can achieve high standards; however, these schools are frequently the exception and any improvements can be relatively short-lived. Taking school improvement out of its social context and focusing only on improving schools can be problematic because 'schools often reflect rather than transform inequality' (Orfield 2000, 401). Perhaps the question should not be about which schools are underachieving, but rather about 'why there is this link between poverty and attainment and what can be done about it' (Gorard and Smith 2004, 216).

Reconsidering underachievement in the USA

In the previous chapter, declining performance on the Scholastic Aptitude Test (SAT) and the National Assessment of Educational Progress (NAEP) tests was examined in light of their contribution to the picture of underachievement in America's schools. Here we reconsider the validity of these claims. As there are no national tests in the USA that would allow for a direct comparison of entire cohorts of students, analysts have to rely on the SAT and NAEP data, which reflect only a sample of the US school population. Both tests have methodological shortcomings that must be borne in mind when any conclusions are drawn from their findings: indeed, such concerns might well present a good case for excluding the data from any analysis altogether, let alone using them to formulate alternative perspectives on school performance. However, both tests play an important role in tracking the state of American education, for the school population as a whole as well as for different subgroups of students. In interpreting the analysis presented below, and indeed any analysis which is based on this data, one needs to bear in mind both the importance of these tests in providing information on the health of the nation's schools, and the methodological caveats which may limit their applicability.

This section reconsiders some of the evidence that has been widely used to explain falling levels of achievement in American schools. In the absence of a national testing programme, these comparisons rely on nationally sampled tests which are not always linked to what is actually taught in school. The evidence for declines in national standards in America's public schools is therefore unclear and can obscure a more fundamental problem, notably the differential achievement of subgroups of students and, in particular, the gaps in achievement between certain minority students and those from white backgrounds. We consider some of the trends and explanations for these achievement gaps before review-ing the implications of the No Child Left Behind legislation for reduc-ing achievement gaps and addressing the underachievement of America's schools.

Re-examining examination scores

Falling scores on the SAT and NAEP have made an important contribu-tion to America's underachievement account. However, recalculations of SAT data indicate that scores have actually risen among black and white groups over the last two decades, despite the fact that more students were now participating in the test (Hochschild 2003). In their re-analysis of SAT performance, Berliner and Biddle (1995) also suggest that because SAT results are reported on a standardized scale, any differences in the SAT scores indicate only very small differences in the number of actual correct or incorrect answers on the multiple-choice paper. They argue that one incorrect answer on a verbal SAT question corresponds to a drop of 50 scale points on the final scale. Thus, the 60–90 point decline in SAT standardized scores, which caused much consternation in the 1970s, actually corresponds to the average student scoring between 6 and 9 incorrect answers. On a 138-item test, this translates to a fall of, at the most, 6.5 per cent in the number of correct answers.

In response to concerns that the grades students are awarded are 'not what they used to be', the College Board who administer the SAT com-missioned an investigation into the relationship between high-school grades and performance on the SAT for different subgroups of college-bound students (Camara *et al.* 2003). The results reveal an increase in both high-school Grade Point Averages (GPA) and scores on the SAT mathematical tests, while scores on the SAT verbal test showed little change over the same period (Figure 3.2). Between 1972 and 2002, the proportion of female students taking the SAT increased, as did the numbers of students from Hispanic and Asian backgrounds, while the proportion of white students declined. Overall, students improved their GPA by 0.31 of a grade point, with students from Asian-American backgrounds showing the largest gains. Students from African-American backgrounds registered an increase of 0.2 of a grade point. For the SAT verbal test, although African-American students achieved the lowest scores of any ethnic group, the increase in their scores between 1981 and 2002 (from 406 to 430) placed them alongside students from Asian-American backgrounds as showing the largest improvements. White stu-dents, although still having the highest scores of any ethnic group, showed the smallest overall increase (from 520 to 528).

Figure 3.2   **Variations in SAT-verbal and SAT-mathematics scores 1972–2002**

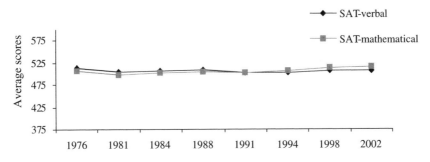

Source: The College Board (Camara *et al.* 2003)

There are, however, methodological problems with the SAT that limit how far we can generalize. One obvious problem with its reliability is that the SAT is taken on a voluntary basis by students making college applications, and therefore is not representative of the entire school population. The purpose of the SAT is to predict the progress of college entrants after one year of their undergraduate course. Indeed, the College Board itself describes the use of the SAT to draw wider conclusions about educational performance as 'inherently unfair' (in Berliner and Biddle 1995, 18). Another reason why some commentators question the usefulness of comparing performance trends using the SAT is that increasing numbers of students, many from very diverse backgrounds, now take the test, thus making comparisons over time very difficult. Of course, as a standardized test the SAT had to be standardized against a particular population of students: those chosen were college entrants in 1941 who were a predominately white, male, middle- or upper-middle class, English-speaking group, thus drawing further into question the validity of longitudinal comparisons using the SAT (Berliner and Biddle 1995; Hochschild 2003).

The NAEP is another domestic large-scale test that is used to monitor national standards and whose long-term performance trends have added to the underachievement debate. Although the test draws upon a national sample of students, the actual numbers of students involved has varied greatly in recent years (Flanagan and Grissmer 2003; NCES 2003). In the 1970s and early 1980s, the NAEP sample ranged from between 31,000 to 8,000 students. From the mid-1980s, this fell to between 5,500 to 3,000 students (Hedges and Nowell 1998). However, in the 2003 data collection period, 343,000 students were assessed in reading in Grades 4 and 8 (NCES 2003). These numbers were much higher than in previous years because they combined samples from each state, whereas previously national samples had been drawn separately from the state samples. Re-analysing the annual and long-term trend data generated by NAEP gives a different account of pupil performance to that presented in Chapter 2, and one that also shows little evidence of underachievement.

Table 3.3 **Average scores and profiency levels on NAEP Grade 8 reading tests (2003)**

Group	Average test Score	At or above basic (%)	At or above proficiency level (%)
All	261	74	32
White	272	83	41
Black	244	54	13
Hispanic	245	56	15
Free meal eligible	247	57	16
Not eligible	271	82	40

Source: NCES (2004)

Table 3.3 gives the results for the NAEP 2003 Grade 8[3] reading tests. The results are shown for the three main ethnic groups, and by students' eligibility for free school meals. The average tests scores show the relatively lower performance of students from the black and Hispanic communities, and those who are eligible to receive free school meals. However, while the annual data does therefore show that there are certain groups of students who perform less well on these tests, whether these students are underachieving is another matter.

In addition to its annual surveys, NAEP also carries out assessments of long-term trends in student progress (NCES 2000). These have provided a gauge of student achievement in reading, mathematics and science for over 30 years. By administering the same assessment to a nationally representative sample of 9, 13 and 17-year-old students, this provides the most accurate longitudinal profile of the achievement of American high-school students and student subgroups. The national trends in the reading performance of 13-year-old students by the three main ethnic groups are given in Figure 3.3.

The general trend for all students has been that average scores increased during the 1970s. Since 1980, scores have fluctuated slightly, but the average score in 1999 was higher than that in 1971. Overall, from 1971 until the mid-1980s, the achievement gap between black and white students narrowed. However, in the 1990s the achievement of all groups slowed, with white students improving their performance relative to black

[3] US Grade 8 is equivalent to National Curriculum Year 9

Figure 3.3   **Reading performance of Grade 8 students, according to ethnic group**

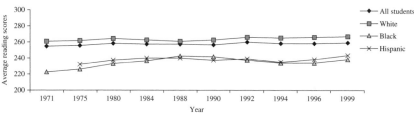

Source: NCES (2000)

students and the achievement gap between the two groups starting to widen (although not to the extent of three decades ago). For students of Hispanic background, there has been an inconsistent pattern of losses and gains between 1973 and 1999: the gap has narrowed but not to the extent of the black–white achievement gap (Hedges and Nowell 1998; Lee 2002). Trends for their achievement in mathematics and science have been similar across all age groups, with the most gains evident in mathematics (NCES 2000). In reading, students from black and Hispanic groups have gained at each age level, with a narrowing of the gap between their performance and that of white students becoming evident (see Table 3.4). In mathematics and science, the overall trend has been one of improvement and a narrowing of the ethnic achievement gap, although their performance remains consistently below that of white students. However, if the proportional changes in NAEP scores over the same period are considered, it seems that the greatest improvements are now being made by students from the black and Hispanic communities (see Chapter 5 for a fuller discussion on the measurement of proportional changes in test data).

Table 3.4   **Proportional increases in Grade 8 reading scores, according to ethnic group**

Group	1971	1999	Change
All students	255	259	1.57
White	261	267	2.30
Black	222	238	7.21
Hispanic	232★	244	5.17

Source: NCES (2000)   ★ 1975 data

However, despite their faster rate of improvement on NAEP, there are real concerns in the USA about the achievement gaps that exist between students from the black–white and Hispanic–white communities. The fear is that legislation like No Child Left Behind will further compound inequalities among the poorer performing students in America's schools. As we have seen, it is often the case that students from black and Hispanic backgrounds perform less well in school than their white peers and, as the following section will explain, these lower performing students are not evenly distributed among schools in the United States: they tend to be concentrated in the poorer urban schools. If these students are achieving at the lowest levels on tests like NAEP, then it is likely that they will also struggle to reach the minimum competency levels on the NCLB tests. As a result, their schools may struggle to achieve adequate yearly progress targets and could end up being labelled as failing or underachieving and subjected to NCLB strict accountability sanctions. The reasoning behind this scenario is described further below.

Achievement gaps and school equality

That African-American students perform less well on standardized tests than European Americans is held as an almost universal truth in US educational research. Longitudinal assessments since the 1960s have shown white students to be ahead in every measure and at every grade. Achievement gaps according to race have also been apparent in international tests (Bracey 2002). Accounting for the fluctuations in this gap has perplexed many researchers, as has the development of strategies to eliminate the gap altogether (Lee 2002; see also Jencks and Phillips 1998 for a detailed account of research in this area). Attempts since the 1960s to desegregate schools, equalize school funding and raise the income of black families have had some impact but not the desired long-term effect: the gap still remains (Jencks and Philips 1998; Orfield 2000). While it may be the case that achievement gaps between black–white and Hispanic–white children have been narrowing, considerable inequities do still remain.

Although the USA is a wealthy country, there exists within it large pockets of poor and isolated groups. With one of the most unequal distributions of wealth of any industrialized country, the USA has large sections of its population living in poverty, mainly in the urban areas of large cities (Orfield 2000). In the first half of the twentieth century, changing patterns of immigration into American cities resulted in large numbers of the more affluent white families, as well as many employers, leaving the city centres for its suburban fringes – the so-called 'white flight' (Anyon 1997). The resultant poverty and racial segregation of America's inner cities have presented many social, economic and cultural challenges to the schools that serve these communities. Today over seven million children are enrolled in elementary and secondary schools in the nation's central cities, while almost a third of all children of school age (over fifteen million) live in the suburban fringes of these cities (Department of Education 2002a). However, the distribution of children within both these communities is uneven. Only 6 per cent of white children attend schools in urban areas, compared with 31 per cent of children from ethnic minority backgrounds (in particular African-Americans and Hispanic children: Department of Education 2002a). Nationally, 16 per cent of children between the ages of 5 and 17 are identified as living in poverty, and almost a quarter of these children live in the inner cities, while 10 per cent live in their suburbs (Department of Education 1999).

Schools in these poorer areas are likely to experience skills shortages among staff, as well as unequal funding, curriculum opportunities and involvement and resources from parents (Orfield 2000). Because of the way that school financing operates, large gaps in budgetary allocations to schools exist and have resulted in many of America's urban districts being funded inequitably. In fact, in only 10 out of the 47 states for which data was available did districts with the highest levels of poverty receive the most state funding. In every other state, it was schools in the wealthier districts that received the most money. For example, in the state of New York, where the funding gap is among the largest, pupils who attend school in districts in the upper quarter for poverty were allocated $2,152 per student less than if they had attended a school in a district in the lower quarter for poverty. This $2,152 equates to a difference of $53,800 for a class of 25 students, or $860,800 for a school of 400 students (The Education Trust 2002).

Not only is there an uneven distribution of students according to their ethnic minority background in American schools, there are also wide variations according to ability. Analysis by Flanagan and Gissmer (2004) suggests that students from both black and white homes who live in the central cities of north-east and midwest USA have among the lowest scores of black and white students nationwide – in fact, 80 per cent of the lowest scoring black students live in these central cities. However, students who live in the suburbs and rural areas of the north-east and midwest have among the highest scores in the country, which are in fact equivalent to the top performing countries in international comparative tests. Therefore, it is in this context of segregation on the grounds of wealth and race, as well as inequities in the funding of the school system that the relative achievement of American public schools ought to be considered. Tracking the academic achievement of samples of the whole school population might well dispute the evidence of falling standards, and this is true for many of America's school children. However, disaggregating the data according to race, income or locality reveals a very different picture.

There appear to be particular trends in the performance of some students in US schools that may not always be clear from test data that is aggregated at the national level. That achievement gaps exist between different ethnic groups is well established. However, there are also discrepancies in the distribution of certain groups of students among different schools and different locations that further question the equity of the whole school system. More seriously, there is a real concern that these inequities will only be increased under No Child Left Behind. The impact of this Act on the attainment of some of the most educationally vulnerable students in America's schools is considered next.

The No Child Left Behind Act and its impact on America's failing schools

The key points of the No Child Left Behind (NCLB) Act were summarized in the previous chapter. One of its strengths is that, as its very title suggests, it demands that the academic progress of every child, regardless of how able, be open to scrutiny. However, many commentators and practitioners take issue with this because the act also states very clearly that not only is every child expected to make progress, they must make sufficient progress to achieve minimum competency levels within twelve years of the Act's inception (that is, by 2014). In many states, these minimum competency levels are relatively high. For example, in New Jersey attaining proficiency levels for Grade 8 mathematics has to improve from 39 per cent of the school population in 2003 to 100 per cent in 2014 (Department of Education 2004).

By January 2003, each state was required to submit a detailed workbook to the US Department of Education outlining the steps they would undertake to ensure compliance with the statutes set out under NCLB. States also had to indicate how both schools and school districts would demonstrate Adequate Yearly Progress (AYP) towards full proficiency in 2014. States are required to make public the results of these tests. This performance data will be disaggregated according to students' sex, ethnic group, special educational need, level of economic disadvantage and English language proficiency. If a school fails to make AYP, a series of sanctions can be administered by the school district (acting on behalf of the state). The form of these sanctions ranges from district-level monitoring through to giving parents the option to transfer their children out of 'failing schools' and providing students who remain in the school with additional tutoring. In more extreme cases, where a school fails to make AYP for four or more consecutive years, that school can be forced to replace staff or aspects of the curriculum or, at the extreme, be re-structured as a Charter school or one run by a private company.

The NCLB act mandates 'much more testing of students than was required before 2001 and has more stringent penalties for failing schools than any federal law' (Hochschild 2003, 109). However, evidence such as that presented above suggests that American schools have been improving, or at least are stable in their achievements: rather, it is the state of urban education and the achievement gap between certain groups that remain the key areas of concern. However, instead of emphasizing the specific need for urban school reform and so focusing attention and resources directly in that area, policy-makers have demonstrated a strong commitment to reforming all schools, regardless of how much they need it (Hochschild 2003). On the one hand, raising the achievement of students in all America's public schools appears both equitable and praiseworthy. However, some of the implications of NCLB's strict accountability rules and sanctions, in particular those that apply to student subgroups, could result in great numbers of schools and their students being labelled as failing and underachieving.

The consequences of No Child Left Behind

The fact that students from different economic and cultural backgrounds are not distributed evenly throughout the USA, and are rather clustered in certain localities, has important implications for the NCLB subgroup rules. Under NCLB, a subgroup is a group of students characterized by their ethnic group, by their limited English proficiency, their special educational need or whether they come from a low-income home. Typically, a subgroup comprises 25 students, although states do vary in their definition (Department of Education 2004).

Many authors claim that the sanctions linked to the subgroup proficiency measures will result in diverse schools, and in schools with large numbers of students being unfairly penalized (Kane and Staiger 2003; Popham 2004). For example, more than 4.5 million students in American public schools (9.6 per cent of the total enrollment) are labelled as having limited English proficiency (NCES 2002). However, they are not evenly distributed among the states: they range from less than 1 per cent of the school population in Vermont to more than 25 per cent in California (NCES 2002). Aggregating these learners into a subgroup for the purposes of NCLB is not without difficulty: English language competency is transient, in that once students have improved their level of English, they will be removed from the subgroup. The students who remain in the subgroup are likely to be those of lower ability, and new students who may only recently have moved to the country. Therefore, it seems unlikely that students in this subgroup are going to demonstrate AYP towards full proficiency (Abedi 2003).

In some states like New Mexico and California, over 80 per cent of schools contain a Hispanic or African-American subgroup, compared to only 5 per cent of schools in Virginia. Additionally, 92 per cent of African-American students and 91 per cent of Hispanics attend schools which have black or Hispanic subgroups, compared with only 33 per cent of white students. The concentration of the lowest performing students in certain schools or in certain locations is likely to present difficulties in meeting NCLB's strict accountability measures for these subgroups. Using data from NAEP, Kane and Staiger (2003) examined the effect of aggregate and disaggregate measures of success for students from different ethnic backgrounds. When looking at the individual level performance of students from African-American backgrounds they found 'considerable overlap' in their scores and the scores of white students. However, when performance is aggregated to the school level, this overlap is reduced. By disaggregating the scores of these students into NCLB subgroups in each school, wide disparities between the attainment of black and white students are likely to be emphasized. Similar trends were reported between the performance of students from white and Hispanic backgrounds. According to the authors, 'the single most important determinant of the difference in failure rates between states is likely to be the racial composition of their schools'.

Holding schools accountable for such large and 'unrealistic' increases in the progress of many of these groups of children could also result in fewer resources and more sanctions for large schools and schools with diverse populations (Kane and Staiger 2003). In the USA, these schools are likely to be those with large proportions of students with limited English proficiency, as well as children from different ethnic minority backgrounds and those with special educational needs. In fact, the reason why almost 57 per cent of Ohio's school districts failed to make AYP in 2003 was either partly or fully because of the progress of students with special educational needs (Chester 2004). In Washington State, it was larger schools with more diverse populations who were less likely to achieve yearly accountability targets (Bylsma 2004).

Texas, one state held up as a model of school accountability reforms, has for some time monitored proficiency targets for subgroups of students. However, the expected targets were different for students at aggregate and disaggregate level: 90 per cent proficiency targets overall, but only 55 per cent for subgroups of students (Kane and Staiger 2003). In 2003, in order to meet AYP targets for proficiency in Grade 8 Language,

Arts, Literacy (LAL) examinations, 58 per cent of students in New Jersey were expected to achieve minimum levels (Department of Education 2004). In comparison, on NAEP reading assessments in 2003, only 37 per cent of these New Jersey students were actually judged to be proficient (NCES 2004). Although it is true that these are two different tests, the difference between the federal benchmarking test (NAEP) and New Jersey's AYP target results remains large.

These strict rules for student subgroups are likely to be the main reason why many schools that would otherwise be successful on state accountability measures might be deemed to be failing under NCLB. Not only must the school make AYP, different subgroups of students must also make the same progress towards proficiency. According to many educators, this is one of the crucial flaws with the NCLB legislation. While few would disagree that challenging the progress of groups of students who have traditionally done less well in school is praiseworthy, the issue lies with the fact that these students must also meet the demanding AYP proficiency targets or the schools will receive stiff penalties. Kane and Staiger consider the use of subgroup rules as 'counter productive in test-based accountability systems', and Linn (2003) argues that 'the goals that NCLB sets for student achievement would be wonderful if they could be reached, but, unfortunately, they are quite unrealistic, so much so, that they are apt to do more to demoralize educators than to inspire them'. Many otherwise excellent schools could therefore be labelled as failing.

So although we have a seemingly equitable piece of legislation, designed to give all students equal chances of success in school, schooling in America's public schools appears to be anything but equitable. Through its assertion that all students must achieve the same minimum competency levels, with no account made of the value-added context in which their schools may operate, the danger is that the No Child Left Behind legislation in its present form could further enhance these inequities and unfairly label children and schools as underachieving.

'Academic paradise' or 'examination hell'? Reconsidering the relative achievement of Japan's schools

The nature of American interest in Japan's schools and the very polarized picture that has emerged from almost three decades of scrutiny offers a cautionary tale for those wishing to 'borrow' educational policies from other apparently more successful nations. America's interest is part of a long tradition of US eagerness to be 'first in the world' in educational, as well as economic, terms. One example of this determination is the Goals 2000 initiative under President Clinton, which pledged that America would be 'first in the world' in maths and science by 2000. In the post-Sputnik era, the gaze of US education reformers turned to the USSR and the education system that was producing much technological and scientific expertise. Previously it was the universities of western Europe that had been scrutinized as models for the US higher education system. With the rise of the economic tigers in the Far East and the ensuing 'wake-up call' for American competitiveness, it was inevitable that the US reformer's eye would turn in this direction and to Japan in particular (Cummings 1989; Orfield 2000). The perceived link between better schools and better economics is apparent in all these comparisons. For example, it is no coincidence that the policy-borrowers' gaze has rested on countries like Japan and Korea that are successful in international tests as well as being economic success stories. The Czech Republic performed well in TIMSS in 1995, ranking second in the world in Grade 8 science and sixth in Grade 8 maths (TIMSS 1996). However, little has been written about education strategies from the Czech Republic that might be adopted for schools in Britain or America. The Czech Republic is not a member of the G8, and until 2004 it was not even in the European Union. Perhaps it is therefore not viewed as a threat to economic competitiveness, and therefore seen as having little to teach about school reform.

According to Le Tendre, this 'desire of many American policy makers to "imitate Japan" by further centralizing curriculum decisions in the US and instituting national standards is not based on empirical evidence' (LeTendre 2002, 31). In fact, American interest in what happens in the Japanese context is, at its most basic, simply a case of 'how do we stack up?': the debate rarely moves to examine the context of education (LeTendre and Baker 1999). Consequently, many of the myths – both positive and negative – that have built up around the Japanese school system have strong links with America's stereotypical view of what Japanese schools *should* be like, rather than what is actually happening in them. Lewis (1999) describes what she calls two 'resilient myths' about Japanese education. The first is that it causes more psycho-social problems among students than exist in students in the USA, and the second is that Japanese education is narrowly focused on academic achievement, rather than on the whole child. Both these myths have been evident in the polarized account of Japan's school system given in Chapter 2: but their contribution to the perceived failure of the Japanese education system will be re-evaluated here.

Tragic stories of Japanese youth blighted by high rates of suicide, bullying and violence in school, burnt out by competition and expectations to conform within a rigid and confining school system have been described in the previous chapter. However, accounts perpetuating these myths like those by Schoolland (1990) and Yoneyama (1999) are heavily based on sensationalized newspaper reports rather than large-scale empirical evidence (Keng and LeTendre 1999). They frequently fail to acknowledge that the suicide rate among Japanese youth has fallen steadily since the 1960s and continue to contend that schools are the root of much that is amiss among young people, thereby disregarding other complex social factors which could impact upon youth development. Many of the horror stories of Japanese youth suicide so vividly portrayed by both the Japanese and the US media conform to America's expectations (formed partially by events during the Second World War), that the suicide rates ought to be higher among Japanese youth than among American youth (Keng and LeTendre 1999). This, however, is not the case. The suicide rate among Japanese 15–24-year-olds is very similar to that for American young people: in 2000, the suicide rate among this age group in Japan was 11.5 per 100,000, compared with 10.2 deaths per 100,000 in the USA. The figure for American males was in fact higher than that for Japanese males: 17.0 deaths per 100,000 compared with 15.8 (WHO 2004). However, it should be noted that international suicide statistics are notoriously difficult to compare and must be treated with caution, as countries differ greatly in how they record and report this data.

Keng and LeTendre (1999) also refute the link between youth suicide and pressure from school. For example, the suicide rate among Japanese youth has been relatively stable in recent years and does not appear to be affected either by the increased pressure to succeed in high-stakes testing nor by seasonal examination patterns. That violence and bullying are worrying features of Japanese schools, just as they can be in schools in many other countries, is not denied by many of those who carry out serious comparative work in the Japanese context. Their concern, however, is that reactionary and sensationalized accounts, which do not draw upon empirical evidence but rather on media representations, are done more to refute the evident achievement of Japanese students in international comparative tests, rather than to contribute to serious contextualized critiques of the Japanese education system. In addition, these over-sensationalized accounts of school suicides serve to further complicate efforts to study the complex problems with violence and bullying which do exist in some schools.

One of the major criticisms of American strategies to policy borrow from the Japanese education system is that the focus has rested almost exclusively on the unproven causal link between high performance in international comparative tests, a (once) competitive national economy, and a highly centalized and structured school system (LeTendre 1999). This brings us to Lewis' second myth about Japanese schooling. Many researchers, both Japanese and western, dispute the existence of a top-down controlling and regulatory school system in Japan, and emphasize the extensive lateral networks that exist between both schools and districts wherein teachers are strongly encouraged to collaborate, as well as the influence teachers have in policy reform and its implementation in schools (Cummings 1989; DeCocker 2002). That the judiciary would have a role in deciding educational policy, as has frequently happened in the USA (particularly with regard to equitable school funding), is unthinkable in the Japanese context, as would be policies which encourage unregulated or unproven school reform such as Charter schools and home schooling (Rohlen 2002; Anyon 1997).

The image of Japanese classrooms as formal rigid environments is also open to contention by comparative researchers, who do much of their fieldwork in these settings. It may be true that the pedagogical style is more formal in senior high school, but junior high schools in particular are described as being creative and active learning environments, where students take tremendous responsibility for their own learning, and teachers have the flexibility to innovate within collaborative and cooperative networks (Cummings 1989; Tsuchida and Lewis 1999; Stevenson 2002). That the Japanese school system is not entirely authoritarian and punitive can also be seen by the large number of Japanese students who remain in education long after they reach the compulsory leaving age: around 98 per cent continue to post-compulsory senior high school, and the statistics suggest that, for the large part, they stay there (Japan Statistical Yearbook 2004).

The differences between the Japanese and American school systems are large, and it seems remarkable that foreign policy-makers ever considered that by taking school policy strategies out of their wider context they could simply transplant good practice into another school system. For example, the present US strategies of top-down coercive accountability, characterized by the NCLB legislation, would not be well received in Japan: 'The Japanese approach makes students accountable, the America approach makes teachers accountable' (Rohlen 2002, 187).

White (1999) describes three stages of reaction to the apparent success story that is Japanese education. The first is 'wow'. This is characteristic of the 1970s and the amazement that greeted the news that superior Japanese performance in international tests appeared to co-exist with formal and structured curricular and national education standards. The second reaction is 'uh-oh' and is the reaction of those who were concerned about American competitiveness in the face of Japanese economic and educational superiority in the 1980s. The third phase, characteristic of the 1990s, is 'yes . . . but'. This response notes the positive aspects of Japanese schooling but also the downside, as in 'yes . . . but would you wish to send your child to a Japanese school?'.

After Japan's economic bubble burst during the 1990s, their apparent continuing success in international tests now has a different context. Rather than highlighting innovative teaching and high levels of student motivation, it is the dark underside of school drop-outs, violence and bullying, now seen as a feature of an authoritarian and coercive regime, which appears to characterize international perspectives of education in Japan (Berliner and Biddle 1995; Bracey 1997; LeTendre and Baker 1999). This section has sought to demonstrate how divisive, sensationalized and inaccurate such polarized accounts can be.

That is not to say that all is well with education in Japan. The Ministry of Education itself notes the need for reform and has looked to the USA as a model – although, ironically, Japan has demonstrated the same stereotypical shortcomings that characterized America's fascination with the Japanese system a decade earlier (Rohlen 2002). In addition to concerns over bullying and school violence, Japan also has to focus on the differential attainment and educational opportunities afforded to subgroups of its students who can be left behind in a (still) male-dominated society, which also has the enduring perception of being racially homogeneous. The next section will focus briefly on three subgroups of students who are perceived to fare less well in Japanese schools. The list differs little from some other countries: children from poorer homes, females and students from certain ethnic minority backgrounds.

Japan is a wealthy country and poverty levels are difficult to estimate. Okan and Tsuchiya (1999) reckon that about 8 per cent of Japanese middle-school children live in relative poverty. It is estimated that the retention rates in senior high school are lower for children from families who receive government low-income allowances. These are mainly children who are either from single-parent families or 'newcomers' – new immigrants to Japan, often from South America.

Throughout high school, girls are afforded the same educational opportunities as their male peers. In addition, around 50 per cent of both male and female students proceed to tertiary education (Japan Statistical Yearbook 2004). However, this figure masks differences in the opportunities afforded to female students in higher education: for example, they are more likely to opt for less prestigious two-year junior college courses rather than a four-year university degree. Furthermore, they remain under-represented in Japan's elite universities and have restricted opportunities in the labour market, particularly with regard to high-status employment (Okan and Tsuchiya 1999). The main reason for this remains embedded in Japan's working culture, where the long hours and job transfers that those with long-term career prospects are expected to undertake still make it difficult for a woman to combine a career and family life. According to Okan and Tsuchiya, girls' educational qualifications still only have 'symbolic value' and they are unable to 'translate their academic achievements into rewards in post-school life in the way that boys can'.

Japan is still considered a relatively homogeneous country, with a low proportion of ethnic minorities (Japan Statistics Bureau 2002). One consequence of this is that students from minority backgrounds are generally not well catered for in Japanese schools, which tend to assume that all their students are Japanese and have knowledge of the language and culture (Tsuneyoshi 2000; Okan and Tsuchiya 1999). In 2002, there were approximately 1,852,000 registered 'foreigners' in Japan – an increase from 1,075,000 in 1990. The largest minority group are immigrants from Korea and China, although in 2002 there were 268,000 Brazilians and an increasing number of immigrants from the Philippines (Japan Statistical Yearbook 2004). Of course, these figures only include people who are registered, and so exclude the increasing numbers of foreign workers who have entered Japan illegally.

As mentioned above, the largest minority group are Korean, and around 80 per cent of Korean students are enrolled in Japanese schools (the remainder may attend Korean schools, in particular those run along lines similar to the North Korean system). Those who attend Japanese schools often remain un-noticed as being 'foreign', as they may be physically unrecognizable from Japanese students, and some may choose to keep their Korean identity hidden for fear of prejudice (Okan and Tsuchiya 1999). Because there is no national testing system in Japan, nationwide data on the achievement of Korean children does not exist. What little data is available is at the prefecture (or district) level, and suggests that Korean children fare less well overall than Japanese children in school. For example, in Kyoto around 90 per cent of Korean children proceed to senior high school; the figure for Japanese students is over 95 per cent (Okan and Tsuchiya 1999). An increase in the number of students from South America, who often do not have even basic skills in the Japanese language, has also presented problems for schools, and these overseas students now occupy a strata the very bottom of the academic achievement hierarchy.

We therefore have an alternative account of the school system in

Japan, one that characterizes it as neither an 'academic paradise' nor an 'examination hell'. That there are intense pressures on Japanese young people to perform well in examinations may well be the case, but allegations that this has resulted in the 'self-destruction of the Japanese education system' (Yoneyama 1999, 20) are simply not backed up by empirical evidence: for example, suicide rates for young people in Japan are relatively stable and differ little to those for young people in America. The second enduring myth about Japanese schooling – that is it a rigid autocratic system – has also been questioned. Researchers who work in Japanese schools praise the flexibility and stability of a system that is able to resist the quick-fix reforms of politicians and at the same time endeavour to educate the whole child. Like many other countries, Japan has its own groups of disadvantaged students. Here, inequalities that persist in Japanese society as a whole have found themselves, as in so many other countries, becoming magnified in the school system.

Summary

In the last two chapters, we have considered two sides of the underachievement debate as it is used to describe the relative failure of the school system in three countries. By drawing examples from these different national contexts, we have sought to demonstrate that the underachievement debate is anything but clear.

In the United Kingdom, recent relatively high performance in international comparative tests by some students has led to accusations of a long tail of underachievement by many others, usually students from poorer homes. However, we have shown that scores on the recent PISA tests indicate that, rather than being highly segregated, the school system in the UK is among the most equitable in Europe, with the achievement of students from poorer homes – although lagging behind that of their peers – nevertheless world class. We have also looked at New Labour's policies for the reform of the education system, and the impact that this mix of high-stakes testing and accountability is having on raising standards in schools, in particular through their (so far) only modestly successful Excellence in Cities programme. Some of the flaws in the theoretical model that underpins New Labour's brand of standards-driven reform have also been described.

Just like the UK, the USA has also developed its own educational 'crisis account'; and just like the UK, it has employed a mixture of high-stakes testing and school accountability in an effort to drive up standards. However, reviewing the evidence for the apparent underachievement of

American school children has found little evidence of falling standards. Rather, it has pointed to the existence of very definite achievement gaps between the performance of students from black and Hispanic backgrounds and that of their white peers. Although these students are improving at a faster rate than their white peers, their relatively lower achievement appears to be compounded by inequities in the structure of schooling, such as unequal school funding. Recent legislation in the form of the No Child Left Behind act, although praiseworthy, appears to offer little by way of solution, and instead may result in large numbers of these students attending otherwise excellent schools which now may be labelled as failing.

The third country we looked at was Japan. Here the underachievement account is very different to that in the UK and the USA. Japan is perhaps unique in that it has developed reputations of both underachievement and overachievement, which characterize Japan as both an 'academic paradise' and an 'examination hell'. The first perspective has come from Japan's ongoing success in international comparative tests and the resulting policy borrowing attempts from other less academically successful nations (and the USA in particular) who wish to emulate Japanese success. The second account can be seen as a reaction to that success by (mainly foreign) researchers who question the high levels of suicide, violence and bullying that they see as being a direct consequence of a high-pressure, rigid and autocratic school system. The reality is somewhere in between. There are concerns in Japan over bullying and violence in schools, but the suicide rate among young people is no worse than in the USA. The school system, although highly centralized, can be flexible and is known for its focus on the 'whole child', particularly at the elementary stages. Of course, there are low achievers in Japan's schools, just as there are in schools across the world. But there appears to be little empirical basis for claims that Japanese schools have worse levels of bullying and violence than schools in the USA.

We have also considered the contribution of international comparative tests to national 'crisis accounts' of falling standards in schools, as well as their usefulness for those interested in policy-borrowing. Frequently, the results of these tests have been used to form international league tables of school effectiveness, rather than to offer us a serious comparative assessment of what actually works in school. According to Nelson (2003), the efforts of researchers to find cross-national relationships between instructional variables and student achievement have, so far, yielded few results. Any relationships that have been uncovered are difficult to translate into direct implications for policy and practice. In fact, Barker (2002) suggests that the failure to discover simple cross-national relationships should send a clear message about the need to avoid the types of policy borrowing strategies that often accompany the publication of results from international comparative tests. This might encourage countries to look beyond simple rankings of success and avoid searching for quick-fix responses to perceived shortcomings in national school systems, and instead to focus on understanding the interactions between variables such as curriculum, resource distribution and accountability, and their impact on student achievement.

From Chapters 2 and 3, it should be apparent that the underachievement discourse, rather than presenting a clear description of one nation's academic performance relative to another, is anything but clear. What we do see is that countries appear proficient in developing their own 'crisis accounts' of failure in their schools, and as a result frequently turn to other, apparently more successful nations, in order to cherry pick the best educational practice. However, the reality is perhaps more complex: not only is it unrealistic to simply transplant one successful educational initiative from one country to another without paying considerable regard to the educational and social contexts, but it is also possible that commentators may be too hasty in labelling schools and societies as failing simply on the basis of examination outcomes – something which we see all too often in commentaries on the underachievement discourse, and which can also be compounded by a resistance, both political and from the media, to hearing good news.

However, considerable inequities do still exist within school systems, as has been seen, for example, by the achievement gaps between white and black/Hispanic students in the USA. In the next two chapters the claims and counter-claims for the underachievement of these different groups of students are considered.

CHAPTER 4

Failing boys and 'moral panics'

The gap between the best and worst performers in our system actually widens as they go through education; and it is both significantly wider and more closely related to socio-economic status in this country than anywhere else.

(DfES 2004, 15)

So far, we have considered the underachievement debate from an international perspective. Its importance in influencing national education policy-making has been established, and some of the contradictions and difficulties which surround national 'crisis accounts' of achievement have been highlighted. In this chapter, the focus is on what is perhaps the most widely used application of the term 'underachievement', that of the individual: and, in particular, the influence of sex, ethnicity and social class on school performance.

Since the publication of national school league tables in 1992 and the formalization of the National Standards Framework in 1994, monitoring the performance of the country's schools has almost become a national pastime. The decision by the Welsh Assembly Government to abolish the publication of school league tables and to limit the scope of National Curriculum testing in Wales (*The Times Education Supplement* 2004) suggests that perhaps things may be changing, but for now it seems that, in England at least, the standards-driven accountability of the present system is here to stay.

While the concept of underachievement is key to many people's understanding of the need to raise standards in school, the focus of the debate has shifted slightly in recent years. This has been subtle but has switched from being on underachieving boys to underachieving *working class* boys; from the underachievement of ethnic minority students to the underachievement of *certain* ethnic minority students, and from a failing nation to a nation successful apart from a long tail of underachievement. This slight refinement of the debate should perhaps be welcomed on the grounds that it reflects an awareness of the problems we encounter in our understanding of what it is that we actually mean by 'underachievement'.

As we have seen in the previous two chapters, alternative accounts of underachievement can exist at national levels, and the story is little different when the focus is on the achievement sweep of groups of students. In these two chapters, we review both sides of the underachievement debate. We begin with the evidence and explanations that support the notion of large groups of students from different groups, in particular male students and those from certain ethnic minority backgrounds, underachieving in school. Before we review this, it needs to be emphasized that although research into school achievement often focuses on a wide range of factors that may or may not contribute to school success – such as family background, sex, ethnicity, personality, school and country – what constitutes success often has a narrow focus relating to either the number of 'good' passes an individual gains at GCSE, or the percentage of pupils who achieve the widely publicized National Targets and/or Key Skill competencies. Unfortunately, this is not the whole picture, and the other aims of education that can help to create well-rounded citizens are often sidelined. In the present educational climate, which seems wedded to the 'allocation of success and failure' (Slee and Weiner 1998, 3), it is performance data that is seen to constitute high or low achievement, and it is within this framework that success in school is now constructed. With this in mind, we begin by reviewing some of the evidence and explanations for the underachievement of boys in British schools.

Sex and underachievement

> Underachieving boys are one of the most disturbing problems facing the education system.
>
> (Woodhead, cited in Dean 1998)

This statement, from the former Chief Inspector of Schools, lent its voice to the plethora of media headlines that have bemoaned the 'failure' of boys in our nation's schools from the mid-1990s onwards. Headlines such as: 'Why teenage boys think success is sad' (*The Times Educational Supplement*, 18 August 1995), 'Girls sweep the board in GCSEs' (*Mail on Sunday*, 1996, 23), 'Outclassed' (*The Times*, 30 March 1996), and 'Girls trounce the boys in examination league table' (*The Times*, 3 September 1994), helped establish underachievement, and male underachievement in particular, as the 'predominant discourse in education in the 1990s' (Weiner *et al.* 1997, 620; see also Salisbury 1996; Arnot *et al.* 1999; Chaplain 2000). The underachievement debate was further defined in 1998 when, in a speech at the 11th International Conference for School Effectiveness and Improvement, the former School Standards Minister, Stephen Byers, used the term 'laddish' to describe the behaviour of boys in school. He argued that boys' 'laddish' anti-school attitudes were impeding their progress at school.

This 'moral panic' (Cohen 1972) surrounding the academic achievement of the nation's boys has come about largely because examination results suggest that the performance of girls, especially at GCSE, has overtaken that of boys. Few headlines commend the improvements in the achievement levels of girls, and the fact that the attainment of all pupils has risen steadily over the last 30 years is barely mentioned unless it is to decry falling standards and a 'dumbing down' of the school curriculum (Smithers and Ward 2004). In short, boys have fallen behind in this crude measure of success and the dominant view is that something has to be done about it. Numerous feminist researchers have drawn attention to this 'backlash' (see, for example, Epstein *et al.* 1999; Salisbury 1996), and have made it clear that any attempts to raise the achievement of boys must not lose sight of the work done over the last three decades to improve the lot of girls in school.

The next section looks more closely at the problem of 'underachievement' as it relates specifically to the performance of boys in school; it considers both the evidence and the explanations that are often given for their relatively poor achievement in school examinations.

Evidence for the underachievement of boys

Table 4.1 shows the proportions of students who achieve five 'good' GCSE passes, and those who achieve at least a grade C in English language. In both sets of results, the performance of boys is consistently lower than that of girls. Trends such as these are used as evidence for the underachievement of boys relative to girls: according to Arnot *et al.*, 'boys have failed to build upon their performance at the same rate as girls in recent decades, especially in the proportion gaining more than five GCSE A*–C grades' (Arnot *et al.* 1999, 23).

Performance trends such as these are not restricted to GCSE, but instead appear at all ages and in all subject areas. According to Younger *et al.* (2002), in England more girls than boys achieved benchmark levels in National Curriculum Key Stages 2 and 3 English tests in 2001, as well as outperforming boys in the once traditional male subjects of physical

Table 4.1   **GCSE achievements according to gender, England (1996–2003)**

Year	5+ A*–C grade (%)			English (%)		
	Boys	Girls	Difference	Boys	Girls	Difference
2003	48	58	10	52	68	16
2002	46	57	11	52	67	15
2001	45	55	10	51	66	15
2000	44	55	11	51	66	15
1999	43	53	10	50	66	16
1998	41	51	10	48	64	16
1997	40	50	10	46	63	17
1996	40	49	9	47	64	17

Source: DfES (1996–2003a)

education, design and technology, mathematics and science. Additional research on patterns of achievement in Wales by Salisbury (1996), and in Scotland by Turner *et al.* (1995), add to a picture of many boys leaving school with poorer academic qualifications than their female counterparts. In 1996, the Equal Opportunities Commission published their analysis of external assessment across all the Key Stages for England and Wales. At GCSE, the trends were similar to those in Table 4.1: 'girls were more successful than boys (with respect to the number of A*–C grades) or as broadly successful in almost all major subjects' (EOC 1996, 6). The Commission acknowledged that the gap between boys and girls has been 'roughly the same' for several years, but suggest that this gap became greater than when the GCSE was introduced in 1988 and note that subsequent changes to the GCSE courses, including the reduction of coursework, have failed to reduce the superior performance of girls.

Explanations for male underachievement

According to Reed, focusing on male underachievement is not a case of debating whether this underachievement exists, because 'its reality is a measure of its productivity in shaping educational policies and practices' (1998, 60). Indeed, there are a plethora of explanations for the apparent 'underachievement' of boys: some of the most prevalent are discussed here.

Changing masculinities

It has been argued that there are innate, natural-born differences between the sexes: boys are more likely to suffer from oxygen starvation at birth, they have poorer verbal reasoning skills, they mature later than girls, their parents do not talk to them as much as they do to their sisters, and so on (Arnold 1997; Cohen 1998). However, according to some authors, these theories are based on 'crude versions of cognitive psychology' and have little basis in published research (Reed 1998, 61).

Mahony (1998, 42), on the other hand, links much of the 'hysteria' surrounding the underachieving youth or 'public burden number 1' to a fear among the male elite that men will lose ground to women in the workforce. The collapse in the post-war boom of heavy industry and the replacement (particularly in some working class homes) of the male with the female as the main family bread-winner has led to what some researchers would call a change in the gender regime of these communities, and is cited as another explanation for the poor performance of young men in our schools (Connell 1994; Arnold 1997; Jackson 1998; Spendlove 2001; Yates 1997).

The influence of the peer group appears to be central to the role boys adopt in school. There are many examples in the literature of boys refusing to work hard in order to avoid being seen as 'gay' or 'spoffs' (Connell 1994; Measor 1999) – Mac an Ghaill's (1989) so-called 'academic achievers' – and this behaviour is seen even in the primary school, where no label is worse than that of being called a 'girl' (Renold 2001). As Epstein points out, 'the rejection of the perceived "femininity" of academic work is simultaneously a defence against the charge of being gay' (1998, 97). Stanworth has described the 'myriad of subtle ways' (1983, 14) in which the school community seeks to instil society's gender stereotypes on its pupils. Connell (1994) has also written about the 'hidden curriculum' which pressurizes males to conform to masculine stereotypes or face being rejected from the peer group: 'when boys try to do their best they get called names and that . . . it's important to keep in with your friends' (from an interview with a Year 9 'achieving boy', cited in Smith 1998).

In response to concerns about male underachievement, a plethora of strategies and initiatives have emerged. These range from experiments with single-sex education to networks of sports clubs encouraging failing students to do better in school (for example, Henry 2001; Arthur 2004; DfES 2004d), and the efficacy of some of these strategies will be considered in the book's final chapter. However, whatever strategies are devised by schools to raise the attainment of boys, it is important not to fall into the trap of reinforcing masculinity in a way that creates and perpetuates an anti-school ethos, and which in turn might precipitate increased disaffection. The problem should not be seen as the reverse of that in the 1970s and 1980s, when concern focused on the educational success of girls.

Assessment and the school curriculum

Although the Task Group on Assessment and Testing (TGAT) did not define gender bias in their formulation of the new GCSE, it recommended that assessment instruments were reviewed regularly for its presence (DES 1987). Nevertheless, Murphy (1988) has found several ways in which gender bias is very much a feature of National Curriculum assessment. The manner in which genders perceive and answer questions is different – boys in isolation, girls more in context; girls tend to express themselves in a more reflective way than boys – and this may give them an advantage in subjects like English and the humanities but less so in science and maths; likewise the types of questions are perceived differently – with boys generally preferring more multiple-choice styled responses.

Millard (1997a) explores the notion of a gendered curriculum where the non-fiction reading practices generally preferred by boys have no place. She sees this as disadvantaging boys in the long term, as the narrative reading practices encouraged by the school curriculum have little relevance in the workplace. However, research into teacher and pupil perceptions and preferences in English suggests another perspective. In her questionnaire study of 300 pupils and 98 teachers, Myhill (1999) asked pupils to rate their enjoyment of different methods of working in English. Her findings point to the existence of fewer gender differences in English than were previously thought. For example, boys and girls equally felt enjoyment in doing narrative and IT based work in English, and also enjoyed reading more or less the same type of fiction and non-fiction. Instead, it was the teachers who held gender-stereotyped views about pupil interests in the subject. Interestingly, complaints by teachers that the 1999 Key Stage 3 English paper question on H.G. Wells' *War of the Worlds* was too boy-friendly prompted a QCA (Qualifications and Curriculum Authority) analysis of the papers that found that boys did no better than the girls on the question (Cassidy 2000).

One of the most contentious methods of assessment has been coursework. This is seen by some researchers greatly to favour the hardworking methodical girl (Arnold 1997; Murphy 1988; Pirie 2001; Sammons 1995; Spendlove 2000; Younger and Warrington 1996), to such an extent that the high coursework element of English was reduced in 1991 in an attempt to reduce girls' lead in the examination stakes. On the other hand, Gorard *et al.* (1999) claim that there is little evidence for the perception that coursework gives girls the advantage. A review on behalf of the Qualification and Curriculum Assessment Authority in Wales provides further support for this view (ACCAC 1999). While acknowledging the complexity of the issue, it notes that the reduction of the coursework element in English did not affect the difference in girls' and boys' performance. Coursework did make a valid contribution to a student's overall mark, but this contribution is greatest at the lower GCSE grades – where many of the 'underachieving' group may be found.

Underlying each of the above assertions is the assumption that our assessment system is gender-neutral and that boys and girls *ought to* achieve the same levels in school examinations. This is a key issue when considering gender equality in examination outcomes. If researchers are writing about how gender differences are encouraged by social conditioning (Millard 1997), how they can be reinforced by schools (Delamont 1990) or, more controversially, how they can arise from innate differences in the structure and development of the brain (Gurian 2001), is it still realistic to cling to the notion that, despite everything that happens in schools, the examination system should somehow remain gender-neutral? As we have seen above, one important example of this is the acquisition of literacy skills and the resulting differential performance of boys and girls in English and language examinations. Throughout school, research tells us that girls are the keener readers who are more likely to be 'devoted' to their books (Millard 1997), and this is confirmed by large-scale international surveys like PISA (OECD 2001). When boys do read, their favoured genres – action and adventure, and non-fiction – can leave them disadvantaged in the school curriculum, where narrative accounts that emphasize personal responses are favoured. However, although the English curriculum may well disadvantage boys, there is little correlation between achievement in English examinations and success in later life (Millard 1997). On the other hand, because success in English examinations can act as a key to education and employment opportunities, the disadvantage that boys have in acquiring the 'right' literacy skills can be compounded.

The classroom, the teacher, teaching and learning

Claims about the feminization of the school curriculum have come hand-in-hand with criticism of female teachers for imposing female values on pupils; but according to Delamont (1999), these claims have a long history and little basis in fact. Nevertheless, they are reworked as an explanation for the relatively poor performance of boys and in calls for an increase in the number of male teachers in our schools (Platten 1999; Hayes 2002; see also Mills *et al.* 2004).

The different behaviour and learning cultures of boys and girls is well documented (for example, in Barker 1995; Holden 1993; Measor 1999). Boys are frequently considered to be 'more concerned with preserving an image of reluctant involvement or disengagement' (Younger and

Warrington 1996, 303) while girls are increasingly portrayed as being 'ideal students'. In the classroom it is the boys who command the 'greater share' of the teachers' attention and time compared with the girls. Boys can bring another agenda into the classroom, asserting themselves as jokers and as risk-takers, with a noisy approach to their work and a dislike of the tedium of writing. As a result, they are frequently the focus of classroom activity, whereas the girls are marginalized on the edges. Some researchers claim that this behaviour has a detrimental effect on the boys' learning; boys react against work they see as inappropriate and find open-ended tasks involving discussion or collaboration difficult. Francis (1999; 2000) offers a different perspective on this behaviour. In her observations of boys, she noted that their behaviour often provided a 'welcome relief' for both teacher and pupil. Many of these pupils were extremely endearing, not loutish, and she found little evidence that their behaviour had a detrimental effect on either their learning or that of the rest of the class.

That pupils themselves have a strong sense of the gender dynamics of the classroom, and in particular of the way the teacher responds to different groups of pupils, has also become apparent (for example see Francis 2000; Smith 1998; Stanworth 1983; Younger *et al.* 1999). In their interview and observational study of pupils and teachers in comprehensive and selective secondary schools, Younger *et al.* (1999) found several differences between the way some teachers *thought* they treated the boys and girls in their class and what was borne out through classroom observation. Their study concluded that boys and girls *were* treated differently in class: boys were reprimanded more, received more direct questioning from teachers and responded more frequently to open-ended questioning. This ran contrary to the perception of some teachers, who believed they treated pupils equally and that gender differences were not an issue in their classroom. The authors also found support for the boys' view that they received more negative attention than girls. However, most of the observations in the study, in particular those which related to the disproportionate amount of teachers' attention that was focused on the boys, related to classroom management issues and not to the learning process. There was, in fact, little evidence from these observations to suggest that boys were given more support than girls in the learning process.

Thus, there are three dominant explanations for the apparent underachievement of boys in schools: the conflict of masculinity in contemporary society; the curriculum and its assessment; and finally the every-day experience of both students and teachers within the classroom. However, the complexity of the gender debate is apparent from a consideration of examination results. For example, the percentages of young men and women achieving no GCSE qualifications at age 16 are similar (approximately 4 per cent and 6 per cent respectively in 2001/02), as are the proportions of pupils gaining an A-level pass across all subjects (90 per cent for boys and 92 per cent for girls in 2001/02). Girls achieve consistently higher results than boys in English, while in mathematics and science there is a 'notable shift' towards both groups achieving similar results (Arnot *et al.* 1999, 17), yet the debate is frequently reduced to the binary notion of underachieving boys and successful girls.

This dichotomous approach to understanding underachievement is not only used in discussions of gender differentiation: it has a strong presence in the underachievement literature when the apparent underachievement of students from ethnic minority backgrounds and from working class homes is examined. The evidence presented and explanations given for the apparent underachievement of pupils from both groups is the focus of the remaining sections of this chapter.

Ethnic minority students and underachievement

According to Gillborn and Youdell (2000), the widespread media attention given to the underachievement of boys has failed to address the real issue: that it is pupils from ethnic minority backgrounds who, along with those from the working classes, experience the most pronounced inequalities in our education system. It is on the apparent underachievement of pupils from ethnic minority backgrounds that this chapter now focuses. In particular, it considers some of the explanations for their perceived underachievement, along with the evidence used to reinforce the debate.

In 1985, the Conservative government commissioned a report that examined the response of the education system to ethnic diversity in its schools. Known as the Swann report, this highlighted concerns over the differential performance of pupils from some ethnic minority backgrounds:

> West Indian children as a group are underachieving in our education system and this should be a matter of deep concern not only to all those involved in education but also the whole community.
>
> (DES 1985, 3)

The Swann report stressed the need for a clearer understanding and monitoring of the factors that contribute to the underachievement of ethnic minority pupils, the experiences of these pupils in school and schools' experience of them (DES 1985). However, despite this rhetoric, educational reforms in the 1980s and early 1990s saw an increase in the 'deracialised discourse that effectively removed ethnic diversity from the agenda and glossed over many discriminatory processes' (Gillborn 1998, 718), a trend exemplified by the lack of school and LEA data on the relative performance of these groups of students.

The election of the Labour Government in May 1997, and in particular the publication of the education white paper 'Excellence in schools' (DfEE 1997), with its emphasis on raising the attainment of ethnic minority groups, was seen as an indication that things were to change. This white paper acknowledged the differential achievement of pupils from the various ethnic groups, going so far as to claim that some were underperforming and that the gap in performance was growing; mention was also made of strategies aimed at tackling racial stereotyping and harassment. However, according to Gillborn (1998), the reality was very different. The Government's failure to standardize methods for differentiating between ethnic groups or to make a full commitment to Section 11 funding (raising finances to support English language tuition), and its continued emphasis on selection and setting, placed at a disadvantage those from lower socioeconomic and minority backgrounds, and suggest only a partial shift away from the Conservative's 'colour-blind rhetoric' (Gillborn and Youdell 2000, 725), so giving little to indicate that young people from minority backgrounds would be better served by a new Labour government.

In 2003, the government published its consultation document on raising the achievement of ethnic minority pupils (DfES 2003). 'Aiming High' sought to address the unequal educational opportunities afforded to many students from ethnic minority communities. Alongside 'Schools Achieving Success' and '14–19: Extending opportunities, raising standards', this was the latest in the government's initiatives to raise standards in schools (DfES 2003). The document advocates developing a whole-school approach to raising achievement, with an emphasis on strong leadership and effective teaching and learning, as well as an ethos of respect and clearer strategies for addressing racism and poor behaviour. In addition, continued support for schools would be provided through the Excellence in Cities programme, and investment would come through the £155 million Ethnic Minority Achievement Grant. Central to these proposals was concern over the differential achievement of pupils from ethnic minority backgrounds. For example, while Chinese and Indian students achieve above average GCSE passes, the performance of black and Pakistani pupils in particular is characterized by a 'long tail of underachievement' (DfES 2003, 1). The following section considers some of the evidence that has underlined these concerns.

The evidence for an achievement gap

Nearly one in eight students in school in England and Wales comes from an ethnic minority background, a figure that is projected to rise to around one in five by 2010 (DfES 2003). Most of these students live in the major conurbations, with around 40 per cent of them attending school in London. The relatively lower academic achievement of these students is often presented as evidence for their underachievement. Unfortunately, longitudinal national-level data on their achievement has only recently started to be collected. From January 2002, schools in England and Wales have been required to provide information on individual pupil characteristics for the Pupil Level Annual School Census (PLASC) (DfES 2004c). This means that for the first time pupil attainment data can be mapped onto student characteristics such as ethnicity, receipt of free school meals, and English language proficiency. Reviewing the data for the attainment of students from different ethnic groups in the core subjects of English, mathematics and science, as well as at GCSE, reveals the extent to which the performance of students from the various ethnic groups can differ (Table 4.2).

Table 4.2 **Percentage of students achieving Key Stage 3 Level 5 or above in the core subjects according to ethnicity in 2002**

Ethnic Group	English %	Mathematics %	Science %
White	70	72	70
Mixed	69	69	67
White/Black Caribbean	62	62	60
White/Black African	69	68	68
White/Asian	78	78	76
Other Mixed Background	71	71	68
Asian	66	66	59
Indian	77	79	72
Pakistani	57	55	47
Bangladeshi	58	57	48
Other Asian Background	70	75	69
Black	56	54	51
Black Caribbean	56	53	51
Black African	56	55	50
Other Black Background	58	55	54
Chinese	80	90	82
Other Ethnic Background	59	64	58
Unclassified[1]	63	67	65
All Pupils	69	71	68

[1]Includes information refused or not obtained.
Source: DfES (2004c)

While the proportion of all students reaching the expected level in each of the core subjects has decreased from Key Stage 2, students from the ethnic minority groups within the black category appear to perform consistently below the national average. For example, at Key Stage 3 mathematics, 53 per cent of black Caribbean students, 55 per cent of black African, 55 per cent of other black pupils and 62 per cent of Mixed white/black Caribbean pupils achieved the expected level, compared to 71 per cent nationally. A similar profile is apparent for students from the Bangladeshi and Pakistani communities. On the other hand, Chinese and Indian pupils, as well as those of Mixed white/Asian heritage tend to perform above the national average at all Key Stages.

Prior to the establishment of the PLASC database, the main source of longitudinal examination performance data for students from different ethnic backgrounds has been the Youth Cohort Study (YCS). The YCS is a longitudinal study that collects data from a nationally representative sample of young people during the two years following the end of their compulsory schooling. It is unique in presenting data on pupils from a range of ethnic, social and geographical backgrounds, although the data available is not extensive and discriminates poorly between the different ethnic groups (DfEE 1996). Figure 4.1 charts the trend in performance for 16-year-old students from the main ethnic groups who achieved five or more good GCSE passes between 1992 and 2002. The data shows that while the trend for all groups is towards improved performance, students from Pakistani, black and Bangladeshi groups achieve below the levels of students from white and Indian groups.

Figure 4.1   **Students achieving 5+ A*–C GCSE passes according to ethnic group (1992–2002)**

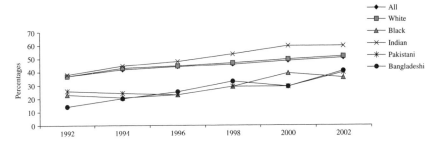

Source: Youth Cohort Study, DfES 2003b

Trends such as these would seem to confirm earlier work by Gillborn and Gipps (1996) and Gillborn and Mirza (2000), whose Ofsted commissioned reviews into the achievement of pupils from ethnic minority backgrounds suggest the following trends in their performance in secondary school:

- regardless of ethnic origin, pupils from advantaged backgrounds achieve the highest grades;
- although there have been widespread improvements in GCSE performances, not all ethnic groups have shared equally in this improvement: for example, African-Caribbean pupils (boys in particular) have not made the same amount of progress;
- in secondary school, Asian pupils make better progress than white pupils from the same socioeconomic group, although there are variations in this trend within the Asian category; and
- studies outside London have shown that white pupils leave school with the highest average qualifications.

The above discussion has suggested that the pattern of ethnic minority achievement in school is anything but clear: while the general trend for all groups is one of improvement, it is apparent that not all groups have shared equally in this success. However, analysing trends in the performance of students from ethnic minority backgrounds is further complicated both by difficulties in separating the effect of the interaction between social class and ethnic group, and by inaccuracies in the methodologies of studies carried out in this area. These are issues we return to in Chapter 5.

Exclusion rates and ethnic background

Figures for school exclusions present further evidence for the under-achievement of students from ethnic minority backgrounds, and of those from the African-Caribbean community in particular. Research by the Social Exclusion Unit (SEU 1998), based on data from the 1991 census, showed that African-Caribbean children were six times more likely to be excluded from school, and that 16 per cent of pupils who were excluded came from an ethnic minority background, nearly half of whom were African-Caribbean (who totalled only 1% of the school population; see also Learner 2001). These excluded pupils often came from single-parent families, appeared to be of average or above average ability, and were not usually considered to have been disruptive during their early school career. However, African-Caribbean pupils were no more likely than other pupils to be persistent truants, suggesting that they were not disaffected with school.

Research by Ofsted in 1996 agreed with the findings of the SEU, and in its survey of 39 schools in 16 LEAs found that more boys than girls were excluded along with a 'disproportionate number of black pupils'

(Ofsted 1996, 6). There has been little research into the underlying factors for these exclusion rates. Gillborn (1997) cites a survey among LEA Directors of Education revealing that while 8 per cent thought the increase in rates of exclusion were due to 'poorer discipline', 42 per cent blamed the trend on increased competition between schools and the threat of poor league table positions.

More recent figures on school exclusions would appear to confirm these earlier trends, although it is important to note that the proportion of all students excluded from school has decreased steadily over the last few years, with some of the largest falls in exclusion rates being among students from the various black ethnic groups (Table 4.3).

Table 4.3   **Permanent exclusions[4] by ethnic group in England (1998–2002)**

	1998	1999	2000	2001	2002
Total	0.19	0.16	0.13	0.13	0.14
White	0.18	0.15	0.12	0.13	0.14
Black	0.58	0.44	0.34	0.31	0.30
Black Caribbean	0.77	0.60	0.46	0.38	0.42
Black African	0.30	0.21	0.17	0.17	0.16
Black Other	0.58	0.50	0.37	0.39	0.36
Asian	0.10	0.07	0.06	0.05	0.07
Indian	0.07	0.04	0.03	0.03	0.03
Pakistani	0.13	0.10	0.07	0.06	0.10
Bangladeshi	0.10	0.07	0.08	0.07	0.11
Chinese	0.05	0.03	0.01	0.02	0.03
Other Ethnic Group	0.26	0.25	0.20	0.15	0.20

Source: Statistics in Education (DFES 2003e)

[4] The number of permanent exclusions of compulsory school age and above as expressed as a percentage of the number (headcount) of all pupils of compulsory school age and above in each ethnic group in primary, secondary and special schools.

As we have seen, the most recent school performance data reveals the existence of an achievement gap in the performance of students from different ethnic backgrounds, coupled with concerns over the relatively high exclusion rates for students from the black community. However, although many accounts of underachievement do distinguish between the various ethnic minority communities, concern exists over the reliability of these, and in particular over the way the accounts have disregarded proportional analysis of trends in achievement scores (White and Gorard 1999). These are issues discussed in Chapter 5; for now, we consider some of the explanations that are given for the underachievement of students from these communities.

Explanations for ethnic minority underachievement

There has been concern over the underachievement of students from ethnic minority backgrounds since the 1960s. Then, attention focused on the performance of students of Caribbean and Pakistani origin, who were not only being outperformed in the curriculum but were also more likely to be excluded from mainstream education. Explanations focused on home background factors, language and cultural problems, and low teacher expectations (Tomlinson 1983). This concern has continued to the present day, when some research has suggested that, despite higher levels of attainment by all young people, there has been an increased divergence between the attainment of ethnic minority groups both at secondary level and in higher education (Modood *et al.* 1997). One ongoing area of concern focuses on the role that schools and teachers play in reinforcing racial stereotypes and in failing to tackle the underachievement of students from minority ethnic backgrounds. Some of the research evidence for this is now considered in more detail.

The Macpherson report on the inquiry into the death of Stephen Lawrence made four specific recommendations for education: that the National Curriculum be amended to incorporate themes of diversity and the prevention of racism; that schools and LEAs develop strategies to address issues of racism in schools; that such strategies be reviewed by Ofsted; and finally that community and local initiatives be developed to promote cultural diversity and prevent racism (in Gillborn and Mirza 2000). The Ofsted document 'Raising the attainment of minority ethnic students', published shortly after the Macpherson report, suggested that schools and LEAs lacked direction when it came to addressing inequalities in attainment of students from ethnic minority groups: 'Despite some pockets of sound practice, many schools and LEAs are not nearly as effective as they should be in tackling the underachievement of minority ethnic groups' (Ofsted 1999, 54).

Indeed, many commentators have criticized schools for failing to address the racism and harassment experienced by some minority pupils, with Ofsted (1999, 4) going as far as to label schools as 'institutionally racist' (although this label has been dismissed as 'institutionally lazy' by a prominent Asian writer, who instead has called for a 'hard and scientifically passionate examination' [Dhondy 1999, 15] of the causes of the apparent failure of some pupils from certain minority groups).

In trying to explain the reasons for the disenchantment of some ethnic minority pupils with the education system, Gillborn and Youdell (2000) point to several factors inherent in what they see as the 'A–C economy' of schools, which specifically disadvantages pupils from minority groups.

They claim that in order to preserve a high league-table position, schools use selection, ability-testing and streaming as a way of maximizing the number of pupils who pass the all-important 5 or more A★–C GCSE grades threshold. In doing so, Gillborn and Youdell claim that schools are not providing all pupils with equal access to the curriculum, because in some cases students are encouraged to sit fewer GCSE examinations. They argue that strategies involving streaming effectively bar pupils for whom English is an additional language from the top sets. Ability-testing, which has predictors based on 'white' norms, can place ethnic minority pupils at a disadvantage, and this has a knock-on effect on option choices and access to the higher-tier examination papers. Thus, black pupils were more likely than their white peers to sit the foundation as opposed to the higher tier GCSE papers.

These findings are similar to those from earlier studies of multi-ethnic inner-city schools conducted in the mid to late 1980s (Mac an Ghaill 1988; Gillborn 1990). These authors sought to highlight the injustices of the education system for pupils from minority backgrounds: 'the education system is part of a wider system of constraints which, often unwittingly, helps to maintain blacks (both Asian and African-Caribbean pupils) in a position of structural subordination' (Mac an Ghaill 1988, 3). In this rather depressing account, Mac an Ghaill describes a racism which was 'prevalent throughout the white staff' (1988, 61), manifesting itself in racist stereotyping which identified Asian students as high achievers who enjoyed the material advantages of the higher sets, and black students as trouble-makers, relegated to the middle and lower sets with less experienced teachers and lower expectations. Gillborn has also commented on the inherently racist actions of some white teachers: 'Afro-Caribbean pupils were in a situation where their very ethnicity meant that they were likely to experience conflict with white teachers no matter how conscientiously they approached their work' (1990, 200).

The recommendations of the Macpherson report and the subsequent Race Relations Act 2000 prompted the DfES to draw up a Statutory Code of Practice for schools and to provide detailed guidance on how to meet the requirements of this new piece of legislation. In addition, the consultation document 'Aiming High' (DfES 2003) specifically sets out a whole-school approach to raising achievement levels whereby 'lessons are planned and delivered as effectively as possible and teachers are equipped to reflect the diverse cultures and identities of communities represented in their schools through their lessons' (DfES 2003, 15). From September 2002, all newly qualified teachers have had to demonstrate that they have high expectations for all students and that they can plan and manage lessons that cater for students from a range of backgrounds. In addition, through a combination of continued professional development for teachers, an increase in the numbers of new teachers from ethnic minority backgrounds, and an improvement of interactions between schools and local communities, the new proposals seek to address many of the concerns raised about the experiences of ethnic minority students in schools.

This section has considered the patterns of ethnic minority attainment in the context of the underachievement discourse. Although the patterns of achievement across different ethnic groups are anything but clear, much research has been carried out into the experiences these pupils have in our schools. Many of these findings make depressing reading, as they suggest that some pupils from ethnic minority backgrounds are disadvantaged and discriminated against in school, and that this continues once they leave compulsory education. However, some of these reports have been contested on methodological grounds by other writers, who suggest that on occasions data has been unrepresentative or ambiguously interpreted. These are important issues, as they have a profound impact on how we understand the nature of any underachievement of these groups of pupils. They are discussed further in the next chapter.

Underachievement of children from poorer homes

'. . . it is poverty, it is the relationship of people from poor backgrounds in deprived circumstances that really is the key to underachievement. Would you agree with that?'

(House of Commons 2003)

The correlative relationship between socioeconomic status and educational achievement has become accepted as an almost universal truth. However, as an area of research, it has become subsumed by a more recent focus on variations in achievement according to gender and ethnicity. Concern by mainly feminist researchers during the 1970s and 1980s into differential learning outcomes and educational opportunities for girls and the ensuing 'moral panics' of the 1990s into male underachievement, coupled with concern about the achievement and increasing exclusion rates and disaffection of students from ethnic minority communities, has moved research into the attainment of working-class students to the margins.

Perhaps this new emphasis is unsurprising – teachers can easily differentiate between the boys and girls in their class, or between students from visible ethnic minority groups. With the current emphasis on raising standards, any differential attainment or behaviours among these groups is much more visible and open to comment. It is a lot more difficult for teachers to identify the students in their classes who come from poorer homes, particularly in the secondary school where one might conceivably teach well over 120 students a day and be less familiar with an individual's home circumstances than would be a colleague in the primary sector. As a consequence, trends in the performance and learning behaviours and trajectories of this group of students might be a lot more difficult to determine. A more cynical reason for the replacement of poverty as a key focus of educational comparisons is simply that there is little schools or society can do about whether one is born female or black. On the other hand, there are clear implications for social justice and equity if academic success is seen to be dependent upon whether or not you come from a home where your parents have never worked.

Evidence for the underachievement of students from poorer homes

According to data from the Youth Cohort Study (YCS), students whose parents were from the highest professional backgrounds are most likely to gain five or more 'good' GCSEs. In 2002, this was achieved by 81 per cent of pupils from professional backgrounds, compared to 32 per cent of those from routine occupational backgrounds (DfES 2003b). Figures from the PLASC database allow the comparison of pupil performance across the Key Stages according to whether or not students receive free school meals (DfES 2004c). Tables 4.4 to 4.6 reveal the extent to which pupils who do receive free school meals lag behind their peers at each Key Stage and in each core subject. For example, at Key Stage 3, fewer than half of students who receive free school meals (FSM) reach benchmark levels, while with students who do not receive free school meals almost three-quarters achieve minimum competency levels. At GCSE, three times as many students who receive free school

Table 4.4   **Proportion of students awarded Key Stage 2 Level 4 or above, according to FSM status**

	English %	Mathematics %	Science %
Non FSM	79	76	89
FSM	54	53	72
Unclassified★	55	53	65
All pupils	75	72	86

★Includes information refused or not obtained
Source: DfES 2004c

Table 4.5   **Proportion of students awarded Key Stage 3 Level 5 or above, according to FSM status**

	English %	Mathematics %	Science %
Non FSM	74	75	74
FSM	44	46	42
Unclassified*	44	48	43
All pupils	69	71	68

*Includes information refused or not obtained
Source: DfES 2004c

Table 4.6   **Achievements at GCSE/GNVQ, according to FSM status**

	5 or more GCSE (A*–C) %	No passes %
Non FSM	55.2	4.1
FSM	24.4	12.2
Unclassified*	0.1	93.3
All pupils	50.7	5.5

*Includes information refused or not obtained
Source: DfES 2004c

meals fail to secure any examination passes when compared with their peers. Monitoring trends across the Key Stages is problematic, but the suggestion that students with free school meals are not making the same amount of progress between Key Stage 2 and 3 as their peers would appear to have some validity.

Explanations for the underachievement of poor students

Monitoring achievement according to socioeconomic status has both conceptual and practical difficulties. Schools rarely record the occupations of their students' parents, and free school meals, the most widely used proxy measure for family poverty, is an imperfect measure of socioeconomic status as it takes no account of families who do not take up their free meal entitlement. Many of the explanations for the relatively poor academic performance of students from poorer homes have focused on family background and composition factors, as well as on parental education levels and their involvement in their child's schooling. There is a long and distinguished research literature on this subject: however, for brevity, an overview of some of the explanations for only two of these factors – underachievement according to family background and parental involvement – are given here.

Family background

Early work by Jencks (1972) suggested that family background was the single most important contributor to success in school, an argument which has prompted a great deal of research focusing on the structural characteristics of families, such as socioeconomic status (SES) and family make-up. Frankel's 1960 study of 'able' boys found that higher achieving students were more likely to come from a higher social class than those he identified as underachieving. These findings are supported by Gold who claimed that 'academic underachievement is no doubt related to SES' (1965, 56). More recent works by Ekstrom *et al.* (1986), Rumberger (1983; 1995) and Paterson (1992) also link low SES to poor achievement and enhanced school drop-out rates.

However, this view is not shared by all researchers: McCall (1992), Raph (1966), White (1982), Whitmore (1980), Mann (1998) and West *et al.* (1998) found little or no link between family SES and school achievement. White, in his review of the literature on this subject, concluded that the traditional and most frequently used measures of SES show only a weak correlation with academic achievement. Paterson also argues that SES is a clumsy term, but one which reminds us that we are not dealing with a single dichotomy of 'working class' and 'middle class'.

The relationship between gender and social class has also received much focus. For example, Arnot *et al.* suggest that while girls have been largely successful in school, 'social class remains a key factor in educational success' (1999, 28). The authors describe how more varied employment opportunities and increased participation in education have presented a 'sea-change in values' for most middle-class girls (1999, 121). However, working-class young women still largely remain 'frustrated' by school and still associate themselves with the traditional pattern of leaving school at 16, getting married and having a family. The same social class inequalities are thought to influence young men: 'class inequalities have been the major factor restricting the majority of boys from achieving access to male elite professions' (1999, 130). The implications of the changing employment climate for the prospects of young working-class boys cannot be underestimated either, as they can no longer expect to follow their fathers into the heavy industry and mining jobs once characteristic of many traditional working-class communities.

Parental involvement

There is a growing body of research into the processes by which family background influences school success, and central to this is the issue of parental involvement. Laureau (1987) and Hughes and Academy (1992) argue that schools are inherently middle-class organizations with corresponding middle-class values; children who are raised in such surroundings are better able to adapt to this environment. It has also been argued that middle-class parents are better equipped to support their children in their studies, and are more able to relate to teachers and the school system. Laureau's large-scale study into the effect of SES on parents' involvement in their children's education found support for this argument. In this study, working-class parents were less likely to read to their children at home, were less familiar with the school curriculum, found interactions with teaching staff awkward, and saw education as the responsibility of the school. In comparison, parents from middle-class backgrounds were more likely to take an active role in their child's education by encouraging them to read at home and closely monitoring their school progress. These parents were more comfortable with informal parent–teacher interactions and viewed education as a partnership between home and the school.

Research by Tett *et al.* (1998) into parental involvement in literacy programmes in Scotland also showed that parents who were of a lower social group had less confidence in their ability to help their children, and were therefore unwilling to participate in school-organized support programmes. This is supported by Stevenson and Barker (1987), who found that better educated mothers were more closely involved in their child's education, and that the children of these 'involved' parents were more likely to succeed at school. Ho and Willms conclude that parental involvement made a 'significant unique contribution to explaining the variation in a child's academic achievement over and above the effects associated with parental background' (1996, 138). They found, however, that family SES had no relationship to the supervision a child received at home and that family background explained only 10 per cent of variation in parental involvement. Nor do Ho and Willms support the notion that working-class parents place less emphasis on school achievement; and this view is supported by Mann's 1998 findings in a study of the impact of working-class mother–daughter relationship on academic achievement.

Summary

This chapter has considered the underachievement debate as it is applied to the performance of three different categories of students: grouped according to their sex, ethnic group and socioeconomic status. Overall, the findings present a rather depressing picture of the state of the British education system, where many leave school with few or no qualifications and large groups of pupils appear to be failing to fulfil their potential. However, while there is seemingly strong evidence in favour of the underachievement discourse, the issue is not so straightforward. The concept of underachievement itself is one which poses little consensus about its definition and measurement. The very notion of underachieving boys, which contributes to most people's perception of what is meant by the underachievement discourse, is open to re-interpretation. For example, emerging from any review of the literature into male underachievement is overwhelmingly a picture of boys leaving school with poorer academic qualifications than their female counterparts. The explanations for this are varied and range from problems arising from changing masculinities in today's society to alternative methods of assessment and pedagogy. It is clear that this is a complex issue: but explanations often present boys as a homogeneous group, when clearly they are not. It is not surprising, therefore, to find that some writers have an alternative perspective on the notion of male underachievement that draws upon some of the difficulties and inconsistencies uncovered when researching the field.

This is not to say that *all* the findings described in this chapter should be re-examined: rather, it urges caution over the interpretation and reporting of some of the 'evidence' – particularly in the form of examination data – that has contributed to the 'crisis account' of failing boys and the underachievement of students from ethnic minority homes. Chapter 5 re-evaluates some of these difficulties and inconsistencies which surround the underachievement debate, and in doing so identifies some more of the difficulties in understanding the concept of underachievement.

CHAPTER 5

Reconsidering underachieving students

> . . . continuing underachievement endangers social cohesion and leaves personal and economic potential unrealised. Further action is needed if the improvement for some is to be translated into improvement for all.
>
> (DfES 2003, 4)

So far, we have outlined some of the evidence and explanations that characterize underachievement at the individual level. In particular, we have raised concerns about the relative achievement of students according to their gender, ethnic minority group and socioeconomic status. Despite presenting a seemingly depressing picture of the failure of large groups of students in school, several issues do arise. For example, if it is the case that boys are underachieving in school, then labelling boys as underachieving does little to help explain or remedy the issue – we cannot change the fact that they are boys. Perhaps it would be more helpful to know *which* boys were doing less well in school, but even that appears to raise further seemingly unanswerable questions.

Another issue is the assumption that our assessment system is gender neutral, and that boys and girls *should* achieve the same outcomes in school examinations. The debate is further complicated by the difficulties in separating the interactions between gender, ethnicity and poverty. For example, it may be the case that students from certain ethnic minority backgrounds appear to be doing less well in school, not because they come from a particular cultural or religious background, but because they are more likely to be living in relative poverty and their lives are influenced by the difficulties and uncertainties that coming from a more economically disadvantaged home may bring.

In this chapter, we re-examine some of the evidence for the underachievement of different groups of students and reveal some of the contradictions and inconsistencies that underpin the discourse. We begin with a re-evaluation of the evidence for the apparent underachievement of boys. It questions whether the fact that, in some areas, boys have *never* performed as well as girls constitutes proof of their underachievement. The second section employs the same rationale, this time in examining the underachievement of different ethnic groups; the third section addresses some of the methodological inconsistencies arising from different studies into the effect of social class and family background on achievement. In the final section, the three main variables – gender, ethnicity and social class – are combined, evidence for their interaction is considered, and two studies which present very different perspectives on their relative impact are reviewed.

An alternative account of male underachievement

Earlier, we summarized several of the explanations given by the media and academics for the 'underachievement' of boys. However, an alternative account also exists. For example, Delamont contends that 'it is pointless to be swept away by a moral panic about "failing", anti-school working-class boys. This is not a new problem' (1999, 13). Schools, she argues, have never been able to deal with the working-class boy. She goes on to claim that the whole standards debate is surrounded by a 'discourse of derision' (1999, 3), compounded by a lack of understanding of the academic gains made by all pupils, and coupled with the media's resistance to hearing good news.

That underachievement is not a new phenomenon has also been demonstrated in an historical study by Cohen (1998). She noted the seventeenth-century academic John Locke's consternation that young men found it difficult to succeed in Latin, while their younger sisters would 'prattle' on in French having had little or no formal instruction. The standard of the young men's English also gave him little joy.

According to Cox and Dyson (1969), standards were reported as being similarly in crisis in the 1960s. Reading was argued to have been of a lower standard than previously, older children did not know their tables, examiners were appalled at the poor levels of English and the standard of the 11+ intake into grammar schools was also reported as being lower. Indeed, in Wales, the 11+ examination results were adjusted so that equal numbers of boys and girls could attend grammar school. If the top 40 per cent had gone regardless of gender, two-thirds of the pupils in grammar schools would have been female (Rees and Delamont 1999). Gorard (2001a) also disputes the fact that boys have attained higher grades than girls in compulsory education at any time over the past 25 years. Through an analysis of past results, he demonstrates that achievement gaps between males and females have remained relatively static and that differential attainment by gender is 'a product of the changed system and nature of assessments rather than any more general failing of boys' (2001a, 10).

Another example of contradictory findings comes from the TIMSS (described in Chapters 2 and 3). The original TIMSS was administered in 1994/95. However, a version of the test was re-run in 1998/99 under the title TIMSS-repeat (or TIMSS-r). This second study found similar overall patterns in achievement in maths and science as the original, but also that performance was *significantly higher* for boys than for girls (Ruddock 2000, own emphasis). Again, these results present no real evidence for the underachievement of any group of students, but contribute to a complex and confusing picture of comparative attainment whether at an individual or an international level.

Nevertheless, it is important to remember that debates surrounding the relative achievement of boys have to avoid over-simplification. Often boys are considered as part of a homogeneous group, and as a result individual differences and diversities are not always taken into account. Indeed, as several researchers have pointed out, differences *within* the gender groups can be greater than those *between* them (Arnot *et al.* 1999; Salisbury *et al.* 1999).

Reconsidering the evidence for male underachievement

In this section, we reconsider some of the examination data that was presented in Chapter 4 as evidence for the underachievement of boys in school. Frequently, changes in examination performance over time are estimated by subtracting one set of percentaged results from another and noting the difference (see Table 4.1). However, the problems with using this simple method to estimate absolute differences in examination scores have been described by several authors (in particular, see Gorard 1999, 2000 and 2001a; Heath 2000). Even so, this is a method that many researchers use (as discussed below). In the discussion that follows, we avoid the pitfall of calculating percentage point changes by simple subtraction and instead use three alternative – and arguably more correct – methods for tracing absolute changes in examination scores over time. These are the notion of achievement gaps, Heath's use of odds ratios, and finally an examination of proportional differences in percentages. We first consider each method separately.

Method 1: Achievement gaps

By adopting a methodology also described by Arnot *et al.* (1996, 1999) in their calculation of performance gaps in achieving GCSE grade C and above, Gorard (1999) explores the calculation of achievement gaps as a means of assessing the relative performance of each sex at each grade level. The achievement gap is defined as 'an index of the difference in an educational indicator (such as an examination pass rate) between two groups (such as male and female)' (Gorard 2000, 203). It is calculated by analysing the gaps in entry and in performance between two groups, as shown in the equation below:

Achievement gap = performance gap − entry gap

$$\text{Achievement gap} = \frac{(GP - BP)}{(GP + BP)} \times 100 - \frac{(GE - BE)}{(GE + BE)} \times 100$$

GP = number of girls achieving that grade or better
BP = number of boys achieving that grade or better
GE = number of girls entered
BE = number of boys entered

(from Gorard 2000, 204)

Gorard also describes what he calls the 'paradox of achievement gaps', whereby two different methodologies for comparing the achievement of groups over time have been used, one employing percentage point differences and the other the notion of achievement gaps. Both methods have presented contradictory results. The first has suggested that differences between certain groups of pupils have increased and that, as a result, the education system has become increasingly polarized: but when the method of achievement gaps was used, a very different pattern emerged. Two examples of how achievement gaps can be used in the analysis of performance differences between boys and girls are given below. Both point to a very different, and perhaps more optimistic, picture of the relative attainment of these two groups of pupils.

Achievement in English at GCSE
Figure 5.1 shows the achievement gap between the number of male and female entrants who gained either a grade C or above at O-level/GCSE or a grade 1 CSE in English between 1970 and 1999. The results for English show a steady achievement gap in favour of the girls, but it is a gap that has hardly changed since the early 1970s. There is little evidence here of any differences over time in the relative performance of boys and girls in English: indeed, the current gap is the smallest since the early 1980s.

Figure 5.1 **Achievement gaps in English language examinations**

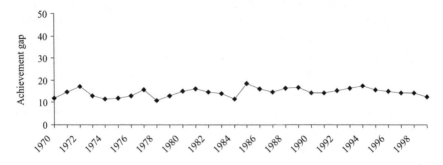

Source: Welsh Joint Education Committee (WJEC) examination board

Similar trends have also been noted for other subjects. For example, in History, French and Welsh, the performance gap has consistently been in favour of girls, with little fluctuation for almost 30 years. Mathematics was one subject that has seen a decrease in the achievement gap. From favouring the boys in the 1970s and 1980s, the trend changed in the early 1990s and both groups now enjoy almost equal success. What caused this change to a well-established trend is not easy to uncover, but it does appear to coincide with the introduction of compulsory coursework in mathematics during the early 1990s (Smith 2005).

Achievement of 5 or more A*–C GCSE passes
Another analysis that used the same technique for determining achievement gaps considers the trends in the proportion of school leavers obtaining 5 or more A*–C grades (or equivalent) (Gorard 2001). This study was different from the one described above in that it examined performance in England in the academic years from 1974/75 to 1997/98. In the period 1974 to 1987, the percentage of boys and girls achieving 5 or more A–C grades had been more or less the same, with the girls marginally in front. However, a change occurred between 1987 and 1989, when the gap between the groups increased in favour of the girls. This trend then stabilized and all pupils made parallel gains, with girls being ahead of the boys by a constant margin (Figure 5.2). Thus, the differential achievement of girls over boys occurred during a brief period from 1987–89 and coincided with the introduction of the National Curriculum.

Gorard offers two explanations for this phenomenon. First, the introduction of the GCSE and the change from 'norm-referencing' methods of assessment (which had previously sought to maintain results at a relatively constant level) to 'criterion-referencing' has meant that standards have been *allowed* to vary, and therefore an assessment of changes in examination results over time has become particularly difficult. Another explanation could be that differential performance according to gender has arisen as a consequence of a changed curriculum and assessment process, rather than from any inherent differences between boys and girls.

Figure 5.2 **Achievement gaps in favour of girls attaining 5+ GCSE grades A*–C or equivalent**

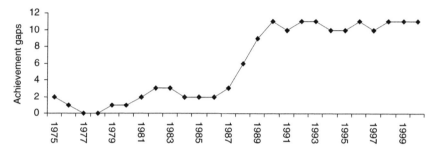

Source: Gorard and Smith 2004

Method 2: 'Odds ratios'

In a paper that used birth cohort data to measure trends in class, sex and ethnic inequalities in educational attainment, Heath (2000) adopts the technique of determining 'odds ratios' to calculate differences between groups. As with the 'politician's error' analysis described below, this method highlights and tries to avoid the drawback of using absolute differences in proportions to monitor changes over time. When applied to measures of class inequality, odds ratios are able to measure the 'relative chances of the members of two classes achieving a certain outcome and of avoiding other outcomes' (Heath 2000, 318). Thus, an odds ratio of 1:1 would indicate complete equality, while a ratio of 14:1 would suggest a more substantial inequality.

Heath's use of the odds ratio in measuring inequalities in the educational performance of groups according to ethnicity and social class is described in the concluding sections of this chapter. In this section, the method is used to illustrate inequality according to sex. For example, by using data from the birth cohort analysis, Heath monitored the trends in candidates who achieved qualifications at O-level or above according to gender for each decade from 1900 to 1970. According to the author, the odds ratio analysis shows a decline in inequality among men and women from the oldest to the youngest birth cohort. A similar trend was evident at A-level and above. These results show that over time the performance between the sexes has become more (not less) equal, thus presenting another alternative account of the achievement gap between male and females. Applying this technique to more recent GCSE performance data reveals the trend shown in Table 5.1 in the proportions of students who achieve the core-subject indicator of good GCSE passes in English, maths and science.

Table 5.1   Likelihood of achieving good GCSE passes in the core subjects, according to gender

Year	Core subject indicator		Odds ratio
	Boys	Girls	
2003	40	46	1:1.3
2002	40	45	1:1.2
2001	39	45	1:1.3
2000	39	44	1:1.2
1999	38	43	1:1.2
1998	37	42	1:1.2
1997	35	40	1:1.2
1996	36	40	1:1.2
1995	35	38	1:1.1

Source: DfES (1995–2003)

These results show that for the most recent cohort of students, boys and girls had almost equal chances (1:1.3) of gaining a grade C or higher in the core subjects. Although the chances slightly favour the girls, the results presented above also show how little the odds have varied over the past nine years.

Method 3: The 'politician's error'

This phrase describes the confusion sometimes, but not exclusively, displayed by politicians between proportional and percentage point differences (Gorard 1999), and can be illustrated by considering the gap between the proportion of pupils who gained 5 or more good GCSE passes in England between 1995 and 2003 (Table 5.2).

Table 5.2 shows that in the period described, both boys and girls improved their score by the same amount (8 percentage points), but that boys were still under-performing compared to girls. However, if the proportional increase is calculated it is clear that the achievement growth of the boys was greater than that of the girls and therefore cannot present any evidence that the boys were underachieving. This is only one example of how different interpretations of percentage changes over time can give a conflicting picture of the relative achievement of different groups: such instances occur widely in the literature. Examples involving the achievement of pupils from ethnic minority backgrounds are considered below.

Table 5.2   **Proportional increase in number of students achieving 5+ good grade GCSE/GNVQ results, 1995–2003**

	1995	2003	Raw change	Proportional change
Girls	50	58	8	16
Boys	40	48	8	20

Source: DfES (1995 and 2003)

Summary

The issue of male underachievement is central to this study and figures prominently in the development of the predictive model for identifying underachievers that is described in Chapters 6 and 7. This 'moral panic' has come about largely through interpretations of examination data suggesting that not only are girls outperforming their male peers, but also that the performance gap between them is increasing. But, as this section has shown, the reality is not so clear-cut. There is no evidence to suggest that the gap in male/female performance is increasing, or that girls are becoming more likely to achieve higher grade passes than boys, or that boys are underachieving in school examinations. What is clear is that the achievement of all students continues to rise steadily and, in addition, what achievement gaps do exist between the performance of male and female students appear to have existed for some time. The most noticeable variation that has taken place in the performance of the two groups did so around 1989 and coincided with the introduction of the GCSE and a movement away from normative towards criterion-style assessment. This has led us to re-consider the assumption that the curriculum is gender-neutral. Should we reasonably expect boys and girls to perform equally well in school?

However, it needs to be remembered that, as Delamont (1999) and Salisbury *et al.* (1999) point out, there are several problems and restrictions thrown up by the analysis of examination results. These are further complicated by the different statistical methods carried out with the raw data and, crucially, in the way the data is reported. The complexity of the debate into gender and performance is also highlighted in an Ofsted report into the relative performance of boys and girls:

> the issues surrounding boys' achievement are real and should not be underestimated but the question of gender and performance is more complex, affecting different sub-groups of boys and girls in different ways and often reflecting the influence of class and ethnicity.
>
> (Arnot *et al.* 1998, 1)

That boys are performing less well than girls in certain subjects is indeed a cause for concern. But the focus should be on which (if any) particular group of pupils appear to be failing to reach their potential and why. This would herald a move away from the traditional binary notion of boys versus girls to include an assessment of other variables such as ethnicity and home background that may have a more profound effect on an individual's learning. One possible implication of a shift away from boy/girl comparisons of performance would be LEAs becoming obliged to provide more detailed examination statistics than are currently available. This might provide us with a very different picture of the performance of pupils in school. The recent publication of the Pupil Level Annual School Census (PLASC) (DfES 2004c) suggests that this may finally be happening.

Before our focus turns to the re-evaluation of the underachievement discourse as it is applied to ethnicity and social class, it is worth providing an example of how the discourse of male underachievement was placed into a relatively simple perspective in one of the focus group interviews (described in Chapter 7). When discussing newspaper articles on male underachievement, one of the boys in the 'underachieving' group suggested that there

> are no differences between boys and girls in class, because you don't really have Set 1 full of girls and Set 4 full of boys, you have top boys and top girls. It's not as if all the boys are no good and all the girls are really good, so I don't think it is true [that boys as a group are underachieving].

An alternative account of ethnic minority underachievement

Chapter 4 has shown us how differing examination performances between various ethnic groups have provided evidence for their levels of achievement. This section re-evaluates this claim in light of some of the difficulties that surround researching this particular group of students. Many of the large-scale research projects into the achievement of minority pupils took place during the 1980s and suffer from several methodological shortcomings (Drew and Demack 1998). There has also been a relative lack of statistical data on ethnic variation in achievement; for example, it is only recently that LEAs have been obliged to include this data in their returns. Many of the recent studies (with the exception of the Youth Cohort Study) have been based in London, are not representative of the rest of the population, often survey only very small populations and can serve to depress the scores of certain groups (Drew and Gray 1990; Haque 2000). Data from LEAs that forms part of their submission to the Ethnic Minority Achievement Grant (EMAG) provides a more recent picture, although this too is not without its limitations (Gillborn and Mirza 2000).

This section focuses first on the problems that occur when categorizing people according to their ethnicity. This is followed by a re-examination of the evidence for the performance gap between white pupils and those from ethnic minority groups.

There has been a great deal of confusion over the categorization of the various ethnic groups both by researchers (DES 1985) and by the respondents themselves (Drew and Demack 1998). The following examples show that a finer division between the different ethnic groups reveals different and sometimes contrasting trends:

- Indian pupils are generally considered to be more likely to achieve higher results than other pupils from South Asia (Gillborn and Gipps 1996; DfES 2004c), but in many studies pupils from this region have been grouped as one (Drew and Gray 1990, 1991; DfEE 1996; Gillborn 1997), which makes further analysis of patterns impossible.
- Despite the large size of its community, information specific to the performance of Pakistani pupils is sparse. This, coupled with the limitations outlined above, has added to a confused picture, but generally research suggests that their performance is lower than that of white pupils (Gillborn and Gipps 1996).
- Pupils from the Bangladeshi community have often been regarded as demonstrating relatively low achievements in examinations, and in Birmingham have been more likely than any other ethnic group to leave school with no qualifications. However, there are exceptions to this pattern, in terms of examination results, qualifications at age 16 and the number of Bangladeshi pupils entering higher education (Barnard 1999; Gillborn and Gipps 1996). For example,

in an Ofsted review of attainment of Bangladeshi students, their achievement at GCSE was higher than that of the other student groups in the schools surveyed (Ofsted 2004).

- The issue of the achievement of black pupils has been particularly complicated by the problems of categorizing ethnic groups. Some returns record three black categories, some two and others one (Gillborn and Mirza 2000). Nevertheless, research has suggested that African-Caribbean pupils perform less well than their broadly-grouped Asian or white counterparts (see, for example, Gillborn and Gipps 1996; DfES 2003b).

- The broad categorization of white pupils is rarely considered. This homogeneous group might include pupils from eastern Europe as well as those from the travelling community. Data specific to these groups is difficult to obtain, but a recent Ofsted document stated that traveller pupils are the group 'most at risk in the education system', whose low attainment in secondary school is 'a matter of serious concern' (Ofsted 1999, 7; see also DfES 2003). The new Pupil Level Annual Census Survey now includes data on this group of students (DfES 2004c).

- The ethnic minority categories in the most recent government publications now differentiate between students of mixed race (DfES 2004c). Although reflecting the ethnic diversity of the UK, this re-categorization further reduces cell sizes and makes calculating trends in performance more problematic.

During the past decade or so, the education research establishment has seen an increase in the volume of research that focuses on the differences between groups of pupils. It is therefore remarkable that ethnic groups do not seem to have been included in this avalanche of data and statistics. Up-to-date, sound research on the relative performance of ethnic pupils is hard to come by, and as the following sections explain, what little does exist is often out of date and fraught with methodological inconsistencies. For example, the Youth Cohort Study (YCS) provides probably the most comprehensive overview of the achievement and employment trajectories of students when they leave compulsory education. Its coverage of students from ethnic minority backgrounds is similarly detailed. However, the cell sizes for many minority ethnic groups are small and make them particularly susceptible to fluctuation. For example, in the 2002 sweep of the YCS, only 106 students gave their ethnic origin as Bangladeshi and 87 as Chinese (Youth Cohort Study 2004). While these figures may well be representative of the number of 16-year-old students in these communities nationally, they are still very small. Disaggregating the data further by gender or parental occupation leads to even smaller cell sizes and an increased likelihood that the data is unreliable.

Reconsidering the evidence for ethnic minority underachievement

The Youth Cohort Study (YCS)

Using YCS data from 1985, Drew and Gray (1990, 1991) estimate that African-Caribbean pupils obtained fewer O-level passes at grades C and above than those from an Asian background. When examination performance over the whole range of grades was examined, the gap between pupils from an African-Caribbean background and those from an Asian or white background was roughly equivalent to one grade C pass (or 5 examination points). Another more recent analysis of YCS data in the 1990s (Gillborn and Youdell 2000) shows year-on-year improvement in exam performance for all the ethnic groups. The authors' analysis suggested that although the number of African-Caribbean pupils achieving the benchmark 5 or more A*–C passes at GCSE had risen to its highest level, the achievement gap between black and white pupil performance had also increased. Data in the appendix of their book shows that in 1985, 7 per cent of black pupils achieved 5 or more A–C grades, compared to 21 per cent of white pupils. In 1996, 23 per cent of black pupils and 45 per cent of white pupils achieved this threshold (Table 5.3).

Table 5.3   **Changes in the proportion of pupils achieving 5+ A*–C GCSE passes**

Pupils	1985	1996	Percentage point increase	Proportional increase
White	21	45	24	114
Black	7	23	16	228
Gap	14	22		

Source: Gillborn and Youdell 2000

This increase in the achievement gap between the two groups, from 14 percentage points in 1985 to 22 percentage points in 1996, was taken as proof that black pupils had not improved at the same rate as their white counterparts and as a consequence were underachieving. However, as Gorard (1999) points out, this over-simplified comparison focuses on percentage point differences, and as a result ignores differences in proportions. This failure to differentiate between percentages and percentage points was discussed above (in the section on gender) and can, according to Gorard, lead to a 'serious misinterpretation' of the data (1999, 236). In the above example, the proportional change in examination scores from 1985 to 1996 between black and white pupils is 228 per cent and 114 per cent respectively. This shows that, while both groups had made significant improvements, it was the black students who achieved the larger increase.

More recent data from the YCS shows both the proportional and percentage point increases in the numbers of students achieving 5 or more good examination passes at GCSE (Table 5.4). Again, this data is unfortunate in aggregating all 'black' ethnic categories. Two trends are immediately obvious from the table. First, that the achievement of students from each ethnic group has risen over the time period presented. Second, the group that has experienced the largest increase is that from the Bangladeshi community, with the 2002 score for the Bangladeshi group representing a large increase over their performance in the previous data sweep (when only 29 per cent of the Bangladeshi sample achieved the base-line level).

Table 5.4 **Achievement of 5+ A*–C GCSE passes, according to ethnic group**

Ethnic group	1992	2002	% change	Proportional change
White	37	52	15	40
Black	23	36	13	56
Asian	33	52	19	57
Indian	38	60	22	58
Pakistani	26	40	14	54
Bangladeshi	14	41	27	193
Other Asian	46	64	18	39
Other ethnic group	37★	53	16	43
None given	18	30	12	67

★ 1994 data
Source: DfES 2003b

It should be noted that the data collection for the latest sweep of the YCS took place in spring 2002 and surveyed students who were eligible to leave school in summer 2001. This group are unlikely to have benefited fully from many of the initiatives now targeted at students from these communities (for example, the Excellence in Cities programme). It will be interesting to see whether these trends continue when the full impact of these new initiatives has been felt in schools.

Local Education Authority data

There has been a consensus among some researchers that while there are different levels of attainment within all the ethnic groups, the attainment gap between the highest and lowest achievers has increased (Gillborn and Gipps 1996; Gillborn and Youdell 2000). This can be illustrated by re-examining the examination results for Birmingham LEA. In Birmingham, around 43 per cent of students are reported to come from an ethnic minority background. It is estimated that by 2008, there will be no ethnic majority in the city's schools (House of Commons 2002). Research conducted by Birmingham LEA into the achievement of its pupils revealed a 'consistently significant gap between the average achievements of black and white young people' (Gillborn 1997). This is supported by data from 1992 to 1994, when the percentage of white pupils gaining five or more higher grade GCSE passes rose from 32 to 36 per cent, while that of African-Caribbean pupils went from 13 in 1992 to 16 per cent in 1993, before falling back to 14 per cent in 1994. However, in the appendix is data for 1995, which when added to Table 5.5 makes the overall picture look very different. While the performance of the African-Caribbean pupils remained below that of their white counterparts, the results for 1995 indicate that not only were they improving but that the achievement gap between the two groups was decreasing. The data for 1995 does not appear in the main body of the report.

Table 5.5   **Trends in the proportion of pupils gaining 5+ A*–C GCSE passes by ethnic group, 1992–95**

	1992	1993	1994	1995	Proportional increase 1992–95
White pupils	32	N/A	36	36	12.5
African-Caribbean pupils	13	16	14	18	38.5

Source: Gillborn 1997

More recent data from Birmingham LEA suggests a sustained improvement in the performance of most ethnic groups. Table 5.6 shows that students from the Indian, Pakistani and African-Caribbean communities made the largest proportional increases in examination scores during the period from 1998 to 2001. In fact, the only group to make no improvement was Bangladeshi boys. Although still one of the highest achieving groups, the rate of improvement of white students was slower than that of many of their peers from ethnic minority backgrounds.

Table 5.6   **Students achieving 5+ A*–C GCSE grades, by ethnic group and gender, Birmingham 1998–2001**

	Percentage achieving baseline levels				Percentage change	Proportional change
	1998	1999	2000	2001		
African-Caribbean boys	13	20	19	17	+4	30.8
African-Caribbean girls	28	30	31	34	+6	21.4
Bangladeshi boys	28	31	30	27	−1	−3.6
Bangladeshi girls	36	40	42	50	+14	38.9
Indian boys	40	43	49	49	+9	22.5
Indian girls	50	55	61	65	+15	30.0
Pakistani boys	21	26	27	31	+10	47.6
Pakistani girls	31	32	41	42	+11	35.5
White boys	34	33	36	39	+5	14.7
White girls	44	45	45	50	+6	13.6
All students	36	38	41	41	+5	13.9

Source: House of Commons 2002

However, there are problems with this data. Not only are pupils from the various black communities grouped together, but the way that the data is disaggregated (both by ethnic group and by gender) means that the numbers of students in each cell can vary substantially. The data presented was only available to the author as percentages, so it is not possible to determine the actual numbers of students in each cell. However, as an indication of the relatively small numbers that can be involved, in January 2003 there were 2,360 students of Bangladeshi origin attending maintained secondary schools in the Birmingham (DfES 2003d). As an estimate, the number of Bangladeshi students sitting for the GCSE examination in a particular year must number only around 400. Disaggregating this data leaves us with increasingly small numbers of students.

Two headlines which appeared three months apart in *The Times Educational Supplement* give additional indication of the confusion surrounding the interpretation of examination data. The first, in October 2000, was entitled 'Gap between black and white expands'. The article describes findings by Ofsted which expose 'a growing gap' between the examination results of ethnic minority and white pupils, and reveals that African-Caribbean and Pakistani pupils have failed to keep pace with their white peers' GCSE improvements (Mansell and Cassidy 2000). This was followed a few months later by the headline 'Black pupils narrow the gap'. This second article presents evidence by the DfEE which claims that the proportion of African-Caribbean pupils getting five A*–C grades increased from 29 per cent in 1998 to 37 per cent in 2000, compared to an improvement by whites from 47 per cent to 50 per cent. This, the authors claim, has narrowed the 'ratio of success between the two groups to 13 percentage points, down from 18 percentage points two years ago'. Both articles use the notion of percentage points rather than proportional differences to describe the variation in results.

Summary

The available data on the relative performance of white pupils and their peers from ethnic minority backgrounds suffers from many inconsistencies and methodological shortcomings. One of the most enduring conclusions of research based on this data is that the performance gap between white students and those from certain ethnic minority groups is growing, and this is used as evidence for the underachievement of students from the latter groups. However, re-focusing the interpretation of the data to look at proportional rather than percentage point changes presents a very different picture. What the data now shows is that the performance of all students is improving and that some of the largest gains are being made by students from certain minority homes, for example by those from the Indian community. The data does not support the argument that there is an increasing performance gap between white pupils and those from an ethnic minority background. However, there are indications that differences *within* certain ethnic groups (for example, between pupils of Indian and Bangladeshi parentage) might exist. Nevertheless, the contribution of different socioeconomic groups to these differences cannot be ignored and future studies will need to take them into account.

An alternative account of the underachievement of students from poorer homes

In their recent five-year strategy 'Children and Learners' (DfES 2004), the government has emphasized the unbroken link between social class and achievement. Endeavouring to enhance social justice by breaking the poverty–achievement link is certainly praiseworthy. However, is there really any evidence that poor children and working-class boys, in particular, are underachieving in school? Although recent data from the PLASC database (DfES 2004c) does suggest that students from poorer homes consistently achieve lower examination results than their peers, this does not necessarily mean that, as a group, these students are underachieving. For example, in Chapter 3 we re-considered the distribution of students' PISA reading scores according to parental occupation. The results showed that although England's scores on this test were widely distributed, overall performance levels were higher than those of many other countries. Interpreting the findings from both the PISA and the PLASC database using the language of the underachievement discourse would suggest to us that poor students were underachieving on domestic assessments but overachieving on international assessments.

This leaves us with a similar paradox to the one we discovered in the discourse of over and underachievement within Japan's schools in Chapter 2 and, if nothing else, should alert us once more to the problems with the term 'underachievement' and with understanding what it is that we actually mean by it. This is an issue that we return to in Chapter 6. For now, the final section of this chapter will re-evaluate some of the evidence and explanations for falling standards among students from poorer homes.

Reconsidering the evidence for the underachievement of students from poorer homes

Data from the YCS reveals the extent to which students perform less well at GCSE than students whose parents are in non-manual employment. However, as Table 5.7 shows, the trend for all students is, once again, one of improvement, with some of the largest jumps in attainment being among students with parents in manual employment.

The DfES-commissioned Coalfields study into the relative achievement of students who live in the former coal-mining communities of the UK also reveals the extent of the relationship between the socioeconomic composition of a region and academic achievement (Gore and Smith 2001). The study linked eighteen areas in the former British coalfields with similar economic regions in order to ascertain whether there was a particular 'coalfields effect' or whether similar patterns of achievement were to be found in areas of similar social composition. The findings reveal the existence of common patterns of attainment in both the former coalfields and in the comparator regions. In both, students' performance is below the national average. The results for boys who reach benchmark levels at Key Stage 3 in the core subjects are given in Table 5.8. Although there are differences in the proportions of students in different economically disadvantaged regions who reach benchmark levels, they are not so great as they are for students who receive free school meals (see Tables 4.4 to 4.6 in Chapter 4, and Chapter 8). Overall, the performance trend for each group is once more generally one of improvement.

Table 5.7 GCSE achievement, according to occupational group

	Percentage of students achieving 5+ A★–C grades								Percentage change	Proportional change
	1989	1991	1992	1994	1996	1998[1]	2000			
Managerial/Professional	52	58	60	66	68	69	69	17	32.7
Other non-manual	42	49	51	58	58	60	60	18	42.8
Skilled manual	21	27	29	36	36	40	45	24	114.3
Semi-skilled manual	16	20	23	26	29	32	36	20	125
Unskilled manual	12	15	16	16	24	20	30	18	150
Other/not classified[2]	15	18	18	20	22	24	26	11	73.3

[1]From 1998, data includes equivalent GNVQ qualifications achieved in Year 11
[2]Includes a high percentage of respondents who had neither parent in a full-time job
Source: DFES 2003b

Table 5.8 **Percentage of boys who achieve Key Stage 3 Level 5 or above in England**

	England (total)			Coalfield Areas			Comparator Areas		
	1998	1999	2000	1998	1999	2000	1998	1999	2000
English	56	55	55	50	49	49	49	50	49
Maths	60	62	64	55	58	60	53	56	58
Science	57	55	61	53	50	57	51	49	55

Source: Gore and Smith 2001

Problems with measuring social class and family background

The difficulties of categorizing students according to receipt of free school meals notwithstanding, there are several other methodological problems affecting research into contextual or background factors that may be linked to underachievement. It seems, for example, that there is little consensus as to the level at which factors such as family background and socioeconomic status (SES) contribute to reduced levels of achievement, and one reason for this may be down to differences in research methodologies. Examples of research programmes that have employed differing and inconsistent methodologies are described below.

In his assessment of using SES as a variable in research, White (1982) discusses many of the pitfalls apparent in establishing a meaningful and widely accepted measure of this variable. Many of the papers he reviewed appear to have similar shortcomings: out of 143 studies analysed, White found over 70 different variables associated with SES. Rumberger (1995), when investigating a wide range of variables in his multi-level statistical analysis of school drop-out rates, identified three determiners of SES: parental education, income and the quantity of reading material in the home. Willms (1986), on the other hand, focused on the father's occupation (as determined by the Registrar General's social class index), mother's education and number of siblings. Another factor that might be viewed as contributing to levels of achievement and where inconsistencies in analytical techniques were again apparent was that of parental involvement. Rumberger (1995) identified five factors determining parental involvement: participation in parent–teacher associations; contact with the school regarding academic performance or behaviour; attendance at school meetings; help with homework, and enforcement of rules regarding homework, while Ho and Willms (1996) considered a total of twelve different items, and Laureau (1987) used only two. Large-scale surveys such as the YCS rely on young people's reporting of their parents' occupations and level of education (DfES 2003b), while international surveys with much younger students also rely on students' self-reporting of their parents' jobs (for example, OECD 2000; DfES 2003c).

There are also differences in the way respondents are sampled. For example, Willms (1986) used a postal questionnaire of Scottish school leavers, while other researchers, including McCall (1992), Pong (1998) and Ho and Willms (1996), have used a national database for analysis. The selection of subjects also sometimes shows inconsistencies in methodology. In a study into the effect of parental involvement, social class and school achievement, West et al. (1998) selected families on an 'opt-in' basis (i.e. they chose to participate in questionnaires and interviews). As a result the sample comprised parents who were actively interested and involved in their child's education, with very few of them coming from the lower social groups. Sampling techniques such as these can only serve to give a biased picture.

The different methods described above for measuring background variables were taken into account when designing the research instrument used in this study for identifying underachievement (and described in Chapters 6 and 7). However, as there is no standard way of measuring factors such as social class and family background, and it might be argued that whatever method is adopted, this may in fact only result in further complicating an already complex field.

Conclusion: Putting it all together – ethnicity, sex and social class

This section considers the relationship between trends in social class, sex, ethnicity and examination performance. It presents two different perspectives, both of which give alternative explanations for the interactions of these variables. The first is a consideration of absolute differences in achievement scores, while the second uses the idea of the 'odds ratio' that was described earlier. As mentioned earlier, one of the problems with considering school achievement according to student group characteristics is simply that these characteristics do not operate in isolation. For example, that Bangladeshi students are doing less well in school on certain assessments may not just be a consequence of Bangladeshi origin – this particular group of students may be adversely affected by other factors such as poverty and limited English proficiency, which may have more impact on their attainment than their ethnic origin. Figure 5.3 shows the achievement gaps that exist between students with the characteristics we have considered in Chapters 4 and 5. It would seem from the results that belonging to the manual social group would mean that you were less likely to succeed at GCSE than if you were male or black.

Figure 5.3 **Attainment inequalities by race, class and gender, GCSE results for England and Wales 1988–1997**

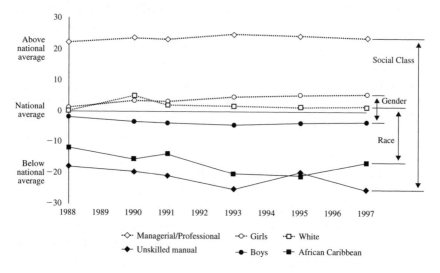

Source: Youth Cohort Study (all pupils), in Gillborn and Mirza (2000)

Using data from the 1985 YCS, Drew and Gray (1990) concluded that the variation in examination results between the respondents was largely due to gender and social class rather than ethnicity. While social class accounted for the largest part of the variance, the three factors together only accounted for about 10 per cent of the total variance (Drew and Gray 1991). However, it is important to point out that the vast differences in sample sizes mean that these trends must be treated with caution. For example, when analysing the achievements of pupils from professional and managerial backgrounds, the number of cases compared for both sexes was 12 for Afro-Caribbean students, 17 for Asian and 2,118 for white (Drew and Gray 1991). When analysing this same data Gillborn focused on gender differences and notes that while white girls outperformed white boys in each social group, only black girls from working-class backgrounds similarly outperformed the boys in their SES level. The author concludes that 'these data suggest, therefore, that national statistics on the achievement of girls at 16 may give a somewhat misleading picture, generalised erroneously from a pattern that may only be true for white students' (Gilborn, 1997, 72). He acknowledges that there was insufficient data to establish whether middle-class African-Caribbean boys were 'still performing more highly than their female counterparts' (1997, 73), but suggests that the superior female performance in the working-class group may be skewed by the large numbers of African-Caribbean students in the lower social classes. While this conjecture is of interest, it must surely be treated with caution when the small number of cases is taken into account (115 African-Caribbean, 189 Asian and 5,218 white pupils of both sexes from the professional/managerial background were used in Drew and Gray 1990). In fact, the sample sizes are not quoted in the Gillborn (1997) article, so it is only by reference to Drew and Gray that the actual number of cases can be determined. Unfortunately, the data as presented by both Gillborn (1997) and Drew and Gray (1990) did not allow the average performance of both boys and girls to be examined, regardless of social class. However, Gillborn later appears to contradict his earlier idea that superior female performance may be a white phenomenon when he states 'that African-Caribbean young women tend to achieve more highly than their male counterparts is not news' (1997, 75).

Both these studies are therefore problematic for two reasons. First, and most obviously, they do not give a clear picture of any trends and it is difficult to draw sound conclusions from them. Second, they are concerned with relatively small and disproportionate numbers of pupils (compare, for example, the generalizability of results generated from comparing 115 African-Caribbean boys and girls with 5,218 white boys and girls, all from different social groups).

This chapter concludes by reconsidering Heath's analysis of birth cohort data (Heath 2000). The use of the odds ratio in Heath's study has been described in detail above. Here, the conclusions of his findings as they relate to ethnic group, social class and gender are described. Heath's results indicate that over the period 1900 to 1970, gender inequalities and those related to ethnic group have declined. His analysis suggests that 'ethnic minorities from less developed countries with modest educational provisions have shown themselves remarkably adept at taking advantage of the educational opportunities available in Britain', while overall 'gender and ethnic inequalities are now smaller than the class inequalities' (2000, 329). This is despite there being a reduction in the absolute differences between the results the different classes achieve at O-level (although this is less apparent at A-level).

These findings serve to add to the confusion surrounding an understanding of differential examination performance over time. There are several examples of this confusion throughout this book, but it is most notable when groups of pupils are compared according to gender, social class and ethnicity. Yet it seems remarkable that there is no consensus over the most effective method to adopt when investigating these changes. It may be that several methods are indeed appropriate: but at present, different methods are being used which yield different results, and this surely is not helpful. It may be that the time has come for a statistical 'rule book' which unambiguously states the appropriate technique for interpreting a particular data-set: what Gorard calls a set of 'relatively standard protocols [which] can be produced for general researchers to use when simply wishing to conduct a "smash and grab" on existing data in preparation for a new study' (Gorard 2002, 3).

Summary

This chapter has reconsidered some of the evidence that has led to suggestions that many students are underachieving in school. By focusing on three different groups of students (categorized according to their gender, ethnic group and socioeconomic status), we have shown that labelling large numbers of students as underachieving can be incorrect. A re-analysis of examination data reveals that for some student groups gaps in attainment have existed for some considerable time, and are likely to be an artefact of the school assessment system, rather than due to any problems that are inherent with (for example) being male. Reconsidering examination outcomes also shows that the performance of all students is improving, with many of the largest jumps in achievement being made among groups who are popularly labelled as underachieving, for example, students from the Pakistani community.

A further issue arising when students are grouped for the purpose of describing educational achievement is that this often leads to the construction of one group as failing (for example, the boys) and the other as succeeding (for example, the girls). Such divisions are unhelpful and give little indication as to which boys are not succeeding in school.

As the above examples have demonstrated, the interplay of three of the factors generally associated with achievement – social class, gender and ethnicity – is extremely complex. Reducing the problem into binary black/white, working class/middle class categories is not only unhelpful but, as this chapter has shown, can also be incorrect.

CHAPTER 6

What is underachievement?

. . . achievement falling below what would be forecast from our most informed and accurate prediction, based on a team of predictor variables.

(Thorndike, 1963, 19)

The previous chapters have established the context for this book. In addition to describing the underachievement debate at international, school and individual levels, they have re-examined some of the evidence supporting the claims that large sections of the school population are underachieving. The key points to emerge from this re-evaluation tell us that not only is this evidence often tenuous at best, it also leaves us with no clear understanding about what it is that we actually mean by the term 'underachievement'. The fact that one group of students does less well than another in an examination is simply insufficient evidence to label the lower achieving group as underachieving, when we do not know exactly what we mean by the term. So far, we have received little guidance to help us understand what underachievement means, let alone to enable us to realize a satisfactory way of measuring it. Before the focus of this book moves towards developing a potential model for identifying underachieving pupils, it is clear that the term 'underachievement' must be examined more closely, and this is the aim here. This is therefore a key chapter, as it moves the debate away from the context in which underachievement is often used, but where little regard is given to its meaning, towards a consensus on its definition and measurement, and eventually to the development of a model for identifying underachievement.

We have already seen that 'underachievement' is a term widely used by politicians, journalists and academics to describe relatively poor academic performance, from that of a nation to a group of students; but a review of the academic literature has found that a consensus on its definition and measurement is hard to come by. Rather than a straightforward concept, it appears that defining and measuring underachievement is fraught with methodological difficulties and inconsistencies. This chapter considers some of the research into this definition and measurement, and includes a discussion about some of the problems researchers have encountered in researching the field, in particular over the use of mental ability testing in the measurement of ability and/or academic achievement. The chapter ends by describing how we might go about measuring underachievement and identifying students who, on this basis, may be failing in school.

Defining underachievement

> The ever-broadening spectrum of our scientific and technological progress, from the harnessing of atomic energy to the conquest of space, has placed a special premium on talent and brainpower in all areas of human thought and endeavour. The young people whose scholastic performance lags far behind their intellectual ability represent a serious loss to society in terms of their potential contribution.
>
> (Frankel 1960, 72).

The concept of unfulfilled potential occupied the forefront of educational research during the late 1950s and 1960s. The intense focus on academic performance during the post-Sputnik era made 'underachievement' almost a household term. Nevertheless, a review of the research literature from that time to the present has revealed that there are many unresolved issues with regard to the definition, measurement and remediation of the problem. One definition of underachievement that figured heavily in the literature was that of 'school performance, usually measured by grades that is substantially below what would be predicted on the basis of the student's mental ability, typically measured by intelligence or standardised academic tests' (McCall *et al.* 1992, 54). This and many other conceptual definitions represent a consideration of the discrepancy between achievement and ability (see, for example, Clark 1988; Gold 1965; Tolor 1969; Whitmore 1980). However, they have all presented methodological difficulties and, according to Shaw (1966, 325), 'no useful solutions'. Many researchers have blamed this apparent lack of consensus on the use of a definition that employs terms which are themselves difficult to quantify. For example, what constitutes a 'bright' or a 'gifted' child? How much of a difference is a 'substantial' difference? How do you measure 'potential'? Can 'giftedness' be defined using IQ? Problems with this conceptual definition of underachievement have led to many researchers operationalizing the definition to include statistical measures of difference (see, for example, Frankel 1960; Kellmer-Pringle 1970; Lau and Chan 2001; McCall *et al.* 1992; Raph *et al.* 1966, Tuss *et al.* 1995).

The role of statistical analysis in defining and measuring underachievement is fundamental. Different techniques of marking out underachievers that have been widely reported in the literature include the 'absolute split' method, used to identify students who 'score higher than a certain minimum (e.g. the top 5%) on a measure of mental ability, but score lower than a certain maximum (e.g. bottom 5%) on a measure of academic performance' (Lau and Chan 2001, 188). The 'simple difference' method of obtaining a 'discrepancy score' by subtracting the standardized performance score on an academic test from the standardized ability score on an IQ test is another widely used technique, as is teacher nomination (i.e. the teacher labels which students s/he thinks are underachievers). Studies using these methods include Carr *et al.* 1991, Lowenstein 1982, and Tuss *et al.* 1995.

However, perhaps the most widely used method of identifying underachievers is the 'regression method'. This involves the use of regression techniques to estimate the deviation of a student's score on achievement and ability tests. The cut-off point for the 'underachiever' label is usually one standard deviation. This method has the advantage that while underachievers are selected from across the ability range, use of the one standard deviation cut-off ensures that the numbers identified remain constant (see, for example, McCall *et al.* 1992; Thorndike 1963).

An unfortunate consequence of using different definitions and techniques for measuring underachievement has been that reaching a consensus on its definition and measurement has proven impossible. These difficulties are further explored by Annesley *et al.* (1970), who considered the four different methods of identifying underachievement that are mentioned above. The authors found that a lack of agreement among the methods resulted in some pupils being labelled differently, depending on which method was used. However, a more recent study of 126 Chinese students (Lau and Chan 2001) found that the same group of 'underachievers' was identified using each of three statistical methods, although the composition of the group identified by teacher nomination was different. Not only are there methodological inconsistencies in the identification of the underachiever, understanding the way in which underachievement actually manifests itself can also be problematic. Authors disagree over the different types of underachievement and also over the frequency with which the phenomenon is thought to exist in the population (see, for example, Shaw 1966; McCall *et al.* 1992; Whitmore 1980).

Therefore, given the range of definitions and techniques used by researchers, it is not surprising that accurate data is hard to come by. To compound the problem, much of the research into underachievement has considered groups of pupils working at different academic levels, with different levels of ability and achievement. For example, Tuss *et al.* (1995) worked with a multi-national sample of 738 10-year-olds; Lau and Chan (2001) with 126 Chinese pupils aged 12 to 15; Tolor (1969) with 1,263 affluent US high school students, and so on. It is left to Newman *et al.* (1990, 139) to sum up what appears to be the root of the problem: 'there is no agreement on the best measure of ability to predict achievement or on the manner in which underachievement should be quantified.'

In search of a consensus

The assertion that achievement ought to correspond exactly to the level of performance on an ability test is, according to Thorndike (1963), one of the reasons why a consensus is hard to establish. He argues that the problem of underachievement is 'one of understanding our failures in predicting achievement and of identifying more crucial or additional factors which will predict achievement more accurately' (1963, 3). Would it then follow that if we were to come up with a perfect model under-achievement would not exist, and it is therefore an artificial phenomenon brought about by the shortcomings in our analytical techniques? As to whether a perfect model that predicts all types of achievement could exist, the answer must surely be no. Consequently, there will always be pupils whose achievement is hard to predict: but whether this group will constitute the underachievers is another question.

In common with other researchers (Carr *et al.* 1991; Cattell and Butcher 1968; McCall *et al.* 1992), Thorndike recognized the need to consider other characteristics of the individual in order to come up with a modified method for predicting achievement. He advocated the use of what he called 'stable, relatively unmodifiable factors' (1963, 18), such as gender, family background, parental education and socioeconomic status. Combining these factors with ability and achievement scores would he claimed, lead to a refined definition of underachievement, understood as 'achievement falling below what would be forecast from our most informed and accurate prediction, based on a team of predictor variables' (1963, 19). It is worth noting that although his work is widely referenced, it has proved difficult to find research that has adopted Thorndike's refined definition of underachievement. Instead, researchers seem to prefer to adopt one of the conceptual or operational performance/IQ definitions widely used by psychologists. However, an approach that brings together a wide range of factors considered to have an effect on academic performance and models them against an accepted outcome appears eminently sensible. It is Thorndike's model that has been adopted by the present study as a method for predicting academic achievement and, as a consequence, academic underachievement.

This section has sought to highlight some of the methodological problems and inconsistencies that underpin research into defining and measuring underachievement. It has attempted to make the argument for the use of a definition that is based upon more than just a measure of academic performance and success in an IQ test, and which also takes into account a whole range of variables that might have some influence on how an individual performs in school. This is certainly not to under-play the role intelligence testing might have in the development of this model; indeed, it is the place of mental ability testing in educational discourse which forms the focus of the next section.

The role of mental ability tests in measuring underachievement

As described above, a key emphasis of the various conceptual and operational definitions of underachievement has been the discrepancy between ability and achievement scores. This has presented methodological concerns not least because of the problems presented by the actual tests themselves. The concept of intelligence and intelligence testing has been surrounded in controversy since the work of Binet and Terman in the early twentieth century (Gipps and Murphy 1994). Various definitions of intelligence exist, with the problems in gaining consensus for a single definition summed up by Gold (1965, 52), who described intelligence as 'ranging from a unitary factor . . . to a group of basic mental abilities to . . . a short-hand term for the layman, covering a multitude of varying uncorrelated abilities that may better not be grouped under a single heading'.

Intelligence-testing was developed in the early part of the twentieth century as a means of distinguishing pupils with special educational needs. Its creators accepted its limitations and advocated care when depicting such a diverse range of skills as a single number: 'the aim of Binet's scale was to identify children in order to help and improve them, not to label them in order to limit them' (Gipps and Murphy 1994, 67). Despite the reservations of its creators, the theory of a measurable form of intelligence took off and the era of mental-ability testing began. This form of testing was most widely used in the USA, where intelligence was seen by some researchers as a product not of the environment but of the genes.

However, by the 1940s intelligence-testing began to attract critics. Gold argued that the intelligence test measures 'far more than innate or developed ability. Much of what it measures is extraneous and obscures the subject's actual intellectual potential' (1965, 72). There was also a growing feeling that intelligence tests were unfair to minority groups, had limited use and were of questionable validity (Whitmore 1980). The nature of intelligence was no longer perceived by many researchers to be a product of the genes, but rather as something whose development was closely related to changes in the social environment. This debate continues today, with researchers such as Herrnstein and Murray (1995) arguing that 40–60 per cent of intelligence is heritable.

Problems with the use of mental ability testing

Part of the attraction of intelligence tests was that they were thought to measure ability independent of schooling and culture: but evidence emerged during the 1950s to suggest that the tests were biased in favour of the white middle-class male (Gipps and Murphy 1994). Since then, attempts have been made to develop tests with no cultural bias. However, eliminating cultural bias would also assume that the subjects have common experiences, and such tests would have to be standardized using a representative sample of the population. As a result, tests standardized in one country may not be valid in another. This issue of validity in mental-ability testing is also problematic: one way of ensuring validity is to correlate it against existing tests, but this method does not address the problem of the validity of the *original* tests. Another possible correlation is with school achievement tests, but here the argument becomes cyclical, because the items on the intelligence test are specifically selected to correlate with school performance.

Another fundamental problem with ability-testing comes with the need to divorce the concepts of ability and achievement. Gipps and Murphy (1994) note the distinction between the two terms and relate ability to a notion of potential, and achievement to actual performance. Such a distinction is fine, but how does one assess ability without allowing the subject to perform a task and so, by definition, assess achievement? For example, an individual who is not well on a particular day when the ability test is administered may perform badly and score poorly. However, this might not reflect the individual's academic ability, merely their performance or completion of the task at that particular moment. Such limitations suggest that it would be difficult to assess ability without assessing performance and consequently achievement. The terms 'ability' and 'achievement' appear to be so inextricably linked that any attempt to distinguish between them in a test which required some measure of performance would question the validity of such an assessment tool.

The case for the use of mental-ability tests

Some of the problems and concerns researchers and practitioners have relating to the use of mental ability tests have been raised in this section, but what of the case *for* IQ tests? Nash (2001) argues for a realization of the importance of IQ testing in sociological research. He explores the apparent contradiction among both researchers who use psychometric testing while simultaneously dismissing its theoretical rationale, and those for whom it is acceptable to study environmental effects on ability by using mental–ability tests, but who at the same time regard ability as a social construct. The 'power' of IQ tests in predicting up to 40 per cent of the variance in academic performance is, according to Nash, central to their importance. If these tests correlate so highly with attainment in an academic subject and are such good predictors of school success then, he argues, researchers have an obligation to acknowledge the 'theoretical ontogeny of the concept and to challenge, rather than contribute to, its ambiguities and contradictions' (Nash 2001, 201). Despite uncertainty about the validity of mental–ability tests among some researchers, there are plenty of examples in the literature of research that have used them in order to identify underachieving pupils (see, for example, Whittington 1988; Mellanby *et al.* 1996; Dobbins and Tafa 1991).

It seems then that mental-ability testing is central in the identification of underachievers. It is true that there is a great deal of concern, confusion and methodological inconsistency surrounding not only the identification of the pupils but also in the actual use of the mental-ability tests. Nevertheless, the role of these tests in predicting academic performance cannot be ignored, and they must be included in any predictive model. They must also be evaluated from a practical standpoint, as schools invest a great deal of time and expense in their administration. It would be foolish to ignore them.

Measuring underachievement

The primary aim of this part of the study was to design the best possible model for predicting a pupil's achievement in an examination and consequently to identify pupils who do not do as well as expected – the underachievers. Several analytical methods were combined in this study, including questionnaires as a means of data collection and assessing children's attitudes and perceptions; examination and test data, and focus-group interviews that sought to gain a clearer insight into any underlying characteristics of groups of students identified here as underachieving. The data that enabled us to perform this analysis was obtained from around 2000 Year 9[5] students attending twelve secondary schools in the South Wales valleys (see Appendix 1 for more detail about the research methods that were used). This study is unprecedented in that it uses individual-level data that covers a whole range of student characteristics, including school attendance and attitudes towards school. The total sample size is of necessity smaller than those of national pupil data-sets, but this detailed data makes it a unique study into the characteristics of 'underachieving' students. The sections below describe the two stages in designing the model for identifying underachievers, while a detailed description of the results from the model is given in Chapter 7.

Stage 1: predicting achievement

This first stage involved developing a preliminary model for looking at the relationship between different student characteristics and the students' achievement at Key Stage 3. Several variables that gave an indication of some of the background characteristics of the students involved in this study were collected, including information on students' academic self-concept and prior attainment; the extent to which their parents were involved in their schooling; and background variables such as gender and receipt of free school meals. The purpose of this was simply to determine which variables were the best predictors of average performance in the Key Stage 3 examinations. The technique most suited to this was multiple regression (Field 2000), which allowed us to predict how a student performs in the end of Key Stage examinations by considering the impact of a range of student variables on examination levels. For example, a student who achieves well at Key Stage 2 is likely to do well as Key Stage 3: in other words, there is a strong positive correlation between these two variables. In this study, rather than considering the correlation between just two variables, multiple regression techniques will allow us to consider how several different variables can make an impact upon average achievement at Key Stage 3.

Two key variables that were used in this analysis were prior attainment at Key Stage 2, and performance in tests of mental ability (here we used

[5] Students aged 13–14 and attending the third year of secondary school.

the Cognitive Ability Test: see Appendix 1 for details). However, the use of both these variables in the construction of the underachievement model is problematic and needs to be highlighted before the model is developed further. The prior attainment measure used was the score on the National Curriculum tests at age 11 (Key Stage 2). Any disadvantage the individual may experience prior to, or at the time of, this assessment (and which could manifest itself in low achievement or underachievement) might affect these results and so bias the model. There are two ways of dealing with this problem in the context of the present study. The first is to ignore the bias that social, or other, disadvantage may have on the prior attainment scores, and to include these scores in the model without adjustment. This can be justified on the grounds that the focus of the study is on identifying underachievement in the secondary school, and realistically secondary schools can do little to prevent underachievement that might already have taken place in the primary school: their influence on any underachievement can only be remedial in response to the needs of their intake. It can also be argued that, although there may well be pupils who have underachieved at Key Stage 2, there may be those that have overachieved, and so the effects cancel each other out. It could also be the case that some older children are more likely to become disaffected at school and so to underachieve, which might suggest that underachievement could be more of a problem in secondary schools than in primary schools. Another way of dealing with the problem is to exclude prior attainment from the model. This would result in a model for identifying underachievers that relied heavily on contextual variables and the results of mental-ability tests. Unsurprisingly, this model is not as strong as one that includes Key Stage 2 scores, and is also susceptible to criticism from those who are uncomfortable with the over-reliance on mental-ability tests in these contexts. The decision was made to adopt the first of these two possible strategies: prior attainment was retained in the model but with its potential for bias noted. The main reasons for taking this decision were related to the strong correlations between prior attainment and the output Key Stage 3 score, as well as the importance of including prior attainment in ensuring the reliability of the underachievement model.

Stage 2: predicting underachievement

Underlying this study is the desire to develop a model for measuring and identifying underachievement. The model that we use reflects the need to take into account factors such as gender and socioeconomic status, as well as estimates of an individual's achievement and mental ability. This leads us to a refined definition of underachievement that can be understood as 'achievement falling below what would be forecast from our most informed and accurate prediction, based on a team of predictor variables' (Thorndike 1963). It is this definition that is used here to help identify a group of underachieving pupils. The method used is exactly the same as that described for our preliminary model in stage 1 above. However, as this is a predictive model, whereby the prediction is made that any group identified as underachieving will mainly comprise working-class boys, the gender and social class variables have been omitted. The motivation for adopting a predictive model at this stage stems from the current popular underachievement discourse that suggests that it is boys, and those from the working classes in particular, who are underachieving in school. This model is simply intended to test the validity of this claim. Here, any student whose actual achievement in the Key Stage 3 tests falls below that predicted by the model is identified as underachieving. It also makes sense for any student whose actual score is better than predicted to be classed as an overachiever. Thus, in this model, two groups of pupils can be distinguished: the underachievers and the overachievers.

However, the modelling process described here can only take us so far. The identification of a group of potentially underachieving pupils using statistical techniques is only the first part of the process. The next step is to determine the features that underachieving pupils have in common and that distinguish them from the other pupils in the sample. In order to do this, the most obvious approach is to speak to them. To this end, four sets of focus-group discussions took place, with two groups of underachieving and two groups of overachieving students; the groups were further separated by gender. The discussions, featured in the next chapter, centred around three themes: attitudes towards school, the influence of the peer group, and the notion of underachievement.

Summary

This chapter has sought to establish not only that a basic definition of underachievement is hard to come by, but also that different researchers have used different methodologies with differing results. As if one methodological uncertainty were not enough, intermeshed with the underachievement debate are uncertainties surrounding the whole concept of mental-ability testing. A discussion of the issues surrounding this form of testing could fill many volumes, and is beyond the scope of the present study. However, schools do use these tests, and invest and expect a great deal from them. Their value cannot be underestimated or ignored, and no investigation into any form of predictive achievement would be complete without them.

One definition of underachievement has stood out: Thorndike's 1963 assertion that the identification of an underachiever was only as good as the model that is used. Only by developing the best possible model, which takes into account a range of background and contextual variables that are accepted as influencing achievement, can a picture of an individual's potential be constructed. By using such a model to compare an individual's predicted achievement with their actual achievement in an examination, individuals who score significantly below their prediction can be classified as underachieving. As the aim of this study is to replicate a model of achievement, thereby making the best possible prediction of an individual's achievement, it follows that the better the model, the less likely any underachieving pupils will be identified. If all the factors specific to an individual's performance could be included in the model, all levels of achievement could be fully accounted for. Obviously, accounting for every single factor is beyond the scope of any study. For example, whether a pupil slept well the night before an exam might have an influence on how well they do on the paper, but cannot be controlled in a universal model such as that described here. The models used in this study do however aim to include as many of the factors which the academic literature tells us might influence achievement, and hence underachievement, as possible.

The first half of this book has described many of the problems that surround the underachievement discourse. Not only is the evidence base for the wholesale labelling of groups as 'underachieving' uncertain, the actual meaning of the term 'underachievement' as applied in these contexts has also been unclear – and note also that not one of the examples of research into identifying underachievers has used Thorndike's (1963) expansive model. However, this is not to say that individuals do not underachieve: rather, there is little evidence to suggest that they belong to a homogenous group of, say, working-class boys.

We have also suggested a model that should help us better understand what it is that we mean by the term 'underachievement'. We began by trying to predict which individual characteristics, such as gender or prior achievement, are the best predictors of academic success. This was then adapted into our final model, in which students who may be underachieving were identified. A great deal of the debate into underachievement has focused on the performance of working-class boys, and we adopted this perspective in our underachievement model in order to predict that the students identified here as underachieving would mainly comprise working-class boys. As a supplement to our model, focus-group discussions with a sample of students from the underachieving and over-achieving groups were carried out in order to determine features that may distinguish between the different underachieving and overachieving groups. The results from both models are given in Chapter 7.

CHAPTER 7

Measuring underachievement

We face a genuine problem of underachievement among boys, particularly those from working-class families. This underachievement is linked to a laddish culture which in many areas has grown out of deprivation, and a lack of both self-confidence and opportunity.

(Blunkett 2000)

The previous chapter pointed out many of the complexities and uncertainties involved in understanding what it is that we mean by the term underachievement. It was proposed that the most straightforward and accurate method for identifying underachieving students would be to design a model that took into account a range of contextual and background variables, as well as the results from achievement and ability tests. This model could then be used to predict performance in the Key Stage 3 examinations. Students who did not do as well as predicted could be considered to have underachieved on this assessment. On the other hand, students who did better than expected could be said to have overachieved. This chapter describes the results of this analysis (for more detail about the research methods used and the characteristics of the student sample, see Appendix 1).

In particular, we are concerned with exploring the characteristics of the underachieving students and examining whether they fit the oft-cited image of underachieving working-class boys. In the second half of the chapter, exploratory focus groups are described, which aimed to uncover any differences between the groups of underachieving and overachieving students. We begin by briefly describing the relationship between the student variables and achievement at Key Stage 3.

Predicting achievement

The purpose of this model was to consider the relationship between achievement at Key Stage 3 and the different variables affecting the students. In particular, we wanted to determine which variables were most strongly related to examination performance. The most effective method of doing this was to run a multiple regression model. In this model, the variables listed in Table 7.1 accounted for 82.6 per cent of the variance in the examination outcome at Key Stage 3. This means that by examining these variables listed below, one can predict an individual's average Key Stage 3 score with 82.6 per cent accuracy.

Table 7.1   **Predicting outcomes at Key Stage 3**

Variable (predictors)	Amount predicted by each variable (%)
Prior attainment	68
Attendance	5.3
Self-concept (reading)	3.4
Free school meals	1.8
School factor	1.1
Self-concept (general)	0.8
Gender	0.8
Family type	0.3
Parent's evening attendance	0.3
Month of birth	0.3
Sibling order	0.2
Working mother	0.2
Parental involvement 1	0.1
Parental involvement 2	0.1
Total amount predicted	**82.6**

One of the most striking findings from this analysis was that the variable for gender was ranked seventh in importance, and explained only 0.8 per cent of the variation in academic achievement at Key Stage 3. This was far lower than the levels of variance attributed to receipt of free school meals, attendance, attitude towards reading and, of course, prior attainment (as measured by an aggregate Key Stage 2/mental-ability test score). Any variables not listed in Table 7.1 were not very strong predictors of Key Stage 3 outcomes and were excluded from the model (see Appendix 2 for a fuller description of the statistical models used in the study).

Table 7.1 tells us that using the student variables listed above, we can predict how an individual will perform in their Key Stage 3 examinations with almost 83 per cent accuracy. Knowing how well a student has performed at Key Stage 2 and on mental ability tests such as the CAT allows us to predict their examination scores with 68 per cent accuracy. Knowing whether they are male or female is less important – the accuracy with which we can predict their scores goes down to less than 1 per cent. Of course, whether they are male or receive free school meals may also effect how well they do in their prior attainment tests, and we see how important this is in the next chapter.

Predicting underachievement

The model for predicting Key Stage 3 achievement described above was used again here. This time, however, the model was a predictive one, with the prediction made that the underachieving group would comprise mainly working-class boys. The aim of this model was to use the variables listed above in Table 7.1 to predict average Key Stage 3 outcomes and to identify pupils whose predicted score was above or below the score that they actually achieved in the examinations. Therefore, if a student's actual Key Stage 3 score was significantly lower than predicted in the model, s/he was designated as an 'underachiever'; if their score was significantly higher than predicted, s/he was designated as an 'overachiever'. However, as the model was a predictive one (predicting that any group identified as underachieving would mainly comprise working-class boys), both gender and social class variables were omitted from the regression analysis. The results from the model indicated that 82.4 per cent of the variance in Key Stage 3 performance could be accounted for by the variables entered into the model or, put another way, that we could use the variables to predict Key Stage 3 results with 82.4 per cent accuracy (more details can be found in Appendix 2).

The distribution of pupils' actual and predicted Key Stage 3 scores was such that definite outliers could be identified. This meant that pupils whose actual score lay more than one standard deviation below what was predicted from the model were termed underachievers, pupils whose actual score was more than one standard deviation higher than predicted were termed overachievers. It is worth mentioning that these parameters are generous and result in relatively large numbers of students falling into either category. The characteristics of the pupils in these two groups are described next.

Who are the underachievers?

Out of a sample of over 2,000 cases, complete data was available for 970 pupils. Within this group, the regression model identified 147 pupils whose residual scores could label them as underachievers, and a further 200 pupils who could be termed overachievers.

Table 7.2 shows the distribution of underachieving pupils within the four social groups, compared to the whole sample. The largest proportion of pupils belonged to the working–class group (43 per cent): this is unsurprising when the geographical region from which the sample was taken is considered. Students were relatively evenly distributed among the four social classes according to their gender. The social class-categories used here are based on those of the traditional Registrar-General groups, but have been collapsed so that Service equals I and II, Intermediate equals IIIa and IIIb and Working Class equals IV and V. An Unpaid category for the long-term sick, unemployed and those in unpaid work was also included.

Table 7.2   **The distribution of pupils in each social class**

	Service %	Intermediate %	Working %	Unpaid %
All pupils	23	31	43	3
Boys	23	28	46	2
Girls	22	34	40	3

Table 7.3 shows how boys in the underachieving and overachieving groups were distributed according to social class. The proportion of each group in the different social class groups reflects their distribution in the sample. For example, 47 per cent of the underachieving boys belonged to the working class, compared to 46 per cent of boys in the whole sample. Over half of the overachieving boys came from the working-class group. However, the scope for pursuing this analysis and drawing firm conclusions from the results is limited, because we are now dealing with relatively small numbers of individuals. Nevertheless, there was little to suggest from this analysis that the underachieving group was composed mainly of working-class boys.

Table 7.3   **Social class of boys in the overachieving and underachieving groups**

Boys	Service %	Intermediate %	Working %	Unpaid %
Underachieving	19	33	47	1
Overachieving	21	22	54	3

The analysis, however, highlighted differences in the distribution of girls amongst the eight categories. One of the most obvious disparities is the disproportionate number of working-class girls in the under-achieving group (Table 7.4). There were correspondingly fewer under-achieving girls in the service and intermediate groups. Here the results clearly suggest that the underachieving girls were more likely to be working class rather than service or intermediate class, and that con-versely there were fewer than expected working-class girls in the over-achieving group.

Table 7.4   **Social class of girls in the overachieving and underachieving groups**

Girls	Service %	Intermediate %	Working %	Unpaid %
Underachieving	16	18	60	6
Overachieving	20	43	34	2

These results present us with two clear conclusions. First, because the number of working-class boys in the underachieving group reflected their distribution in the sample, and there were also correspondingly more of these working-class boys in the overachieving group, there was no suggestion in this study that, the working-class boys were under-achieving. The second finding concerns the distribution of girls in the underachieving group according to their social class. In this analysis, there were a disproportionate number of working-class girls in the underachieving group. There were also correspondingly fewer of these girls in the overachieving group. Therefore, while the results indicate that the prediction that the working-class boys would be underachiev-ing cannot be upheld, it does raise questions over the achievement of working-class girls.

Now that the students have been identified who, on this model, could be described as having underachieved or overachieved in the Key Stage 3 examinations, the next step is to carry out an exploratory anal-ysis to better understand any characteristics that might distinguish the two groups. The results are described below.

Focus-group discussions

Exploratory focus-group discussions were conducted with small sub-groups of those pupils who had fallen into the different categories of underachievers and overachievers. Although the students who feature below are only a sub-set of the 247-strong group of underachieving and overachieving pupils as identified by the model, they were selected because they gave an indication of the diversity of both groups (profiles of some of the underachieving students are given in Appendix 3).

Four groups were selected, each comprising six students. The students were grouped by gender and by whether they were designated as under-achievers or overachievers. For some of these pupils, it is clear to see why they may have been labelled as underachieving. For example, two failed to improve their National Curriculum levels from Key Stage 2 to 3, and two others had difficulties with spelling which might make practical sub-jects more attractive but could disadvantage them in the core subjects. The reasons for the placing of the two other students in the underachiev-ing group was less clear. Both pupils achieved 3 Level 6s at Key Stage 3[6], well above the Government's targets for 14-year-olds. They were placed in the higher sets where they sat the highest tiered papers and yet, on this model, they were identified as 'underachieving'.

The aim of the group discussions was to try to elicit any features that might characterize, or distinguish between, the groups of underachiev-ing and overachieving students. The complex interactions of factors like ability and social class within these groupings made significant findings difficult to uncover. Nevertheless, the discussions did reveal several inter-esting findings about the way different groups of pupils perceive school. The pupils' responses form the focus of the remainder of this chapter and are structured around three themes: the students' attitudes towards school, the role of the peer group, and the notion of underachievement.

Attitudes towards school: Creative subjects and joke subjects

Here the pupils were asked to describe what they thought were the best things about school. Both groups of girls gave seeing their friends as the best feature, with the overachieving girls qualifying this by mentioning the need to study for a job and equating the importance of friends with the need to work hard in school:

> I wouldn't say being with your friends was the most important but that's what makes you want to get up in the morning – to go and see your friends. (Bethan)

---

[6] National targets require that the majority of 14-year-old students achieve at least a Level 5 by the end of Key Stage 3. The highest level generally awarded at this Key Stage is 7.

Being with friends, enjoying yourself every day, working to get a
job.   (Melanie)

This was in contrast to both groups of boys, who struggled to find anything good to say about school. Paul (underachieving boy) felt that 'it
stopped you being bored because if you were at home you would just be
sitting there'; other boys said they liked the food, break time, home time
and opportunities to play sport.

When the groups were asked to list their favourite subjects, there was
little evidence to suggest that their choices were gendered, particularly
among the girls, who reported enjoying IT, maths and science. These
findings were similar to those found by Francis (2000) and show that boys
and girls see themselves as being good at the same subjects. Here, both
groups of boys were able to list several subjects they enjoyed, including
maths, physical education, art, technology, geography and business
studies, as well as 'anything you don't have to write in' (Paul, an underachieving boy). They also said that they would try their best in these subjects: 'the ones you enjoy, you might as well do them tidy' (Andrew, an
overachieving boy). Generally, the boys preferred subjects which involved
'making stuff' (Simon, an overachieving boy) and which they saw as
being more active. It was not the case that the overachieving boys showed
more enjoyment of academic subjects than the underachieving boys.

The underachieving girls had more difficulty in naming their favourite lessons:

I don't know . . . I enjoy maths . . . um . . . I can't really . . . I don't
really have a favourite subject, its more that I just like them or . . .
you know . . . its just difficult so I don't enjoy them as much.
                                                                    (Julie)

Clare (an underachieving girl) who enjoyed games and art qualified
this by saying that in these subjects, you can 'just enjoy yourself, it's more
fun . . . you can talk and that (ha ha). . .'. The other girls in this group
linked their enjoyment to the relevance of the subject in every-day life:
'I like ICT, because most jobs have got computer skills involved so it will
be good to do well' (Joanne, an underachieving girl).

The overachieving group of girls had similar difficulties in listing their
favourite subjects, but were conscious of the fact that they chose subjects
which allowed them the freedom to be creative and have greater responsibility to make their own decisions about which direction they wanted
the work to take, for example music, art and media studies: 'I like the
fact that they are less structured and that. I like media studies for the same
reasons' (Bethan). Their more sophisticated reasons for enjoying a subject

did not reflect the need to be with friends or even the subject's practical application in the world of work, although the need for good GCSE grades was, as ever, evident. When asked to name a subject they disliked, most of the pupils in each group said Welsh and R.E. Both subjects are compulsory for all these students and were not taken seriously or seen to be worthwhile by many of them:

> 'I don't like Welsh, its just so boring, no one needs to learn Welsh, who cares that we live in Wales.'
>
> (Julie, an underachieving girl)

> 'RE is a joke subject – no one takes it seriously.'
>
> (Elaine, an overachieving girl)

> 'Welsh is a dying language.'
>
> (Robert, an underachieving boy)

Among the overachieving girls, the way a subject was taught and presented appeared to be more important to their enjoyment than the actual content:

> Alice: I hate physics . . . I give up the will to live half way through . . .
> Bethan: Yes she does, she's like 'Kill me now!'
> Nicola: I know . . . I don't like physics either.
> Interviewer: Why not?
> Nicola: Well there's not enough practical it's just sitting down all the time whereas in biology and chemistry there's a lot more practical . . .
> Bethan: (interrupting) . . . yeah there's a lot of learning . . .
> Nicola: . . . it just seems pointless, just sitting there writing.

All the pupils said that they valued the opportunities for practical work in the sciences but this exchange may represent less of a gendered difference in attitudes, and rather one which reflects the pupils' desire to be given work which was less structured and allowed them to be more creative.

Seeing a subject as pointless was frequently given as a reason for not enjoying it, but during the discussion all of the underachieving pupils said that they didn't like a subject because they found it boring, although the girls also admitted to disliking a subject because they found it difficult – a reason none of the boys gave. When asked whether or not they still tried their best, even if they didn't enjoy the subject, most – although not all – of the pupils in the underachieving groups said that they did not. One of the underachieving boys described his own strategy for overcoming the 'boredom' of Welsh:

In Welsh I just mess around because I don't want the subject, I don't want to learn it so I mess around and get into trouble in Welsh more than anything. The lessons I don't like I get into trouble in because I can't be bothered.

(Paul)

However, not all of the underachieving boys took this view: Robert said, 'I still try hard in every subject. I still do the work even if I don't like a subject', and Luke, who said that 'I can't do my best [in English] because I find it hard to concentrate because it is so boring', was quite (rightly) adamant that he still did not 'mess around' in class. A similar response came from the overachieving group of boys, who admitted to being 'more relaxed' and 'not paying much attention' in their least favourite subjects. However, they did have a more serious approach to tests: 'You do try your hardest in a test because they all add up in the end to have a good job' (Andrew).

In contrast, the overachieving girls took a different view:

I find that if I am not particularly good at something, then I am more determined because if people think you are not very good then you are expected not to do it, so then you feel more determined to succeed.

(Bethan)

Connell (1994) has suggested that some boys have dealt with changes in the way that masculinity is constructed in society either by working hard to promote themselves into good careers, or by rebelling against the boundaries imposed by school. The discussions above suggest that in this study neither was the case. These pupils have become sophisticated consumers of education: they realize the importance of achieving high grades and securing a good job, and at the same time, they understand that some subjects would be more 'useful' to them. Therefore, they had become more selective about which subjects they were prepared to work at and in which subjects they could get away with putting in less effort. This way of discerning between subjects that were useful and those that were not was not confined to the boys. The girls were just as able to distinguish between such subjects; however, the difference here was in the way that the overachieving girls reported being still willing to try their best to succeed in all lessons. The desire, particularly among the boys, to maintain a 'middle way', where they were seen as being sociable in class while still continuing to produce work when necessary, is important in explaining the way the boys behaved in school, and is discussed later.

Friends and the 'ideal' student

There is a large body of literature about the influence of the peer group in the classroom situation and its potential effect on examination success at school (see, for example, Francis 2000; Frosh *et al.* 2002; Mac an Ghaill 1989). In this study, the group discussions attempted to explore whether these interactions were based around either gender or differences in achievement, or whether they were, in fact, a combination of both or neither of these factors.

Each group was asked to describe their notion of an 'ideal' pupil. In Francis' study (2000), the pupils suggested 37 different characteristics for this pupil. However, the most popular features were having good social skills and being able to have fun as well as being hardworking – features which were important for boys as well as girls. While the pupils in our study shared this consensus, being 'brainy' was not as important for the overachieving girls as someone who 'tries their hardest' and was 'prepared to do the work outside school'; according to Bethan, 'some people are really brainy, they just can't be bothered to work to their full potential'.

Both the underachieving groups also disagreed about the relative advantage of being effortlessly brainy and working hard. According to Paul, his 'ideal' pupil was '. . . someone who is like born clever, like they are good in every lesson but don't have to bother trying. They are just clever . . . someone who doesn't revise as much but still does well'.

Many of the other pupils felt the 'ideal' pupil had to be sociable but also enjoy lessons – 'has fun but does their work' (Luke, an underachieving boy), or 'someone like me and my friends, working most of the time but having a mess about and a laugh as well' (Andrew, an overachieving boy). The ideal pupil was summed up by Julie (an underachieving girl):

> 'I think that it is good to be sociable and not too talkative but – you know – openish because otherwise, you'll just sit there and do the work and not really get involved, just copying things down.'

This construction of the 'ideal' pupil as someone who maintains popularity through being sociable but not working excessively is a common one in several studies (see, for example, Francis 2000; Frosh *et al.* 2002). Often it is coupled with the ability to succeed at sport, although the desire to be seen as particularly sporty was not apparent among the pupils in this study. However, sporting prowess did feature prominently in the construction of the friendship group among boys interviewed at the same school a few years previously (Smith 2000). Here, when describing their version of an ideal pupil, there were once again differences within the groups: according to Robert, (an underachieving boy), 'I think a pupil who tries hard in a subject is better than a pupil where it just comes naturally, it shows that they are keen.' Neither of the underachieving groups saw themselves as the ideal student because they 'don't enjoy all the lessons'.

In contrast to research by Younger and Warrington (1996), none of the groups saw girls as being generic ideal students. Rather, they all selected a type of student, who in the case of the overachieving boys was quite specifically someone like them who recognized the need to work but was also willing to have a good time. In this they were seeking to establish a 'middle way' between being seen to be sociable and 'have a laugh' while still recognizing the need to work hard in class, a construction that appeared to feature more prominently among the more able pupils (whether they were classed as overachieving or underachieving). However, this notion was not common throughout the groups, with some pupils characterizing an 'ideal' pupil as someone who worked hard, a concept that was perhaps most strongly felt among the overachieving girls.

Being a swot and ruining your rep.

According to Frosh *et al.* (2002), the boys in their study perceived the unpopularity of being viewed as 'clever' or a 'swot'. Many of these boys counter-posed schoolwork and sport, because being good at schoolwork marked you out as being unpopular but being good at sport was acceptable. Most of the boys in the present study did not consider themselves to be 'swots', and this was explained by some of the 'overachieving' boys:

> Andrew: That's not saying that we are not very bright, its just different with swots, they're like 'yes miss', they put their hand up straight away. We know the answers most of the time it's just that you don't have to show it . . .
>
> Lee: (interrupting) . . . you just don't put your hand up . . .
>
> Andrew: . . . you can write it down and get full marks you just don't have to show it, some people are overenthusiastic.
>
> Interviewer: Why don't you put your hand up if you know the answer?
>
> Andrew: Because sometimes people will make fun of you for answering all the time isn't it?
>
> Interviewer: And is it important not to be seen doing that?
>
> Andrew: Yes, it ruins your rep (ha ha)

Several of the other boys hinted at the pressure of belonging to the friendship group and the need not to been seen to be hardworking. John, an underachieving boy, said: 'It's not that important but you don't want to be embarrassed because all your friends will be having fun and if you try to be a swot they will call you "teacher's pet" and all that.' However, a more pragmatic response was given by one of the more able under-achieving boys: 'If you just want to get your work done and you are really keen, then good for you, you should not have to worry about being picked on' (Luke, an underachieving boy).

The ability of certain boys to maintain their position in the friendship group while still recognizing the need to succeed in school is described by Frosh *et al.* as their 'jockeying for position in hegemonic masculinity' (2002, 41), wherein the successful were able to maintain a middle way between being cool and being conscientious. A common strategy when boys tried to negotiate this middle way was for them to do their school-work, but in such a way that it did not draw the attention of the other boys, a strategy that was implicit in some of the responses by these over-achieving boys.

Being 'one of the gang'

According to Pickering, 'peer pressure is the most significant single factor in the underachievement of boys' (1997, 41). This pressure to be part of the group was touched upon by the girls as an explanation for the relatively poor performance of the boys in examinations. However, the desire to fit in and be a group member was something that the under-achieving boys thought the girls were under more pressure to do: '. . . some gangs of girls class themselves as nice and attractive or thick/brainy and they have to fit into their gang and only if you are like them do they accept you' (Luke, an underachieving boy).

The boys themselves said they felt no pressure to be part of a group and act in certain ways. The difference between the structures of the male and female friendship groups was explained by some of the over-achieving girls and confirmed to some extent what Luke had just said:

> We value different things really because girls . . . I mean I hang around with people who are in my class, the same ability as me, we do structure our friendship groups by what set you are in. But with the boys, they all just laugh . . . they look for different things in friends really. It doesn't make such a big difference if they are not in the same sets and things . . .
>
> (Alice)

The boys saw the girls as being more mature, 'swotty' and sensible; and according to the underachieving boys, the pressure on them to conform to a group was more significant than that experienced by boys, who they felt were less inhibited and just joined in:

Luke: 'You can see the boys messing around on the yard dinner time and the girls will *just* be walking around and talking, but in primary school the girls would join in and play football and all that.'

John: 'Now they'd probably just get humiliated and that, they are more interested in their looks and getting boyfriends.'

Paul: 'It's because they [the boys] are more into sport and stuff or like running around but the girls are like, not fragile, but are just not into running around because other girls don't do it, so if they tried running around they would stick out.'

In this schoolyard, as in many others, boys dominate the physical space with games of football and touch rugby. Outside the organized netball practice, the girls are very much sidelined around the edges of the yard. In this extract, the boys seemed not to recognize this and suggested that the girls were at fault for not joining in as they had done in primary school. Similar responses were found among the boys by Frosh *et al.* (2002). Here, the boys derided the girls' lack of interest in sport, considering their pastimes to be boring and unimportant. This was particularly true of the way the boys referred to the girls as 'just' walking around or 'just' talking, which interestingly is exactly what they did in this study.

A very complex picture of the effect the friendship group has on these pupils has emerged through this discussion. The results are far from conclusive with regard to the differences between overachievers and underachievers. Instead, friendship group interaction appears to be defined by equally complex gender relationships, with the perhaps more subtle workings of the female friendship group becoming apparent in this discussion. Once again, the security of the friendship group, which allowed the overachieving girls to be themselves and to work hard, was clear.

Underachieving boys?

Newspaper headlines were given to the groups to facilitate a discussion about achievement, and more specifically to provoke a reaction to the notion of male underachievement. It is worth emphasizing that none of the groups knew the basis for their selection (apart from their obvious separation according to gender), and nobody in any of the groups linked the discussions on underachievement to whether their particular group was overachieving or underachieving. The newspaper headlines that were given to the groups were similar in nature to those used to illustrate the origins of media accounts of the male underachievement discourse displayed at the start of Chapter 4.

Pupils were given six newspaper headlines that had been collected from the national press over the past few years, and were asked whether or not, in their experience, these reports were fair and reflected their experience in class. They were also asked to suggest reasons for any differences between boys' and girls' achievement. The responses to the headlines by the boys were more muted than when this exercise was tried previously, when some of the boys had been quite outspoken and suggested that 'sexist women reporters' (Smith 1998, 86) had written the articles. In this new study, one of the overachieving boys commented that 'newspapers lie a lot don't they' (Lee), and another that 'they want people to buy the newspapers so they blow things out of all proportion' (Alex).

The underachieving group of boys were more pragmatic: 'Well they can't just guess it, they have the results so it must be true' (Paul); other comments were that 'you just have to accept it' and (sarcastically) 'well apparently I'm stupid' (Robert). However, it was generally felt among these boys that it was not fair to label a boy as stupid and a girl as brainy.

Both groups of girls had several explanations for the apparently poorer performance of the boys, with the underachieving girls focusing on the role of the peer group:

> Clare: The boys act like it is sad to do well.
> Joanne: The boys like to show off around their friends, they say 'oh I'm hard and I don't like school', but if they are on their own with you and none of the other boys are around they are normal.
> Julie: . . . yes it's like if you are on your own with a boy, they can be like girls, they can be normal. When they are around their friends they won't be like 'oh I have to do homework by tomorrow'. They're all like 'oh I don't think I will bother tonight, what's the point' and stuff like that. Then sometimes they say 'oh I might as well do it, there's not much on the TV'.

This difference between the collective and individual identities of boys was also apparent in the interviews Frosh *et al.* conducted with groups of girls. They implied that boys were 'more authentic on their own' (2002, 139), and that their anti-social behaviour when with their male peers was a negative feature of being collectively male.

The overachieving girls' explanation had a different focus – that of the changing position of women in school, as well as in society in general:

> Alice: Different values really, before we weren't actually expected to do well in school and we weren't going to go out into the world. They expected us to leave school at 16, get a job and then get married, whereas now we are more motivated.

Nicola: . . . they don't like the competition . . .

Bethan: I think they are backing down and finding something more important to do and make that the focus of their lives, like having friends and making that more important than schoolwork and so it doesn't really matter to them.

Alice: They do make a big deal now boys aren't doing better but they didn't when it was the girls. But it is a big deal because it is such a big change, but they are only doing it now because boys aren't doing as well, when girls weren't doing so well, they didn't really care and now that boys are the underdogs, they are making a big fuss about it.

However, the overachieving boys, while maintaining that the girls chat as well as doing their work, pointed out that 'not all girls are like the same, there are some in class who are cheeky and talk a lot' (Lee): indeed, the general feeling of this group was that the boys and girls were becoming more similar and that both groups will do well if they work. This assertion by the pupils that boys and girls have similar ability was reflected in research by Francis (2000), for whom 84 per cent of her sample of boys and 66 per cent of girls agreed that subject ability was not gendered. Both groups of girls took on a 'mature' adult role while deriding boys for their relative lack of academic application, while the boys asserted that there was little difference between the genders. Nevertheless, these pupils had a strong sense of equal opportunities – if you worked hard, you would do well, regardless of whether you were male or female.

That ability was not gendered and that boys could not all be underachieving, was summed up in our study by Andrew, one of the overachieving boys:

'If you look at Sets 1 and 2, they have boys and girls in them. It's not like Set 1 is full of girls and Set 4 is full of boys, is it?'

Conclusion

As suggested in the introduction to this section, analysing these group interactions just on the basis of gender and achievement is fraught with difficulty. There are simply too many other factors that, in interaction, can subtly influence the responses of the individuals involved. However, the aim of the focus-group discussion was to try to elicit a group consensus on any underlying factors that might distinguish these four groups, either on the basis of their gender, achievement or a combination of both.

Some of the academic literature on the subject of underachieving boys would describe boys and, in particular, those labelled as underachieving as 'laddish' risk-takers who crave the 'lion's share' of the teachers attention (Younger and Warrington 1996). However, there was no evidence from these interviews that this was the case; only one boy (Robert) admitted to 'messing around' in some lessons, but he does not stand out from the rest of the year group as being disruptive. The attitudes of the underachieving boys (and girls) towards school were no more negative than those of the overachieving groups: they recognized the importance of a good education and wanted to do well in school. There were similarities across all groups over the type of subject pupils enjoyed; those that were practical, creative and seen to be worthwhile were rated highly by all the pupils. But as a group, only the overachieving girls said they would persevere over a subject they didn't enjoy (although two of the underachieving boys did agree with them).

The majority of the pupils agreed that boys in general were noisier in class but that this was not necessarily a bad thing, as it could make the lessons more entertaining. The pupils also felt that generally boys did not stand out as underachieving (although many were aware of the debate and had seen newspaper articles on the subject): they felt that while some boys did not work hard enough, there were girls who were guilty of the same thing.

One of the main findings from the group discussions was the way in which the overachieving group of girls distinguished themselves from the others. This group comprised mainly high-ability girls, while the other three groups were more mixed in ability. It became clear from the discussions that the way these girls constructed their friendship groups differed from that of the boys and the underachieving girls. The other three groups appeared to seek a middle way in which they were able to retain a popular position among a wider group of peers while still not appearing to work hard at school. All the pupils involved in the interviews recognized the need to succeed in school but were able to adopt this middle way with greater or lesser degrees of success: none of the pupils wanted to be called a 'swot' and many adjusted their behaviour to avoid the label.

While there was a certain stigma attached to being called a 'swot' for girls as well as boys, the overachieving girls, secure in their friendship groups, were free to achieve and even admitted that it was acceptable to be called a 'swot' among their friends, suggesting that 'a learning-orientated approach may sit less problematically with constructions of femininity than with masculinity' (Francis 2000, 71). However, the focus-group discussions did not draw out a similar response for the underachieving girls, who clearly did not position themselves as 'swots' because they 'didn't enjoy school', and for whom it was perhaps less acceptable for them to be seen as working hard – unlike the overachieving girls, for whom it was acceptable to do well in school. In this, the underachieving girls were more similar to the majority of boys in the study, suggesting that for some pupils this 'learning-oriented approach' may transcend gender boundaries and be influenced to a greater or lesser degree by an individual's achievement. A similar situation was observed by Frosh *et al.* (2002) who, in their observations of male public school pupils found that as these boys had no alternative but to get on with their work (on account of an obligation to their parents who pay the school fees), they constructed their masculinities in such a way that allowed them to work and achieve examination success, while still retaining their popularity.

It is worth reflecting on the composition of the overachieving boys' group. The girls in the overachieving group were among the most academically successful in the year group; this was not the case for the overachieving boys. The fact that there were no high-ability boys in this group is very interesting; while it is difficult to ascertain the reasons for this, consider the following possibility. Perhaps these high-ability boys had succeeded in achieving the much sought after middle ground, where they were able to do sufficient work to maintain their position in the top sets but were not achieving high enough grades to identify themselves as overachieving – rather, they were merely achieving. While the high-ability girls constructed their friendship group, and to some extent their femininity, around a situation where it was acceptable to overachieve, the high-ability boys defined their friends in different ways, possibly through common interests in sport and music. Thus, they sought popularity in ways external to the classroom that were not related to their ability or what sets they were in, while at the same time maintaining their position in the highest sets. If this was the case, then it could be suggested that it was *these* boys who were the more 'successful' in school.

Summary

This chapter has been principally concerned with understanding which groups of students underachieve in school. However, the predictive value of all the variables as they relate to Key Stage 3 performance has also been of great interest. Most noteworthy was the amount of variance gender contributed to the examination score: accounting for less than 1 per cent of the variance in examination outcome, the apparently poor relationship between gender and achievement in these results should exercise a cautionary note to the proponents of the 'failing boys' debate.

In our underachievement model, 174 individuals were identified as underachieving, along with 205 overachievers, using relatively generous parameters of one standard deviation. The nature of the overachieving and underachieving groups was examined with respect to their gender and social class. The results gave little support to the predictive model that the underachieving group would be mainly working-class boys, but rather indicated that there were more working-class girls in this group than were expected from the statistical analysis. When the profiles of the underachieving pupils were drawn up, the reasons for some students being included in the underachieving group were easier to discern. For example, some pupils achieved the same levels at Key Stage 3 as they had done at Key Stage 2 three years previously, while others achieved three Level 6s at Key Stage 3 rather than the Level 7s that the model predicted (see Appendix 3). The issues that these results raise regarding the expectations we should have for our pupils are examined more closely in Chapter 9. Discussions with a sample of underachieving and overachieving students also revealed few characteristics that differentiated the two groups.

The use of a 'best possible' model for predicting academic achievement, and consequently academic underachievement, has revealed that the students identified here as underachieving were a very heterogeneous group with little in common, apart from the fact that they did not do as well as perhaps they ought in the Key Stage 3 examinations. There is little evidence here of large groups of students underachieving in school. Results such as these bring further into question the usefulness of the underachievement label: it is true that there were some students who did not do as well as expected but these were not a clearly defined group of, say, working-class boys.

Frequently the terms 'underachievement' and 'low achievement' are used interchangeably. However, the findings described here, both from the modelling process and our use of Thorndike's definition of underachievement, suggest that this cannot be the case – underachievement and low achievement are not the same thing. In our model, students who achieved 3 Level 6s at Key Stage 3, rather than their predicted Levels 7s, were identified as underachieving – in no way could they also be described as low achievers. Therefore, if attempts to identify students who are underachieving leave us with a very heterogeneous group, could the same be said of students who are low achievers? Exploring the characteristics of students who do less well in school – the low achievers – is the aim of the next chapter.

CHAPTER 8

Measuring low achievement

> We recommend that the causes of low academic achievement be more rigorously analysed so that remedies, across and beyond the range of educational services, may be developed.
>
> (House of Commons 2003, 36)

Throughout the earlier sections of this book, there have been numerous examples of how students who appear to perform less well in school are labelled as underachieving. These students usually fall into one of three groups: they are either male, are from a particular ethnic minority group, or come from poorer homes. However, as the first half of the book has sought to demonstrate, underachievement is a difficult term to conceptualize. That boys have been out-performed by girls in GCSE English examinations by a consistent margin for almost 30 years cannot be taken as evidence for their underachievement, neither can the fact that, despite higher than average improvements in performance, students from certain ethnic minority communities are still performing below national averages. One consequence of the uncertainty that surrounds an accepted definition for underachievement is simply that underachievement is used interchangeably with low achievement. Thorndike's model for underachievement tells us that this cannot be the case: students who do their best in an examination, when a realistic number of the variables that are known to influence attainment are accounted for, cannot be labelled as underachievers.

In this chapter, the aim is to examine the characteristics of students who do less well in school – the low achievers. By looking at students' performance in Key Stages 2 and 3 National Curriculum assessments, it is possible to gain an understanding of which students are the least successful in school in terms of examination outcomes. The data-set that has been compiled allows us to look at examination performance according to several individual characteristics – namely gender, receipt of free school meals, family type and parental occupation – as well as other factors such as motivation and attendance in school. The small (but representative) number of students from ethnic minority homes in the sample means that findings based on the achievements of this group are particularly unreliable and are not considered here.

Identifying low-achieving students

Here we simply consider whether any differences exist between groups of students, both in their attitudes towards school and in their achievement in National Curriculum tests and in the Cognitive Ability Test (CAT) (a test of mental ability). In this discussion, the students are grouped by their gender and by receipt of free school meals. Further aggregations of students are also possible for example, according to whether they come from families where parents work, or by the type of jobs their parents do. Very often, these categorizations can operate as proxies for family wealth, and in this study, they produced the same trends as those we describe for groups of students who receive free school meals. We begin by examining the differential attainment of male and female students in national tests and in tests of mental ability.

Achievement according to gender

The purpose of this part of the analysis was to examine whether or not there were any significant differences between the performance of boys and girls on the end of Key Stage examinations and in the CAT. The results are summarized below:

- No significant difference in the achievement of male and female pupils was found on the non-verbal and quantitative batteries of the CAT. In the verbal test, there was a significant difference at the 0.05 level in favour of the girls. The average standardized score for all pupils was below 100 (the designated average score).
- There was no significant difference between the performance of boys and girls in Key Stages 2 and 3 in maths and science, but a highly significant difference in favour of the girls in English at both Key Stages. Table 8.1 presents the mean points score achieved in the core subjects at Key Stage 3.

Data was also collected from the schools and through pupil questionnaires on aspects of pupil motivation, parental involvement and attendance at school. The key findings are summarized below:

Table 8.1   **Key Stage 3 results according to gender**

Test	Gender	Number of Students	Mean Points Score	Standard Deviation	Significance
English	Male	915	30.2	6.8	0.00
	Female	908	33.1	6.4	
Maths	Male	902	32.7	7.1	0.08
	Female	901	33.3	6.9	
Science	Male	907	32.0	6.5	0.29
	Female	916	32.3	6.4	

- *Attendance:* there was little difference in the number of days that the boys and girls attended school. However, the mean percentages of 89.1 and 88.7 for boys and girls respectively were below the 92 per cent target all pupils are required to achieve under the Compact scheme that was run between all the schools in the area and the local Education and Business Partnership (EBP).
- *Motivation and attitudes towards school:* differences between the attitude and motivation of boys and girls were found in the majority of the aspects assessed, with the exception of general academic self-concept where the difference was not found to be significant. The results suggest that the boys were more confident in their ability and enjoyment of maths while the girls favoured reading. Both groups had similar feelings about non-specific subjects.
- *Parental involvement:* there were no significant differences in response to the pupils' estimation of how involved their parents were in their schooling, but there was a significant difference (in favour of the girls) with regard to how often parents asked about schoolwork and to whether or not they controlled pupils' going out on a school night. However, any differences in this final question might have more to do with parents' concern over girls' safety, and the restrictions placed upon them – what Francis (2000) calls a discourse of 'female fear' – than a link with school. Interestingly, very low numbers of all pupils said that their parents frequently regulated the amount of television they could watch.

Achievement according to receipt of free school meals

Pupils who receive free school meals tend to come from the poorest families, and approximately 20 per cent of the sample fell into this category. It is worth noting that not all families who are eligible actually receive free school meals. At both Key Stages 2 and 3, pupils who received free school meals performed significantly lower than their peers ($p<0.000$). A similar pattern of results was obtained for performance in the CAT. Table 8.2 gives the results for Key Stage 3 performance.

Table 8.2   **Key Stage 3 results according to receipt of free school meals**

Test	Free school meals?	Number of students	Mean points Score	Standard deviation	Significance
English	No	1464	32.7	6.6	0.00
	Yes	359	27.4	5.9	
Maths	No	1449	34.1	6.7	0.00
	Yes	354	28.8	6.6	
Science	No	1461	33.2	6.2	0.00
	Yes	362	28.0	6.0	

According to national targets, 70–80 per cent of pupils should achieve Level 4 (points score: 27) at the end of Key Stage 2, with a similar proportion achieving Level 5 (points score: 33) at the end of Key Stage 3. Table 8.3 shows how the percentage of pupils achieving these benchmark levels is distributed according to whether or not an individual receives free school meals. In each case, higher proportions of students who receive free school meals fail to reach benchmark levels. In fact, at Key Stage 3, almost two-thirds of these students do not achieve these levels.

Table 8.3   **Percentage of pupils who achieved Key Stage benchmark levels, according to receipt of free school meals**

Subject	Receive free school meals?	Percentage who achieve benchmark level or above
Key Stage 2 English	Yes	48
	No	71
Key Stage 2 Maths	Yes	41
	No	70
Key Stage 2 Science	Yes	44
	No	75
Key Stage 3 English	Yes	33
	No	65
Key Stage 3 Maths	Yes	38
	No	71
Key Stage 3 Science	Yes	35
	No	69

It would seem then that, with regard to the academic variables, pupils who receive free school meals do less well than their peers in aggregate terms at every level. The pupils' scores on the contextual variables are described next.

- *Attendance*: unlike the comparison between boys and girls, there was a statistically significant difference in the attendance rates of those who received free school meals and those who did not. At 84 per cent, the mean attendance of the children who receive free school meals was below the 92 per cent target all pupils are required to achieve in order to meet their Compact goals. The attendance figure for students who were not entitled to free school meals was 90 per cent.
- *Parental involvement*: pupils who received free school meals reported lower levels of parental involvement than their peers. In all aspects of parental attitude towards schoolwork there was a significant difference in the levels of involvement, with the parents of those who did not receive free school meals appearing to be more positively involved with certain aspects of their son or daughter's school life ($p<0.05$). As with gender, there was no significant difference between the control parents had over the amount of time spent watching television, although parents of children who do not receive free school meals were more likely to control their going out on a school night.
- *Motivation and attitudes towards school*: pupils who received free school meals had lower self-esteem than their peers. Differences in self-concept were less pronounced but, overall, these pupils had a lower academic self-concept. They were, however, just as positive as the others about their ability in maths.

The results of this analysis suggest that, with regard to academic performance and school attendance, receipt of free school meals appears to be more of a barrier to academic success than gender. Although only the results for those receiving free school meals are reported here, they reflect the findings for other variables which, in this study, were proxies for poverty – for example, whether pupils had a working father or mother, or came from a single-parent or working-class family. In each case, pupils from more economically disadvantaged homes were less successful in school.

Examining the distinction between low achievement and underachievement was an important aim of this study. By dividing the sample into groups – for example, according to their social class or gender – it was possible to analyse and compare performance. As a result, academic achievement could be considered from the perspective of which groups of pupils succeeded in school – the notion of high or low achievement. The findings of this analysis are quite clear. It comes as little or no surprise that the poorer families in this study were more likely to receive free school meals, have no working mother or father, have a working-class background or a single parent as head of the family. However, what was most striking was that children from these families were more likely to be disadvantaged in the school assessment system in aggregate terms at *every* level. These pupils obtained significantly lower examination results at Key Stages 2 and 3, lower scores on the CAT, were poorer attenders and generally received less parental support than pupils from more economically advantaged homes.

On the other hand, when examining differences according to students' gender, the differences between boys and girls were less apparent. It was true that the girls achieved higher scores in the English examinations and had a more positive attitude towards reading, while the boys scored more highly on the self-esteem scale, but on every other measure, there were few differences between the two groups.

Summary

In this chapter, we have explored the concept of low achievement. By considering the performance of groups of students in the Key Stage 2 and 3 examinations, it was possible to gain an understanding of which groups are less successful in school. The results show us that students from economically disadvantaged homes (characterized here by receipt of free school meals) do less well in school in aggregate terms on every examination outcome. Although girls outperform boys in English assessments, the achievement gaps according to gender were not as pronounced as those according to poverty. For example, fewer than half the students who received free school meals achieved benchmark levels at Key Stage 2, while at Key Stage 3 only around one third of these students achieved the benchmark Level 5 or above.

Bringing together the results from the analysis of low achievers and underachievers it would seem that many of the pupils popularly labelled in the media as underachievers should actually be labelled as low achievers. That the relatively poorer working-class pupil generally does not do as well in school as their more affluent counterparts may well be the case, but there is little to suggest that this group of pupils was underachieving. Thus, we have two parallel concepts – low achievement and under-achievement – that can be framed within the broader issue of achievement at group and individual levels. Therefore, it might be possible to have a high-achieving underachiever (for example, someone who failed to convert their three Level 6 outcomes at Key Stage 3 to Level 7s), or a low-achieving underachiever (for example, someone who achieved the same lower levels at Key Stages 2 and 3). Indeed, what this study has suggested is that applying the underachievement label to a diverse group of individuals is incorrect, and so an alternative label should be sought.

CHAPTER 9

Understanding underachievement

We believe that in all its pronouncements the Government should distinguish between low achievement and underachievement. We are concerned that the present use of the term underachievement frequently fails to distinguish between children who could have achieved more and those children who have worked hard to fulfil their potential but have been unable to achieve high academic results.

(House of Commons 2003, 35)

This chapter will review some of the key findings to emerge from this book. The focus throughout has been on understanding what it is that we actually mean by the term 'underachievement'. The first section provided many examples of how underachievement has been used to describe the relatively poorer examination performance of nations, schools and groups of students. Given the wide application of the term, it is perhaps unsurprising that an alternative perspective also exists, which questions the validity of the whole underachievement debate. Reviewing both aspects of the discourse as it describes the phenomenon at each of these three levels leaves one with the impression that the term 'underachievement' might really not be telling us very much at all about what is happening in schools. Much of the evidence used to explain the phenomenon is open to re-interpretation, and many of the initiatives adopted to try to address the issue appear to have little empirical basis and may do more to reinforce inequities rather than to raise the attainment of groups of students who are disadvantaged in school.

In addition, it seems that we are unclear about what it is that we mean by 'underachievement'. In the absence of an accepted definition, two questions arise: what is underachievement meant to be relative to, and do we really mean low achievement instead? These are issues considered in the second part of the book. In addition to offering a definition for under-achievement that aims to provide the best possible model for predicting achievement in an examination, we also attempted to identify groups of students who may be underachieving in school and to distinguish these students from those who are achieving at the lowest levels. This has left us with two concepts – underachievement and low achievement. Both are often confused and conflated, but being able to distinguish between them offers us a possible way forward through the underachievement discourse.

This chapter draws together the key findings to emerge from this study. In particular, it looks at the work on defining and measuring underachievement, and considers its implications for research into the differential attainment of students, schools and nations. We begin by drawing attention to some general issues about the methodology of researching underachievement.

Researching underachievement

Two particular features of this study set it apart from previous work conducted in this area. First, it is unusual in that it has considered underachievers from across the ability range. This makes it conceptu-ally possible to have a high-achieving underachiever as well as a low-achieving underachiever. Second and perhaps more crucially, it has involved the manipulation of a comprehensive set of background factors that have been cited in the literature as being closely linked to academic performance, in order to produce an arguably more refined model for identifying students who might be underachieving in school. The approach taken here has avoided focusing solely on the psycholo-gist's use of the term 'underachievement' (as the mental-ability test/school performance discrepancy) that characterizes much of the research reported in this area. In contrast, the use of background factors, such as motivation, along with indicators of economic wellbe-ing in the identification of pupils who might be underachieving, is a considerable improvement upon other studies.

Before summarizing the findings of this study and considering their wider implications, it is worth drawing attention to some of the method-ological difficulties encountered when researching this topic. There is a growing body of research that looks critically at the value and reliability of studies in the field of educational research. Indeed, it has become appar-ent from studying the existing published research in this area that some of the confusion surrounding the underachievement discourse has arisen because of difficulties on the part of some researchers in interpreting the mainly quantitative research findings and methodologies. These difficulties have arisen for several reasons, and all have implications for further studies. Moreover, they also present important implications for educational policy at national, regional and even local levels.

Concern over the effective use of statistics in educational research has also been expressed by Gorard (2002), who has highlighted and drawn attention to the ways in which researchers, Chief Inspectors and even Ministers of Education have in the past made 'naïve' readings of data (see, for example, Gorard et al. 1999). Within the research community there may be what Gorard has called a 'methodological schism', where the enforced distinction between quantitative and qualitative methods has led to some researchers avoiding the use of statistics in their own research and, instead, over-relying on analyses conducted by others (Gorard 2002). The relative abundance of qualitative studies in educational research, to the possible detriment of quantitative methods, has two consequences that may have implications for researching school achievement. The first is the relative reduction in the numbers of skilled researchers willing to read, critique and (if necessary) challenge the results of statistical analysis (Gorard 2002). The second is the growth in ever-more sophisticated computer-based statistical models which have resulted in the development of advanced methods of analysis (for example, multilevel modelling techniques) which few outside the specific field are able to understand, let alone challenge (Fitz–Gibbon 2000). Both of these issues are particularly pertinent to the current study, as several of the contradictions in the interpretation of research findings were related to statistical methods, all of which tended to reinforce the picture of underachievement in schools.

As a relatively new researcher, it has been quite perplexing to find so little agreement over the acceptable methods for analysing certain statistical data, especially that which relates to changes in examination performance over time. Clearly, if the numbers had been more critically and effectively analysed when they had first appeared, then perhaps the issues that gave rise to the underachievement phenomenon might have been addressed sooner.

Defining underachievement

As already suggested, one of the unexpected outcomes of this study has been to highlight methodological inconsistencies in the design and reporting of some research into pupil underachievement. These problems were particularly evident when evaluating published research into defining and measuring the underachievement of different groups of pupils, and Chapter 6 described some of the different methods adopted by researchers when investigating this issue. However, what has been fundamental to this problem is that there is little apparent consensus on even a definition for the term 'underachievement', let alone on how it should be measured. Yet, as the early chapters of this book have demonstrated, 'underachievement' is one of the most readily used terms in education today – both inside the staff room and outside it.

One of the problems with the notion of underachievement is quite simply in understanding what the underachievement is in relation to. Is it related to some kind of innate ability on the part of the individual, or is it achievement relative to that of a larger group? Perhaps here a more apposite term might be 'low achievement', or 'differential achievement.' This confusion, together with frequent conflation of the terms 'underachievement' and 'low achievement', was a recurring theme in this study and one that is considered later. Much previous work on defining and measuring underachievement has relied on what can be termed the psychologists' definition of underachievement: that is, 'school performance, usually measured by grades, that is substantially below what would be predicted on the basis of the student's mental ability, typically measured by intelligence or standardised academic tests' (McCall *et al.* 1992, 54). However, the problem with adopting this method is that it does not take into account other factors that are widely acknowledged to contribute to achievement, for example, social class and pupil attitudes towards school. Neither does this method fully compensate for errors in the design and measurement of commonly used standardized ability tests and school examinations.

The wider perception of what is understood by the term 'underachievement' has been further complicated by its adoption by the media as a synonym for much of what is perceived to be wrong with education in this country. In this guise, the term is frequently confused with that of low achievement. For example, when we read that smaller numbers of students from the Bangladeshi community are achieving the benchmark number of GCSE A*–C grades compared with white students, it is suggested that the Bangladeshi pupils are 'underachieving' (DfES 2003). Whether these pupils are underachieving or not, is not evidenced by these results: what the commentators should have made clear was that on this basis, the achievement of Bangladeshi pupils at the benchmark GCSE level was lower than that of white students (although even then there are problems with this relatively simplistic notion of comparing groups of students according to their ethnic background – concerns discussed in more detail in Chapter 5).

This study has sought to broaden the definition of the term 'under-achievement' to take into account the contextual factors that many researchers believe are fundamental to explaining the differential performance of pupils in school. Consequently, this desire for a broader meaning for the term has led to the adoption of Thorndike's classic definition of underachievement as 'achievement falling below what would be forecast from our most informed and accurate prediction, based on a team of predictor variables' (Thorndike 1963, 19). This definition has provided the basis for the model with which groups of underachieving pupils were identified in the current study. Of course, it must be stressed that no model is perfect, and the one offered by Thorndike is unable to take into account *all* of the factors which could influence a particular individual's performance in an examination on a given day. Nevertheless, Thorndike's model does provide a more innovative approach for discussing, understanding, and perhaps rejecting the notion of underachievement.

Measuring underachievement

Thorndike's definition of underachievement has implied the use of a statistical model for assessing the impact of a range of variables on a single dependent variable: here, this was performance in the Key Stage 3 examinations. In this study, multiple regression techniques were used to predict examination performance. A comparison was then made between the predicted and actual examination results in an attempt to identify an underachieving group.

Where multiple regression techniques have been used elsewhere in the identification of underachievers, they have relied almost exclusively on the school performance/mental-ability test discrepancy described earlier. In this new study, a large number of additional variables that are related to academic performance (such as gender, poverty, motivation and school type) were used to enhance the model and hence predict the Key Stage 3 examination result. In its methods, this study is similar to the work of School Effectiveness researchers; both have used a wide-ranging set of contextual variables to account for variations in academic performance, and both have typically found that these variables have accounted for over 80 per cent of the variance in the academic outcome. However, the studies differ in the use to which the findings are put. Here the focus is on the 80 per cent of the variance attributed to background and other factors. In contrast, the School Effectiveness researchers have concentrated on the (at best) 20 per cent of variance attributed to the school effect. As a result, this study has considered the school effect from a somewhat different perspective.

By adopting Thorndike's method for predicting academic performance, this study has presented a novel and arguably more reliable technique for identifying a group of underachieving pupils than the mental ability/school performance discrepancy method described earlier. In doing so, we have found no evidence for the claim that underachieving students are mainly working-class boys. Rather, the students identified as underachieving, on this model, belonged to a very mixed group, comprising students from across the ability range.

The concept of low achievement is different to that of underachievement, and can imply that it is beyond the control of the individual pupil. Very often, when discussing the examination performance of different groups, the notion of low achievement is conflated and confused with underachievement, particularly in media accounts of the phenomenon. Examining the distinction between low achievement and underachievement was an important aim of this study. By dividing the sample into groups according to, for example, their social class or gender, it was possible to analyse and compare the performance of these distinct groups. As a result, academic achievement could be considered from the perspective of which groups of pupils succeeded in school – the notion of high or low achievement.

The findings of this analysis were quite clear. It comes as little or no surprise that the poorer families in this study were more likely to receive free school meals, have no working mother or father, have a working class background or a single parent as head of the family. However, what was most striking was that children from these families were more likely to be disadvantaged in the school assessment system in aggregate terms at every level. These pupils obtained significantly lower examination results at Key Stages 2 and 3, lower scores on the CAT, were poorer attenders and generally received less parental support than pupils from more economically advantaged homes. On the other hand, when examining gender, the differences between boys and girls were less apparent. It was true that the girls achieved higher scores in the English examinations and had more positive attitudes towards reading while the boys scored more highly on the self-esteem scale, but on every other measure there were few differences between them.

Underachievement, on the other hand, is a more disparate concept, and there was little to suggest from this analysis that a particular group of pupils were underachieving in school. Where pupils do appear to underachieve, they do so for a range of reasons, some transient, others more profound. On the one hand, the underachievers were pupils who achieved the same National Curriculum levels at Key Stage 2 as at Key Stage 3, and who might be described therefore as having made no progress over the interim three years between these statutory assessments. However, they were also pupils who achieved good levels at Key Stage 3 (perhaps three Level 6s) but who had been placed in the underachieving group because they had not managed to convert those Level 6s to the predicted Level 7s. This latter group of underachievers would be unlikely to be labelled as such by their teachers, and were probably distributed in the higher class sets and performing well – but maybe not quite as well as expected. Indeed, what this study has suggested is that applying the underachievement label to a diverse group of individuals is incorrect and perhaps an alternative label should be sought.

These particular findings raise important questions about what we want our children to actually achieve at school, and of the real value of the underachievement label. Clearly, it is an overused and misconstrued item in the vocabulary of teachers and educationalists. A number of questions arise. For example, in the attempt to raise educational standards should we strive to create a population of overachievers who are under pressure always to do their maximum best? When do A grades become a disappointment because the candidate was predicted A*s? If we are happy with the notion of overachievement, must there by definition be underachievement – and how much achievement (under or over) is acceptable?

Also of interest is the impact of gender on school performance. In this study, few differences were found between the male and female pupils' scores on the academic and contextual variables: for example, girls were no more likely than boys to attend school regularly, or to have a higher score on the CAT or end of Key Stage tests in maths and science. The only consistently different results were in the examination scores in English. This was in contrast to the results for pupils who received free school meals, who were disadvantaged on *all* of the above outcomes compared to pupils who were able to pay for their school meals.

In the regression model that assessed the impact of each variable on examination performance, the relationship with gender was once again very weak. Here, gender accounted for less than 1 per cent of the variance in examination outcome. These findings have implications for commentators who place gender, and the underachievement of boys in particular, at the heart of the standards debate, and should provide a cautionary note to all those who perpetuate the binary notion of boys versus girls.

Therefore, in terms of underachievement and low achievement, this analysis has shown two things. It has shown that the pupils who were identified as underachieving were a mixed group, comprising boys and girls from each social class who appeared to share little in common. And it has shown the relatively weak influence of gender on achievement, which appears in stark contrast to the clear disadvantage pupils from poorer homes experience in school.

Implications of the study

The following discussion is framed by the context of policy implications from the perspective of a school seeking to become more inclusive for all of its pupils, while at the same time ensuring ongoing improvement in examination results. In addition, we examine the wider implications of the use of examination results as indicators of school success, and the notion of what constitutes a desirable outcome from a fair and equitable state education system.

Implications for schools

In common with previous work, this study incorporated mental-ability tests into the underachievement model. These tests are popular, and their use in this study has several implications for schools. The debate surrounding the validity and desirability of mental-ability testing was rehearsed in Chapter 6. Their use in this context is important, not only because they give reasonable predictions for performance at Key Stage 3 but also because they afford schools an additional instrument for tracking and analysing the performance of their pupils. Nevertheless, it must be remembered that their use is not without difficulties. It has been clearly shown here that pupils from more economically deprived backgrounds perform less well on these mental-ability tests. If pupils' results are relied upon to form the basis of predictions that will follow them throughout school, then there is a danger that pupils from these more economically deprived backgrounds will be set lower targets for their attainment at school, and hence lower pupil and teacher expectations could result. The recent introduction of individual pupil identification numbers makes this issue of labelling pupils as high or low achievers in the early years of their education even more pertinent.

Adjudicating on the relative merits of these mental-ability tests is beyond the scope of this study. As a tool for informing school target-setting, pupil monitoring and even highlighting discrepancies that might uncover fundamental literacy problems, they are invaluable. On the other hand, when in some parts of the country bookshops are selling the tests to ambitious parents in order to allow their children extra practice, their use as a measure of mental ability must be questioned. This is particularly important if schools rely solely on the results of such tests to dictate streaming and target-setting, to the possible disadvantage of pupils from less financially well-off backgrounds.

As this study has demonstrated, identifying a neat homogeneous group of underachievers is not possible. Where such homogeneity does exist, it may be due to a range of reasons – some transient, others more deep-rooted. Does this mean then that schools should forget about the whole notion of underachievement and focus on those pupils who are the *low* rather than *under*achievers – those who receive free school meals, for example? This is an important issue for schools; teachers can easily identify the pupils who are boys in their class, and if they do not appear to be doing as well as 'expected', the underachiever label is not far away. But how many teachers can identify the pupils in their class who receive free school meals and who consequently are at greater risk from educational failure? The answer is probably very few – which in many ways is a good thing. On the other hand, if pupils are at risk of education failure simply because they are poor, this is a grim reflection of comprehensive state education. Perhaps some of the vast resources that have hitherto been put into schemes and initiatives to counter the (now increasingly questionable) underachievement of boys, such as mentoring and reward programmes, should be diverted into strategies to promote and, crucially, to support the achievement of pupils from economically disadvantaged backgrounds. This might generate more noticeable gains in terms of measurable assessment outcomes.

One of the enduring myths about standards in schools has come from the perceived underachievement of boys, particularly in English. However, it is possible that differential attainment by gender is a product of the changed nature of school assessment, rather than of some inherent failure of boys to do well in school exams. In our interrogation of examination data, we assume that the assessment system is gender neutral and that we ought to expect boys and girls to achieve the same results in examinations. Given that we are often told that men and women inhabit different planets, are equal outcomes in school examinations a realistic expectation?

It has been suggested earlier that the most economically disadvantaged pupils do not do as well in school as their wealthier peers but that this relative lack of success is not a result of their *under*achievement, but rather their *lower* achievement. However, the pre-eminence of social factors in affecting academic achievement does not sit happily with the well-documented findings of the School Effectiveness Research movement (see the discussions in Chapters 2 and 3). As described earlier, despite the fact that this study and School Effectiveness researchers have used similar approaches in determining the factors that influence academic performance, the application of the results have differed. The dominant role of background factors in effecting the academic performance of the pupils who attend a particular school raises two issues that are directly relevant to the standards debate. First, if examination results are relatively easy to predict from effects that are external to that of the school, then what effect do schools have? It can be argued that an over-reliance on examination results as the sole indicators of school performance may lead to the wider benefits of schooling being ignored or at least sidelined. It would be somewhat extreme to claim that schools have no effect, but perhaps their effect is not in whether they produce a certain proportion of 16-year-olds with five A*–C GCSE grades. It may be that examination results are not as important as was once thought, and that there are broader social benefits which might be the very thing that makes individual schools stand out as being more or less 'effective'. Of course, examination results and qualifications are easy to compare and measure, unlike some less tangible, but also important, school outcomes, such as citizenship and lifelong learning.

The second issue is that although schools might wish to raise the standards of their lower achieving pupils, the amount of difference they can realistically make is questionable. Providing expensive remedial programmes to support the learning of lower achieving pupils who, as the results of this study suggest, are more likely to come from poorer backgrounds does not reach the root of the problem. As Orfield writes, 'Schools often reflect rather than transform inequality' (2000, 410): schools alone cannot compensate for wider social inequalities, nor can they solve the problem in isolation. This is perhaps an overly pessimistic view of the impact schools can have. It is true that there are shining examples of schools achieving academic success in challenging circumstances: however, these are a much vaunted minority and it is questionable whether their success is sustainable beyond the short term. On the other hand, how many failing schools are situated in areas of economic and social deprivation or conversely how many schools in relatively more affluent areas are in special measures? There are numerous examples of interventions and initiatives that act as concrete reminders that the 'schooling game' is not a fair one and that pupils' experiences are far from universal.

Wider implications

This section considers the implications of this study that go beyond the influence of the school. It is clear that there are pupils who are disadvantaged in schools in terms of academic success. However, is this a natural and acceptable consequence of rewarding educational success through exam performance? This leads us to ask questions not only about the practical value of making comparisons based on such indicators, but also more philosophical questions about the kind of education system we are striving to achieve in this country.

In 1981, Reynolds suggested that pupils in Wales were being 'schooled to fail' (Reynolds and Murgatroyd 1981); more recently, the *Daily Mail* newspaper has implied that British schools are 'the worst in Europe' (Halpin 2001). Much of the evidence that has contributed to these 'failing nation' debates has come from the results of international comparative tests such as TIMSS and PISA, which suggest that pupil achievement in the UK is dogged by a long tail of underachievement. This 'crisis account' of falling standards and failing pupils has led to calls for policy borrowing from more academically successful nations. Whether it is school choice policies from Sweden or curriculum standards from Japan, the assumption has become: if it can work in those countries, it can work in our own. In describing the discourse of over and underachievement in Japan's schools, Chapters 2 and 3 sought to point out some of the pitfalls in removing school policy from its social and cultural context. Alongside stories about the success of Japan's schools, an alternative perspective has emerged which has exposed the 'dark side' of Japanese education, where tragic cases of youth suicide, violence and bullying are symptomatic of a school system where success has come at a high cost. However, many comparative researchers are concerned that these myths about the Japanese school system have little empirical basis and lead to an oversimplified view of a complex issue.

The school accountability and high-stakes testing measures that have emerged as a reaction to the standards crisis in the UK and the USA are another example of policy-makers reacting to the perceived underachievement of students and schools. In the United States, in particular, the strict school accountability measures attached to the No Child Left Behind legislation, although ostensibly equitable, have led to fears that many schools serving diverse and disadvantaged communities will be labelled as failing and subject to potentially punitive school improvement sanctions.

The use of the results from high-stakes tests is fundamental to the evidence base that leads to accusations of the underachievement of different groups. The notion that examination performance is *the* most desirable school outcome was discussed earlier, but this reliance on raw examination results presents other difficulties. First of all, comparing examination results over time is notoriously difficult; tests are changed every year and examination scores are themselves artificial relative values. At GCSE level, the switch in the late 1980s from norm-referenced assessment (where a similar proportion of pupils gained a particular grade year-upon-year) to criterion referencing (where candidates were required to show evidence of meeting a particular grade requirement) has meant that standards have been allowed to vary, and an accurate and clear assessment of whether any changes are due to rising standards or easier tests is particularly difficult. These difficulties are magnified when comparisons are made at international level.

The fact that examination scores are an absolute rather than a relative value also presents problems for researchers who wish to monitor trends in examination performance. Rationalizing the debate only seems to raise more seemingly insoluble questions: does improving the attainment of the lowest achieving pupils mean that the distribution of pupils at the higher end should remain the same in order to allow the others to catch up? Does raising the achievement of all pupils mean that all groups will get proportionally better and that there will always be a group of relatively low achievers (whether individuals, nations or schools) who will never catch-up? Or, alternatively, is it more desirable to raise the achievement of all pupils but allow less variance between the highest and lowest achievers? This might reduce the apparently long tail of low achievers, but it could also mean that there are fewer very high achievers and a lot more average ones.

The above questions can be framed in the issue of what is most desirable in an examination system, equity, equality, or both? No one would argue against having an equitable system, but the fact that large numbers of pupils with particular social backgrounds do not succeed at school suggests this might not be the case. It could also be realistically argued that the distribution of examination results itself discourages equality – there will always have to be pupils who succeed and pupils who fail. A more equal or inclusive system could result in having a group of very average pupils; or put another way, in having practically *all* pupils achieving at least a required standard.

In short, this study has suggested that the way forward might be to reject the notion of underachievement as it is applied to the attainment of groups of students in school. What might be of greater importance is the issue of low achievement among many pupils from economically disadvantaged backgrounds, and understanding quite simply why it is the case that poorer children do less well in school. However, the implications of this study are such that in the absence of joined-up policy-making, realistically there is very little that schools can do alone to address the problems of low achievement. Schools are being judged against indicators over which they have little influence, and which use artificial measures of relative success. If what we want are higher standards in our schools, then perhaps we first need to decide what our priorities are – relatively higher examination scores for some, or a holistic approach to creating a more equitable system where groups of pupils are not disadvantaged merely because they might be poor? This latter approach clearly seems to be more socially inclusive and ameliorative.

Summary

Researching underachievement has been rather like carrying handfuls of sand over an obstacle race. Once you have completed all the obstacles – read the literature, designed the study and analysed the results – you find that the sand has trickled through your fingers and that there is not much left. What started out as being a 'predominant discourse' that labelled sections of the school population as failing has been reduced to a description of a largely heterogeneous group with few unifying characteristics, apart from the fact that at their own level they probably have not done as well as they might on a particular assessment on a particular day. Whether this constitutes evidence of a failing generation is unlikely: some of these 'underachievers' will go on to achieve perfectly respectable GCSE grades and take their place in further or higher education, if they feel that is the appropriate place for them. With all its negative associations and stereotypical connotations, it must be asked whether 'underachiever' is the appropriate term for them.

CHAPTER 10

So, what works? Strategies to close the achievement gap

... given the 15,000 hours of compulsory treatment meted out to the young in the name of education, it is important that we get things right by examining the problems and approaching solutions scientifically.

(Fitz–Gibbon 2000, 1)

This book has argued that the term 'underachievement' is not really very useful in helping us understand what is happening with regard to the relative achievement of students in school. Rather than being a synonym for describing patterns of attainment, it is a concept over which there is little consensus about what it actually means or how it should be measured. Attempts to identify students who may be underachieving have left us with a relatively heterogeneous group of individuals with little in common other than that on a particular day, and in a particular type of assessment, they have perhaps not done quite as well as they ought. We were, however, able to identify a group of students who did appear to be doing less well in school, a group that we called the 'low achievers'. This low-achieving group comprised a disproportionate number of students who come from poorer homes, and who, at aggregate level, were performing less well than their peers on national assessments from Key Stage 2 to 4. Despite these achievement gaps between the most and least economically advantaged students, evidence does exist that suggests the achievement of all students is improving and that long-standing achievement gaps – for example, between majority and minority ethnic groups – are becoming smaller. Even so, inequities still exist, and it is clear that strategies that are proven to close the achievement gap should be developed, refined, or supported in wider practice.

So, what works? In addition to large-scale projects, often undertaken by professional researchers and funded by external research bodies, there has been a plethora of small-scale strategies to raise attainment levels in schools around the country. Some are initiated by LEAs, some by schools themselves: only a few are reported in the research literature, and many are of such small size that it is unlikely they will have influence outside a particular school. On the other hand, others may be singled out and used (rightly or wrongly) to inform national policy. What all these projects have in common is that they are trying to raise the achievement of all pupils, in particular that of boys, low achieving students, and those from certain minority backgrounds. Some of the strategies that are widely used in schools include a focus on assessment data (knowing just where your pupils' strengths and weaknesses lie); awareness-raising for staff through in-service training; mentoring schemes for selected, targeted pupils; segregating pupils by sex for certain (or all) lessons; changing the classroom structure (for example, seating pupils boy–girl), and altering classroom pedagogy as well as syllabus materials in order to make them more 'boy-friendly' (see, for example, Lawrence *et al.* 1997.

However, what is the evidence that these strategies actually produce appreciable learning gains among students, or in other words: how do we know what works? Unfortunately, because of the *ad hoc* nature of many of these initiatives, proof of their relative merits is often hard to come by, and what evidence does exist can be difficult to generalize and may never find its way from the academic journal to the practitioner's desk. Research *does* exist that can tell us something about what works to raise standards in school, although the findings can often conflict with other agendas. For example, class-size reduction programmes can be too expensive to implement, and formative assessment techniques can detract from an exam-based assessment system.

The purpose of this final chapter is to present four strategies that purport to offer some answers about how to close achievement gaps and raise the attainment of students. We begin by describing the main features of each strategy before examining the evidence for its effectiveness. The examples are meant to be illustrative rather than exhaustive: clearly more than four strategies for raising achievement do exist. They are simply meant to show some of the best, and possibly the worst, uses of research evidence to support attempts to raise the performance of students in schools.

Two of the strategies come from the USA, and two have been pioneered in the UK. According to the available research evidence, it is not at all clear that all these strategies actually work; but nevertheless, schools do experiment with them, and indeed are encouraged to do so by government initiatives to raise standards (Blunkett 2000).

We begin by describing the high-stakes testing programme in Texas. Of all four strategies, this one has probably had the widest impact, but it is also the most controversial, both in its overt attempts to make schools accountable for the performance of their students and the evidence it presents that repeatedly testing students can close achievement gaps and improve schools. The second strategy is an excellent example of how academic research can be used to make an impact in schools. The 'black box' research into formative assessment techniques encourages teachers to rethink how they assess their students' work. It is an approach that appears to have met with much success, but it is also one that can come into conflict with the demands of the existing examination-based school assessment system. Reducing class sizes in infant schools is another strategy that has been adopted by the UK government to assist in the drive to raise standards. However, reducing class sizes to below 30 students, as recommended by the government, is a far cry from the optimum 15-per-class recommended by the researchers in the Tennessee STAR class-size reduction study. The final strategy is the use of single-sex classes in mixed sex schools. This is an approach that has been adopted widely, even though there is little evidence to show that it actually works. Many of the studies that have researched this initiative have been small-scale and have often lacked a suitable comparator group. Nevertheless schools use it, and are encouraged to experiment with it.

For each of the four strategies, we describe their main features before considering briefly the evidence for and against their perceived effectiveness at raising standards and closing achievement gaps.

Can you fatten the cow by weighing it? High-stakes testing in Texas

There are numerous examples of school accountability models linked to high-stakes testing. In the USA, many states have initiated their own sanctions-linked testing initiatives – for example, in North Carolina and Kentucky – and, of course, there is No Child Left Behind. In the UK, we have a long pedigree of national testing linked to school performance. However, this section will focus on just one example of a high-stakes testing programme – the Texas Accountability System (TAS).

Now the model for the 2002 federal education plan No Child Left Behind, the TAS measures and holds schools and districts accountable for student performance in assessment tests and drop-out rates (TEA 2003). Each year schools and school districts receive an accountability rating that is based on the percentage of all students and the four student sub-groups (white, Hispanic, African-American and economically disadvantaged) that pass the state's assessment tests. Grounded primarily in the percentage of students passing each test on the Texas Assessment of Academic Skills (TAAS), as well as the overall student drop-out rate, the more than 6,000 schools in Texas have been rated since 1994 as 'exemplary', 'recognized', 'acceptable' or 'unacceptable' (Haney 2000). Schools and school districts that achieve above and beyond the requirements of the TAS can receive monetary awards and exemptions from certain accountability measures. On the other hand, low performing schools and districts receive sanctions and increased scrutiny. Parents also have the option to transfer their children from these 'failing' schools. In addition, school principal and even teacher salaries have increasingly been linked to TAAS success (Haney 2000).

First administered in 1990, the TAAS is a criterion-referenced test that is designed to assess the essential elements of the school curriculum (Toenjes *et al.* 2003). The test mainly comprises multiple-choice elements, and is sat by students in Grades 3 through to 8 (ages 8 to 14) in reading and mathematics, and by students in Grades 4 through to 8 in writing. Each subject is assessed again in Grade 10 (age 15 or 16), and students need to achieve a pass in order to be able to graduate from high school. In the 2002–03 school year, TAAS was superseded by the Texas Assessment of Knowledge and Skills (TAKS), a test designed to be more rigorous than TAAS which also includes science and social studies assessments, and is also the requirement for a Grade 11 high-school diploma (TEA 2003). Additional assessments are also available for students with SEN and those for whom English is an additional language.

Not only have some educators praised the TAAS for closing achievement gaps and raising school performance, it has also been credited with creating what amounts to little short of a miracle in Texan education reform. Four areas of improvement are widely cited as evidence for the success of the initiative: sharp increases in the overall pass rates on TAAS, a closing of the achievement gap between white and minority students, a decrease in the number of students dropping out of high school, and improved state-wide scores on the National Assessment of Educational Progress (NAEP) (Linton and Kester 2003). Indeed, such plaudits seem well placed: the pass rate for students on the TAAS has risen from 55.6 per cent in 1994 to 78.3 per cent in 1999, for example (Toenjes *et al.* 2003). In the 2001–02 school year, the proportion of Texas students dropping out of high school in a longitudinal assessment of retention rates across Grades 9 to 12 was 5 per cent, a decrease from 6.2 per cent for 2000–01 and 7.2 per cent in 1999–2000 (Texas

Education Agency 2003). In the NAEP, Texas Grade 4 students were credited with making more progress on NAEP mathematics tests between 1992 and 1996 than students in any other participating state (Linton and Kester 2003).

Figure 10.1 shows the trends in achievement of Grade 8 students in the TAAS reading test. The rise in the proportions of students passing the assessment seems laudable. Indeed, in 2002 over 90 per cent of all student sub-groups, with the exception of students with limited English proficiency, achieved a pass grade in the assessment.

Figure 10.1 **Texas Assessment of Academic Skills: trends in achievement of Grade 8 students (reading)**

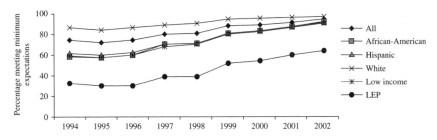

Source: TEA (2003a)

The increasing proportion of students achieving a pass grade across all subjects is similarly impressive. Between 1994 and 2002, the proportional increase in the numbers of Grade 8 students achieving the minimum competency levels required to register a pass was around 190 per cent for students of African-American heritage and those with limited English proficiency (Table 10.1).

Table 10.1 **Texas Assessment of Academic Skills: trends in achievement of Grade 8 students (all subjects)**

	1994	2002	Percentage point increase	Proportional increase (%)
All students	47	81	34	72
African-American	25	72	47	188
Hispanic	32	74	42	131
White	61	89	28	46
Low income	29	72	43	148
Limited English proficiency	12	35	23	192

Source: TEA (2003a)

The lowest increases were among students from the white group, who are traditionally those who have demonstrated the highest scores in these tests. That the rate of improvement of these students does not appear to have kept up with their peers may be due, at least in part, to the consequences of a ceiling effect. For example, in 2000 over 60 per cent of white students scored in the upper 10 per cent of the test score range, while only about 27 per cent of African-American students and 35 per cent of Hispanic students achieved these levels (Linton and Kester 2003). As a larger proportion of white students achieved the maximum range of scores on the test, it is possible that the white students' scores could be underestimating their true achievement levels. In other words, their achievement has reached an artificial ceiling, above which it is difficult for them to progress. At the same time, the scores of their peers from the African-American and Hispanic groups have continued to improve and so present the illusion that they are 'catching up' and hence closing the achievement gap. This is a problem inherent in examinations that achieve almost universal currency, as the TAAS appears to have done.

Although these apparent gains in school performance in Texas have been widely praised and imitated by other states, and indeed by national accountability programmes, there are those who suggest that the TAAS trends may be misleading, and who criticize the 'myth' of the Texas achievement miracle (Haney 2000). One of the most enduring criticisms of the entire TAS is that its emphasis on standardized testing contributes to a narrowing of the curriculum, an over-reliance on test-preparation and teaching to the test, and a reduction in the development of higher-order thinking skills, particularly for students from disadvantaged groups, who are often to be found in the schools under the greatest accountability-linked scrutiny (McNeill 2000; Toenjes et al. 2003; Haney 2000). Such standards-based reform has done little to promote the equity of schools, and according to some commentators is 'structurally misdirected and treats the symptoms of school failure (e.g. poor achievement) rather than the cause (e.g. inferior schools), (Valencia et al. 2001, 319).

While these concerns appear to have gained some consensus among educational researchers on both sides of the Texas standards debate (McNeill 2000; Toenjes et al. 2003), there remains one key area of contention: the impact of TAAS on school drop-out rates. According to Haney (2000), the increase in the TAAS pass rate for minority high-school students is at least partially explained by higher drop-out rates among these groups (although this is disputed by some researchers, for example Toenjes and Dworkin 2002). This controversy is of particular interest not only for its educational impact, but also for demonstrating the difficulties inherent in interpreting official data. Depending on how drop-out is measured – for example, which students you include and whether you track it longitudinally – the dropout rate for high-school students in Texas in 2002 can vary from 0.9 to 35.5 per cent of the school population (TEA 2003b).

The Texas school-accountability reforms have had a phenomenal impact on the education reform programme in the USA. As a means of raising test scores and also of improving basic skill levels among all students, their efficacy appears to be hard to dispute. However, the pay-off – a narrowly focused curriculum and teachers teaching to the test, as well as the sidelining of many of the wider benefits of education – is unacceptable to most commentators. In addition, the absence of a prior assessment of achievement trends among theses groups makes it difficult to determine whether basic skills levels would have improved anyway, without the need for expensive and prescriptive standardized tests.

Is smaller really better? Debating class sizes

Reducing the number of students in a class is a popular and easily visible, although potentially expensive, strategy for raising standards in schools. In England, the School Standards and Framework Act of 1998 required that schools and LEAs limit the size of infant classes that were taught by one qualified teacher to 30 or fewer pupils (HMSO 1998). This limit became statutory from the start of the 2001/02 school year. Funding of around £775 million was made available from central government between 1998 and 2003 to implement these class size limits, and was sufficient to employ 6,000 new teachers and create 2,000 additional classrooms (Teachernet 2004). The legislation certainly appears to have had some impact. For example, in England, the proportion of students at Key Stage 1 (3–7-year-olds) who were taught in classes of 31 and over fell from 29 per cent in 1998 to 1 per cent in 2003 (DfES 1998a, 2003a).

Some of the impetus for class-size reduction programmes in the UK has arisen from academic studies by the University of London's Institute of Education. For example, in a longitudinal multi-method study, the researchers found appreciable gains in children's academic achievement among those who were taught in smaller sized classes (Blatchford 2003). However, the importance of the Institute of Education researchers' findings notwithstanding, the seminal piece of research into the impact of class-size reduction programmes has been the Tennessee Student/ Teacher Achievement Ratio (STAR) Project. The main features of this piece of research are described below, and some of its key findings and implications are outlined.

In 1985, the Tennessee legislature funded an experimental investigation into the impact of small-sized classes on student achievement from kindergarten through to third grade (Finn and Achilles 1999; Project STAR 1990). This study was revolutionary in its method use of experimental research techniques in which teachers and students were randomly allocated to different sized teaching groups. Over 6,000 students in 79 Tennessee schools were involved in the experiment in its first year, a number which expanded to almost 12,000 students over the four-year duration of the study (Finn and Achilles 1999; Project STAR 1999; Grissmer 1999). Students were randomly assigned upon entry to school into one of three different types of class: a small class (13 to 17 students), a normal-sized class (22 to 26 students) or a normal-sized class with a full-time teaching assistant. Each school that participated in the study was of sufficient size (i.e. with 57 students or more enrolled in each grade) to ensure that they could accommodate at least one small-sized, one normal-sized and one normal-sized with teaching assistant class, so reducing any potential bias to the study that might be created by within school differences (Project Star 1990). All students remained in their assigned class for four years, from kindergarten until they reached the end of the third grade (ages 5–8). In Grade 4, all students were returned to a normal-sized group. The random nature with which the students were allocated to each group allowed differences such as those between student populations and instructional resources to be controlled. This meant that the study aspired to a true experimental design in which all variables except one – class size – were held constant. Student progress was monitored throughout the study and their achievement on standardized tests such as the Stanford Achievement Test was recorded.

The Tennessee STAR project has been described as 'one of the most important experiments in education reform' (Chubb and Loveless 2003, 2). Its results have spawned class-size reduction programmes in over twenty American states – most notably in California – as well as in many other countries throughout the world (Project STAR 1999; Hanushek 1999). Its findings continue to be subject to intense academic scrutiny, long after the original STAR students have graduated from high school. The results from Project STAR demonstrated that at each grade level (kindergarten through to third grade) and across all school locations, students who were taught in small classes achieved the highest scores on standardized achievement tests. In addition (as we see below), impressive gains were made by students from ethnic minority groups who were taught in small-sized classes. These achievement gains for all students remained long after the students had been returned to normal-sized groupings and resulted, for black students in particular, in higher numbers from the small-sized classes sitting college entrance exams (Krueger and Whitmore 2003).

Any gains in student test performance, as reported by the designers of the Tennessee STAR project, tend to be presented as 'effects sizes'. These are calculated by taking the differences in the mean test scores of students in the small classes and students in the normal-sized classes and dividing this difference by the standard deviation in test scores for students in the normal-sized classes (Coe 2002). For all students combined, the effects sizes for students in the small classes were 0.18 for reading and 0.15 for maths in kindergarten, an advantage that had increased to 0.26 for reading and 0.23 for maths by the third grade (Finn and Achilles 1999). This means that around 60 per cent of third-grade readers in the normal-sized class would have an average reading score below that of an average reader in a small-sized class.

Although some evidence does exist that points to lasting effects throughout the period of the experiment, the most pronounced effects occurred in kindergarten and the first grade, suggesting that any policies to reduce class sizes should focus on students of this age. In contrast, adding a full-time teacher's assistant to a normal-sized class of students did not confer the same educational advantage. Moreover, students who had been taught in smaller classes responded more positively in terms of the effort and initiative they showed to their learning, as well as in their classroom behaviour (Finn and Achilles 1999). Improvements in the students' behaviour were also apparent in that fewer students in the small-sized classes were held back a year because of unsatisfactory progress. Indeed, over the four years of the project, 19.8 per cent of students in small-sized classes were retained, compared with 27.4 per cent of students in normal-sized groups (Project STAR 1990).

The group that appeared to have benefited most from the initiative to reduce class size was that of students from ethnic minority backgrounds, and specifically those of African-American origin. According to Krueger and Whitmore (2003), on average black students in small classes outperformed their peers in normal-sized classes by 7–10 percentile points, while white students in small classes outperformed their peers by only 3–4 percentile points. Expressed as effects sizes, across the four years of the study the effects size for black students in reading was almost twice that of white students: 0.40 compared with 0.17 (Finn and Achilles 1999). However, the findings for low-achieving students and those from poorer homes suggest that the small-sized classes do not confer the same educational advantage for these groups (Project STAR 1990; Nye et al. 2002).

When the students were returned to normal-sized classes in the fourth grade, those who had been taught in the smaller classes still achieved higher test scores than their peers. Although the effects sizes were diminished, these students retained some advantage throughout elementary school, demonstrating higher achievement gains in reading, mathematics and science than their peers who had been in normal-sized groupings (Nye *et al.* 1999).

For such an influential and closely examined study, it is perhaps inevitable that criticisms of the Tennessee STAR project exist. Many of these centre on its use of an experimental design. For example, Hanushek cites several possible flaws with the research design and implementation of the Tennessee STAR study. He considers evidence from several non-experimental investigations into the impact of class size on student achievement and concludes that they provide 'no consistent or clear indication that overall class size reduction will lead to improved student performance' (Hanushek 1999, 149). Why then should the results from a single experimental study supersede all those from previous non-experimental works?

Among Hanushek's concerns were problems of student attrition. Of the initial experimental kindergarten group, only 48 per cent remained in the experiment for its four-year duration. Students who left the programme from the normal-sized groups tended to be of lower ability than those who left from the small-sized classes, so introducing further possibilities of sample bias. An additional problem was that the schools involved in the experiment were not selected at random: they were invited to participate and smaller schools, with fewer than the minimum numbers of students, were excluded from the study. The sampling of schools is particularly important if, as has been suggested, some students are particularly susceptible to changes in class sizes. For example, in the schools involved in the study 33 per cent of the experimental students were black, compared with 23 per cent of students in all of Tennessee's public schools. However, empirical tests on the results of STAR have shown that problems of non-randomness, student attrition and teacher quality have not adversely effected the overall results (Krueger and Whitmore 2003; Flanagan and Grissmer 2003), and the Tennessee STAR Project remains an important example not only of an experimental intervention in education, but also of what can happen when the political world and the educational world combine to produce a piece of evidence-based research.

In conclusion, the Tennessee STAR Project is an important example of an experimental intervention. It shows that being taught in a small class (with an optimum number of fifteen students) does convey some educational advantage to children in the very early years of their education, and that these effects can remain with the students for some time.

Crucially, this reduction in class size was shown to overwhelmingly benefit black students, and may contribute to closing achievement gaps between these students and their white peers.

However, class-size reduction programmes are costly and, as the Tennessee STAR project has shown, really only impact when the class numbers become very small, around fifteen students. Indeed, many class-size reduction initiatives focus on reducing the student numbers to levels that are still much higher than those of the small-sized classes involved in Project STAR. For example, despite several years of class-size reduction initiatives in England, in 1998 only 6 per cent of Key Stage 1 students were taught in classes of fewer than twenty students. By 2003, this figure had risen slightly to 9 per cent (DfES 1998a, 2003a). In 1999, Brewer *et al.* estimated that to reduce class sizes to eighteen students in Grades 1 to 3 across America would require hiring approximately 100,000 teachers at a cost of about $5–6 billion. The opportunity costs of implementing class-size reduction policies are also high, not only because of the high initial costs of employing more teachers and building more classrooms, but also because the strategy would be expensive to reverse if future methods of raising achievement prove to be more cost effective (Grissmer 1999).

Looking inside the black box: the role of formative assessment in raising achievement

In 1988, the National Curriculum Task Group on Assessment and Testing (TGAT) recommended that assessment should be an 'integral part of the education process, continually providing both "feedback" and "feedforward" and ought therefore to be systematically incorporated into teaching strategies and practices at all levels' (DES 1988, paragraphs 3 and 4). The system that the group advocated combined both formative and summative approaches. However, ensuring parity of esteem for teacher-led both formative and summative assessment has long been a contentious issue in the politics of National Curriculum assessment. According to some commentators, this has derived at least in part from 'political concerns for accountability, rather than by educational concerns for learning' (Torrance and Pryor 1998, 10). This section will briefly outline the place of formative assessment practices in the National Curriculum in England and Wales before describing a seminal piece of research that puts formative assessment techniques into practice.

While the positive role of formative assessment has now apparently been widely accepted in mainstream education circles, there has been, according to Black (2000), an absence of a coherent programme of research to underpin both the theoretical and practical development of the formative assessment process. For example, a review of research into formative techniques found that key work in this area showed little overlap and collaboration – 'it seems that most researchers are not studying much of the literature that could inform their work' (Black 2000, 409) – and these difficulties have been compounded by different notions about what the term 'formative assessment' actually means (see, for example, Harlen *et al.* 1992; Stobart and Gipps 1997). Indeed, a conflation of both the terms and ideas underpinning 'formative' and 'teacher assessment' has led to the gradual replacement of the term 'formative assessment' in the lexicon of assessment policy.

Formative teacher assessment has had a somewhat limited and indirect role in the evolution of National Curriculum testing. Its original conception through TGAT was as a major part of a two-pronged national assessment system with a commitment to 'formative assessment as the best way of achieving this raising of standards, tempered by the recognised need for valid and robust summative approaches' (Shorrocks–Taylor 1999, 165). Its current position is on the fringes of the national testing programme and, although schools are still required to report teacher-assessed levels at the end of each Key Stage, its status is now far from what TGAT had envisaged.

Even so, the success of formative assessment techniques in raising the achievement of students, particularly those of lower ability – who, we are told, constitute the UK's long tail of underachieving students – has been demonstrated by recent research, particularly that carried out by the King's College Formative Assessment Group (Black *et al.* 2003). The evidence this research has produced to demonstrate the efficacy of formative techniques is compelling. Indeed Black (2000) cites research where the use of formative assessment techniques produced learning gains with effect sizes of between 0.4 and 0.7, larger than those produced by some other significant educational interventions. Researchers who have studied formative assessment techniques and their impact on the learning process recommend that schools and teachers should consider implementing four changes in their work: question-and-answer interactions, providing effective feedback, peer and self-assessment by pupils, and involving the pupils in their own assessments (Wiliam and Black 2002). Implementing these 'assessment for learning' strategies should be considered as a long-term initiative, which 'calls for changes in their [teachers'] practice which are radical in scope and nature' (Black 1998, 112). Each of the four strategies is outlined briefly below, and all are considered in detail in Black *et al.* (2003).

- *Developing rich questioning:* for example, by asking questions that are worth answering and which provide students with the opportunity to develop their understanding. In addition, teachers were encouraged to wait several seconds to allow the students to think about their answers, rather than expecting rapid-fire superficial responses.
- *Feedback by marking:* in particular the use of comment-only marking. This provided students with the opportunity to identify what they have done well and what still needed to be improved.
- *Peer and self-assessment:* this enabled students to have ownership over their learning. By providing students with clear criteria about what is expected from them in a piece of work, as well as teaching them the skills needed for collaborative work in peer assessment, they are enabled to develop an objective perspective over their work which helped them better understand its aims and what is required to complete the work satisfactorily.
- *The formative use of summative tests:* for example, by enabling students to set and mark their own test questions, as well as encouraging them to think about how their work might be improved, perhaps by giving them the opportunity to have another attempt at answering examination questions.

In putting these strategies into practice, the King's College researchers worked with 24 mathematics and science teachers in six secondary schools over a two-year period (Black *et al.* 2003). Initially, two mathematics and two science teachers were selected from each school. The teachers were provided with in-service training in the principles underlying formative assessment techniques, and were given opportunities to work collaboratively to develop their own assessment strategies. In addition, the King's College researchers visited the schools to observe classroom teaching and the assessment processes at work. These observations helped to refine the in-service programmes. For the teachers involved in the Black box study, it was very much a case of them adapting and refining their own assessment techniques, rather than relying on the research team to impose a model of assessment (Black and Wiliam 2003).

In the study, the research team were of the opinion that 'results of research studies cannot provide ready-made recipes for practice' (Black *et al.* 2003, 119): rather, they ought to stimulate and support the work of teachers in adapting the findings to their own practice. In this sense, the research takes on a strongly developmental as well as research role. This approach differs from that of the Tennessee STAR Project, where students were allocated to control and experimental groups and efforts were made to ensure scientific rigour. In the formative assessment work, the focus was on innovation and development that was rooted in the realities of classroom life. In addition to its potentially positive impact on learning, the research carried out by the Formative Assessment group also provides us with an important example of how academic research has been translated into practice and adopted by schools across the country. Indeed, the popularity of formative assessment techniques among practitioners, as shown by its prevalence in in-service training courses and sales of the pamphlet 'Inside the Black box' (Black and Wiliam 2001), which has sold around 40,000 copies in the five years since its publication, should provide researchers with valuable lessons on how academic research *can* be translated into classroom practice (Black and Wiliam 2003).

However, a recent evaluation of a school's attempt to initiate 'Black box' style assessment reform does bring a word of caution to attempts to replicate research, however practical its findings may be, in classroom practice (Smith and Gorard 2005). In this study, which was conducted along similar lines to the intervention described above, a contextualized evaluation of the progress made by students who had been assessed by formative methods actually showed them to have been disadvantaged by the intervention compared with their peers. Although in the original study (Black *et al.* 2003) the six participating schools were given greater support and attention by the researchers than was possible here, this smaller study does give an indication of what can happen when a scheme is 'rolled out' into wider practice. Despite the initial enthusiasm among the staff in the school, interviews carried out with the students portrayed misgivings about both the approach and how it was implemented in practice. This throws up an important concern for advocates of evidence-based policy and practice. Even where, as here, there is reason to believe that original research has produced an intervention capable of leading to student improvement (and that in itself is rare), its wider application by policy-makers or practitioners can lead inadvertently to student and school decline.

Together or apart? The merits of single sex teaching

'Single sex classes aim to close exams gender gap'
(*The Times Education Supplement*, 19 August 2004).

Teaching boys and girls separately in a mixed-sex school has become a popular strategy for schools concerned with raising the achievement of boys and closing the gender achievement gap. Since 1998, all LEAs have had to include proposals to tackle boys' underachievement in their Education Development Plans and, alongside other initiatives such as mentoring programmes, have been encouraged to experiment with single-sex teaching (Blunkett 2000; Cassidy 2000).

In their DfES-sponsored study of single-sex teaching within mixed-sex schools, Warrington and Younger (2003) were able to identify over 50 English schools that had experimented with this method in recent years, and the DfES website and the pages of *The Times Educational Supplement* describe the single-sex teaching experiences of many others (DfES 2004e; Shaw 2003; Stokes 2003). For many of the schools that have adopted this strategy, while the subjects and students targeted may vary, the usual reason given for instigating the initiative is to raise the achievement of boys. In some schools, it is achievement gaps in Key Stage 3 English that are the issue; in others, it is concern over GCSE performance in modern foreign languages or science (see, for example, Warrington and Younger 2003; Jackson 2002; Sukhnandan 2000). Often, single-sex teaching initiatives have been adopted alongside other strategies to raise achievement, such as literacy programmes, alternating male/female seating in class and the promotion of positive male role models (DfES 2004e). In some schools, adopting single-sex teaching methods has been viewed as a strategy for making the school different and hence more marketable and attractive to parents (Swan 1998).

Much of the interest in replicating single-sex settings in mixed-sex schools has stemmed from the apparent success of schools that select all of their students on the basis of their sex (Ofsted 2003). In England, around 5 per cent of the school population are taught in 418 maintained primary and secondary single-sex schools (DfES 2003d). According to Ofsted, students who attend single-sex maintained schools out-perform their peers in mixed schools at GCSE, regardless of the proportion of students in the school who receive free school meals and their prior attainment. For example, in 2001 44 per cent of boys in single-sex comprehensive schools achieved five or more good GCSE levels, compared with 41 per cent of boys in mixed-sex schools (Ofsted 2003).

However, research by Robinson and Smithers (1999) into the achievement of students who attend mixed or single-sex institutions provides little evidence that either type of school conveys an academic advantage on their students. Rather, the relatively higher performance of single sex schools, in particular independent schools, has more to do with academic selection and the socioeconomic characteristics of their intake than on separation according to sex (Spielhofer *et al.* (2004) has an analysis of the National Value-added Dataset that has produced similar findings).

Some of the arguments that favour teaching the sexes separately have their roots in feminist thinking that boys should be removed from the classroom setting as a temporary strategy 'until women have constructed their own theories and are prepared to confront rather than to defer to men' (Sarah *et al.* 1980, 56). Single-sex groupings are also thought to enhance the learning experiences for girls by allowing them the space to gain a clearer picture of their own abilities, as well as to develop their self-esteem and confidence (Elwood and Gipps 1999). But there is also an argument for single-sex settings to be used to redress male sex stereotypes and improve their social skills and attainment (Riordan 1990; Sukhnandan *et al.* 2000): this is particularly apparent among those who favour single-sex teaching as a strategy for raising male achievement levels.

Many of these small-scale studies also canvas the opinions of the students themselves. Here too, thoughts differ over the relative merits of the approach. Some girls report enjoying being able to concentrate on their schoolwork without the distractions of boys, but others find an all-female environment over-competitive and bitchy (Robinson and Smithers 1999). A government-funded three-year research programme at Manchester University into the causes of underachievement found that single-sex classes boosted pupil performance (Henry 2001). However, the boys missed the 'civilizing' influence of girls who would also help them with their work. Many of the girls, while missing the presence of the 'class clown', welcomed the opportunity to get more work done without the disruptive presence of the boys.

According to Jackson (2002), studies into the efficacy of single-sex teaching methods in the UK have been largely anecdotal and are often initiated by individual schools in response to their concerns over differential achievement rates or uptake of certain subjects, such as A-level physics. With possible advantages for all pupils, mixed-sex groupings have been the subject of several studies (Kruse 1992; Warrington and Younger 2003; Younger and Warrington 2002, 2003). However, largely because of the small-scale nature of many of these studies, who actually benefits – boys, girls or both – is still open to question. Many schools that implement single-sex teaching methods adopt what Jackson (2002) calls a 'curriculum-only' approach. This means that students are segregated for certain lessons, but the strategies teachers use to teach the lessons remain the same as before. Certainly according to Sukhnandan *et al.* (2000) and Warrington and Younger (2003), single-sex teaching strategies appear to work best in situations where teachers have adapted their approach and where schools have taken time and care in planning the initiative. Even so, conclusive evidence to support the initiative remains sketchy.

Why is it so difficult to study the impact of single-sex teaching in the mixed-sex school and produce clear evidence to support or refute the strategy? One answer lies in the type of initiatives that are usually undertaken: these are often small scale, focusing only on a small number of schools, and perhaps lasting only for a limited period of time (Swan 1998; Sukhnandan *et al.* 2000), and they are frequently *ad hoc*, often established in response to concern over a cohort of purportedly under-achieving boys (Younger and Warrington 2003); they may coincide with a range of other initiatives, thus making the relative impact difficult to determine (Warrington and Younger 2001), and also often lack a comparator group against which any success can be measured (Jackson 2002). In short, they are often not very scientific.

Conclusion

'Underachievement' is a term that has probably outlived its usefulness. The lack of clarity in its use has led to multiple meanings that sometimes disguise the true nature of patterns of learning in schools. What is not in dispute is that many in the student population can, and should, learn more easily than they do. The key problem for the future is that, as educators, we have no clear evidence-based strategy to make this happen. Some of the strategies for closing achievement gaps described in this concluding chapter do give us reason for optimism: they demonstrate that well-conceived research which involves practitioners and policy-maker perspectives from the outset *can* produce findings that can make an impact in the classroom.

However, there is also much to be concerned about. These four examples are from among the best, or most widely advocated, projects of their kind. What they have in common is that each displays flaws that should prevent us from simply rolling their conclusions out into policy and practice but, even so, each has been used, to a greater or lesser extent, to influence governments' strategies to raise standards in schools. For example, the impact of high-stakes testing is far from proven. There are no comparable trends for achievement gaps available from before the policies went live. We have, therefore, no way of knowing what would have happened in the absence of the testing. Yet, high-stakes testing programmes linked to strict school accountability sanctions is a central tenant of the 2002 No Child Left Behind Act – arguably the most important piece of US educational legislation for the past 35 years. The Tennessee STAR study does not tell us what will be the long-term impact of class sizes of 15, and it cannot tell us even about the short-term impact of infant class sizes of 30 – as imposed by the UK government at time of writing. Yet, between 1998 and 2003, the UK government allocated around £775 million to implement these limits on infant classes (Teachernet 2004). The *Black Box* work on formative assessment has yet to be tested rigorously by sceptics, rather than implemented by advocates. Yet the Assessment for Learning techniques that the *Black Box* work pioneered have been endorsed by the UK government as being at the 'very heart of good teaching and learning' (Miliband 2004) and constitute a key element of the new national assessment framework in Wales (Daugherty 2004).

Such problems are best exemplified by the research into single-sex groupings in co-educational schools. Work here has been uncontrolled, or else passive and reliant on the *post hoc* dredging of school results (Arnot *et al.* 1996; Sukhnandan *et al.* 2000), with all the potential to mislead that ensues from both approaches (Gorard 2000). There is clearly an interest among practitioners to adopt this approach in their classrooms; there is clearly a desire among politicians to explore different approaches to raising standards in all schools; and there is clearly money available. One research programme alone has had around £30 million available for Teaching and Learning Research since 2000. So why do we still not really know whether single-sex teaching is effective in raising the achievement of students? Perhaps that is the problem with research in education: the field is simply too broad and there is so much to study that we are forced to prioritize. But what could be more important than finding out what works in this way? Indeed, the scarcity of *hard scientific evidence* as to what works in education, despite the relatively large sums of money invested in research programmes, prompted the chair of the House of Commons Education Select Committee to query what the money was being spent on, and to ask whether it had gone down a 'black hole' (House of Commons 2003, Ev. 12).

What is even more remarkable is that vast sums of public money are spent on initiatives for which little evidence exists to show that they may work. For example, Education Action Zones have recently been phased out and replaced by the Excellence in Cities programme. The evidence for their effectiveness was mixed, having had a 'good effect on primary schools, but not a profound effect on secondary schools' (House of Commons 2003, Ev. 44). However, this was irrelevant, as the programme had come to the end of its statutory life and the political focus had shifted. Such changes will, presumably, always happen, because policy-makers work on different timescales to research programmes and are, perfectly properly perhaps, basing their judgments on factors other than evidence.

What could we do to improve the situation? I end the book by suggesting a number of ways in which public investment for research in educational achievement could be re-directed with almost immediate benefit. In future, publicly-funded research in this area should:

- use an active approach to hypothesis-testing, such as a randomized controlled trial, whenever possible;
- have to explain why an active approach to hypothesis-testing, such as a randomized controlled trial, is not possible before even considering a passive approach;
- have appropriate comparison groups – in the form of before and after evidence, or control group(s);
- make use of the potential for natural experiments wherever possible (because these are cheap, practical and ethical);
- be prepared to use data in any form, numeric or otherwise, to answer the research question;
- and, therefore, look to new and potentially powerful designs for studying achievement at school, including complex interventions and teaching experiments, that routinely mix the kinds of data too often referred to as 'qualitative' and 'quantitative'.

Clearly, these criteria are neither exhaustive nor perfectly evolved. But a concerted programme of research relevant to teaching and learning, which moved funding from work that did not match these criteria to work that did, would in my opinion be cost-effective, good for the research community and, most notably, provide much clearer evidence about what we really can do about the phenomenon currently labelled 'underachievement'.

APPENDIX 1

Further details of research methods

A brief outline of the methods of data collection and analysis drawn upon in the second part of the book was given in Chapter 6. For the interested reader, a fuller description of the main methods used and an outline of some of the characteristics of the students involved in the study are given below. Further details can be found in Smith (2002).

Data analysis and data collection

A primary aim of this research was to design the best possible model for predicting a pupil's achievement in an examination, and consequently to identify pupils who do not do as well as expected. In this study several statistical analytical methods were combined, including questionnaires as a means of data collection and assessing children's attitudes and perceptions; examination and test data, and focus-group interviews which sought to gain a clearer insight into any underlying characteristics of the underachieving group. The questionnaire was administered to Year 9 pupils during the two months prior to their end of Key Stage 3 examinations. This period coincided with preparation for these examinations, and may be thought of as a time when the majority of pupils were well-motivated in anticipation of the forthcoming tests. Prior to the actual administration of the questionnaire it was piloted twice, each time with different groups of students from the same school. The response rate for the final version of the questionnaire was very high (typically more than 85 per cent).

In order to build the best possible model for predicting academic achievement, information on 30 variables that the academic literature cites as influencing achievement had to be collected from the students and schools in the sample. The main method of data collection was by questionnaire, the aim of which was to obtain biographical and motiva-tional information from each pupil. Information on the following vari-ables was sought:

- ethnicity
- gender
- parental employment
- self-esteem
- self-concept
- parental involvement in school
- family type
- age and number of siblings

In addition to the questionnaire, other data was obtained directly from the schools. This included Key Stage 2 and 3 examination levels, CAT scores, attendance figures and data on receipt of free school meals. Attendance was defined as the percentage of days an individual had attended school from September to June of the academic year in which the research was conducted.

In addition to the models that were used to predict underachievement and low achievement using statistical techniques, it was also appropriate to determine which features these pupils had in common and which dis-tinguished them from the others in the sample: this was particularly appropriate for the students who had been identified as underachieving. For this purpose, exploratory focus-group discussions were carried out with four groups of students, split according to their sex and whether they had been identified as underachieving or overachieving in their Key Stage 3 examinations. Fuller details and analysis of the students' responses is given in Chapter 7.

The region of the study

In order to place the results of this study into a wider context, it is worth describing briefly the geographical region from which the sample was taken. The study was located in the area of the South Wales valleys that has now become the Unitary Authorities of Rhondda Cynon Taff and Merthyr Tydfil. This region is bordered by the M4 motorway to the south and the Heads of the Valleys road to the north, and includes many of the former mining and heavy industrial areas of the old Mid Glamorgan. The contraction of the coal industry from the 1960s onward, coupled with further economic changes from the early 1980s, was acutely felt in this part of Wales. In January 2001, unemployment in

Rhondda Cynon Taff was 5.2 per cent and in Merthyr Tydfil it was 8.5 per cent, compared with 4.8 per cent for the whole of Wales (Brooksbank 2001). There has, however, been a great deal of recent inward investment into this region, most particularly from foreign companies. As a result, there are pockets of relative affluence within the region, most notably in the areas bordering the M4 motorway.

The ethnic minority mix of the Valleys is often described as being more than '99% white' (Scourfield *et al.* 2002, 3). This disguises what is in fact a rich mix of Italian, Spanish and Irish families who moved to to the valleys during the Industrial Revolution. The large post-war immigration into Britain by citizens of the Commonwealth came at a time of economic decline in the valleys, which as a result have stayed 'mainly white' (Scourfield *et al.* 2002, 3). This accounts for the very small (but representative) proportion of pupils from ethnic minority backgrounds in the study. The 12 schools that took part in the study were drawn from a sample of the region's 24 secondary schools. The entire range of school types are represented, including church schools and schools who teach through the medium of Welsh.

Characteristics of the students

Students were sampled from Year 9 classes and were drawn from across the ability range. The reasons for selecting Year 9 students were two-fold. On the one hand, they would provide very recent Key Stage 3 examination scores that could be incorporated into the modelling process: but there was also a desire for a practical application for this research. By targeting Year 9 students, any who were identified by the model as underachieving could be brought to the attention of the school and be more likely to benefit from intervention and support as they began their GCSE courses. An outline of some of the academic characteristics of the 2,124 students involved in the study is given below.

Achievement at Key Stage 3

All pupils in state sector schools in England and Wales sit end of key stage examinations. The Key Stage 2 examinations in English, maths and science are sat at the end of Year 6, before transition to secondary school. The Key Stage 3 examinations are taken by 13- and 14-year-old pupils towards the end of Year 9. While end of key stage performance is reported in all subjects, it is only in the 'core' subjects that formal assessment through examination takes place. Results are reported as 'Levels', which at Key Stage 3 range from 2 to 7 (with exceptional performance awarded through teacher assessment). Unfortunately, these levels are broad and, as the pupils sit different tiered papers (except in English), a direct comparison of raw marks is not possible. However, the DfES suggests the use of a system of Points Scores when comparing levels at the end of Key Stages 1–3. The rationale behind the use of this 'Point Score' is that it would 'establish a slightly more sophisticated mechanism' (DfEE 1999, 66) for comparing performance at each Key Stage.

Table A.1 gives the percentages of pupils in the sample and nationally who achieved Level 5 (or Points Score 33) or above in the Key Stage 3 examinations. Both the results for the sample and for Wales were below the National Assembly's target of between 70–80 per cent of 14-year-olds achieving Level 5 (or Points Score 33) or above by 2002 (ETAG 1998). In maths and science the sample's results are higher than those achieved throughout Wales; their English results are lower.

Table A.1   **Percentage of pupils achieving at least benchmark Level 5 at Key Stage 3**

Subject	Sample	Wales
English	58.8	61.0
Maths	64.4	60.0
Science	62.0	55.0

The Cognitive Ability Test

The relationship between scores in reasoning tests and school performance, as measured by public or other national examinations, is well established (Fernandes and Strand 2000). One of the mostly widely used mental-ability reasoning tests in British schools is a commercially produced test called the Cognitive Ability Test (CAT). The NFER, who produce these tests, claim that they were used with over 800,000 pupils in the UK in 2000 (Strand 2001). The test's importance in evaluating the nature of a school's new intake is such that the CAT was taken by 65 per cent of Year 7 pupils in England and Wales in the last academic year (NFER 2001). The tests are age related and comprise a battery of reasoning tests designed to 'tap a general set of prior experience and emphasise the perception and manipulation of relationships' (Strand 2001, 4). In this study, CAT results were obtained for 1,250 pupils from nine of the twelve schools involved in the study, and the relationship between CAT score and Key Stage 3 performance is shown in Table A.2.

Table A.2 **Correlations between CAT and Key Stage 3 Level (sample)**

Examination	Mean CAT score	Verbal	Quantitative	Non-verbal
Average level	0.85	0.80	0.77	0.65
English	0.71	0.71	0.63	0.51
Maths	0.86	0.73	0.82	0.69
Science	0.77	0.75	0.67	0.58

APPENDIX 2

Multiple regression model for identifying underachieving students

A key aim of this book is to model predicted against actual Key Stage 3 examination performance, in order to identify pupils who could be described as underachieving. We based this model on the prediction that underachieving pupils would be predominantly working-class boys, and so the final underachievement model was predictive in nature, omitting gender and social class. However, before describing the final model it is worthwhile investigating any relationships between the *entire* group of predictor variables and Key Stage 3 achievement (Table A.3).

Multiple regression techniques were best suited to undertaking an analysis of this type (Field 2000). Multiple regression can be defined as 'an inferential statistical procedure used to investigate linear relationships

Table A.3 **R^2 values for all variables – stepwise entry**

Variable (predictors)	Adjusted R^2	Beta	Significance
Prior attainment	0.680	0.740	0.000
Attendance	0.053	0.146	0.000
Self-concept (reading)	0.034	0.104	0.000
Free school meals	0.018	0.078	0.000
School factor	0.011	0.098	0.000
Self-concept (general)	0.008	0.103	0.000
Gender	0.008	0.093	0.000
Family type	0.003	0.064	0.000
Parent's evening	0.003	0.051	0.001
Month of birth	0.003	−0.054	0.000
Sibling order	0.002	0.048	0.000
Working mother	0.002	0.048	0.002
Parental Involvement q5	0.001	−0.038	0.005
Parental Involvement q2	0.001	0.038	0.007
Total value for R^2	**0.826**		

between three or more variables. It indicates the extent to which one variable can be explained or predicted by one or more of the other variables' (Brace *et al.* 2000, 257). Regression analysis enables one to fit a predictive model to the data and use that model to predict values of the dependant variable (or outcome variable) from one or more independent variables (or predictor variables). In this study, the outcome variable was achievement in the Key Stage 3 examinations. The predictor variables have been selected from past research into the factors thought to contribute to an individual's examination performance. For further details about the construction of this model for identifying students who may be underachieving, see Smith 2002, 2003.

In the predictive model, the multiple regression analysis was repeated using stepwise entry. Table A.4 shows the results. It is worth re-stating here that this predictive model did not include gender and social class. The results in Table A.4 involve 989 complete cases, and show that 82.4 per cent of the variance in Key Stage 3 performance could be accounted for by the thirteen variables listed. In common with the analysis of all the variables (described in Table A.3), the most important predictor was prior attainment, followed by attendance. The variables not listed in Table A.4 were not significant predictors of examination performance.

Table A.4 R^2 values for predictive model – stepwise entry

Variable	Adjusted R^2	Beta	Significance
Prior Attainment	0.684	0.745	0.000
Attendance	0.052	0.140	0.000
Self-concept (reading)	0.035	0.116	0.000
Free school meals	0.018	0.076	0.000
School factor	0.012	0.102	0.000
Self-concept (general)	0.009	0.097	0.000
Parent's evening	0.004	0.056	0.000
Family type	0.004	0.066	0.000
Month of birth	0.003	−0.050	0.000
Sibling order	0.002	0.047	0.001
Working mother	0.002	0.047	0.003
Parental involvement q2	0.001	0.036	0.011
Parental involvement q5	0.001	−0.032	0.020
Total value for R^2	**0.824**		

An alternative technique for measuring the relative impact of both school- and student-level variables on academic achievement is multilevel modelling. This technique has the advantage of enabling differences at the school as well as the individual level to be examined. However, in order to use this technique effectively, it would have been necessary to include a larger number of schools in the sample. This would have increased the sample of schools from 12 to nearer 30. Therefore, a choice had to be made between gathering data on a relatively small number of pupils (perhaps as few as 30) from a large number of schools, and using multilevel modelling to build the underachievement model, or alternatively using a smaller number of schools but gaining information on the whole year group of pupils and adopting the multiple regression technique. After much consideration it was decided that the latter technique was more within the scope of this study.

Further justification for not using the multilevel technique was given by Fitz-Gibbon (2000). When comparing the use of multilevel modelling (MLM) and a simple Ordinary Least Squares or regression method in the analysis of primary and secondary school data-sets, the author found very high correlations (typically 0.99) between the two techniques. This suggests that there is little to be gained by using MLM techniques in certain situations, since the findings they produce may not add anything to the final results.

Profiles of students who were identified as underachieving

There follow profiles of some of the pupils who have been placed in the underachieving group. All these pupils attended the same school and participated in the focus-group interviews described in Chapter 7. The profiles are based on information the students provided in the questionnaire, as well as on general information obtained from the school. Although these pupils were only a subset of the 147 strong 'underachieving' group, they were chosen because they give an indication of the group's diversity.

Paul: male, working class, both parents at home and in work, youngest child (2/2); average range verbal and non-verbal CAT; above average quantitative (120); Key Stage 2 Levels 4(E), 4(M), 5(S); school attendance 92.3 per cent; parental involvement score high (8/10), parents attend parents evening; reading and general self-concept slightly above average, maths self-concept slightly below, self-esteem below sample mean; Key Stage 3 levels 4(E), 6(M), 6(S).

Paul had a fairly negative attitude towards school, he admitted to 'messing around' in subjects that he did not enjoy or thought to be unimportant, but was well aware of his ability to control his behaviour. He had a reputation in school of being rather silly and talkative in class, but not as being a disruptive character. Paul also admitted to disliking subjects that involved a lot of writing. This might be due to him having difficulties with spelling and a low National Curriculum level in English. He was generally placed in the middle sets. Paul's responses to the focus-group discussions might have characterized him as more of a 'typical underachiever' than many of his peers.

Luke: male, working class, both parents at home and in work, elder child (1/2); above average range CAT for each battery; Key Stage 2 Levels

5(E), 5(M), 5(S); school attendance 99.3 per cent; parental involvement score very low (0/10), parents attend parents evening; self-concept very low on each scale (2.5 reading, 2.6 maths, 2.6 general); self-esteem average; Key Stage 3 Levels 6(E), 6(M), 6(S).

Luke had a fairly laid back attitude towards his work, he was quiet in class and was in the higher sets for many of his subjects. He had a reputation among staff for being an underachiever, although whether they would predict him to achieve Level 7 at the end of Key Stage 3 is another matter. Like many of the other underachieving pupils, Luke had achieved respectable levels at the end of Year 9 and these gained him a place in the highest sets for maths and science. Whether he will do enough to translate these good Key Stage 3 results into the highest GCSE passes remains to be seen. Luke's attitude towards school was typical of many of the pupils interviewed (in both underachieving and overachieving groups). He did not particularly like school but saw its value in helping him obtain a good job or a place at university.

Robert: male, service class, single-parent family, mother works as a nurse, middle child (2/3); average range CAT for verbal and non-verbal, quantitative score above average; Key Stage 2 Levels 5(E), 5(M), 5(S); school attendance 97.9 per cent; parental involvement score 5/10, parents attend parents evening; self-concept and self-esteem was above sample average; Key Stage 3 Levels 5(E), 6(M), 6(S).

Robert had a very positive attitude towards school; he frequently disagreed with many of the other pupils' negative attitudes in the focus group discussions and had a mature attitude about the value of school and the need to do well. He was a very quiet pupil, who could be described as being 'laid back'; his spelling skills were weak although his verbal CAT score was well within the average range. He was in Sets 1 and 2 for science and maths and Set 3 (out of 5) for English.

Clare: female, intermediate class, single-parent family, mother works as a receptionist, youngest child (3/3); average range quantitative CAT, other batteries below average; Key Stage 2 Levels 4(E), 4(M), 4(S); school attendance 91.44 per cent; parental involvement score 8/10, parents sometimes attend parents evening; self-concept and self-esteem all below average; Key Stage 3 Levels 4(E), 4(M), 4(S).

Clare had a fairly negative attitude towards school. She recognized its importance in getting a job, but she was not particularly optimistic about her chances of getting a good one. She was in the lower ability sets for most of her subjects (Set 5 of 6 for science). She would be described as a quiet but not particularly enthusiastic individual. Her inability to improve her National Curriculum levels from Key Stage 2 to 3 is an indication of her relative lack of academic success in secondary school.

Julie: female, service class, step-parents who both work, eldest child (1/3); above average range CAT for each battery; Key Stage 2 Levels 5(E), 5(M), 5(S); school attendance 94 per cent; parental involvement score 6/10, parents attend parents evening; self-concept and self-esteem scores above average; Key Stage 3 Levels 6(E), 6(M), 6(S).

Julie's teachers would probably describe her as a 'high flier', and it would be very unlikely that she would be placed in this 'underachieving' group by teacher nomination. The reason for her apparent underachievement was her inability to achieve any Level 7s at Key Stage 3. However, her Level 6s have ensured her place in Set 1 for most, if not all, of her subjects. Julie was interviewed with the underachieving group and her attitudes were not markedly different from the others in this group. Although Julie did not appear to be inhibited by the group's opinions and was one of its more vocal contributors, it is possible that if she had been placed with her peers in the overachieving group a different perspective might have emerged.

Matthew: male, working class, single-parent family, mother works as a child-minder, eldest child (1/2); average range quantitative and non-verbal CAT, low average verbal; Key Stage 2 Levels 4(E), 4(M), 4(S); school attendance 81.82 per cent; parental involvement score 7/10, parents sometimes attend parents evening; self-concept scores well below sample average; self-esteem above sample average; Key Stage 3 Levels 4(E), 4(M), 4(S).

Like Clare, Matthew's inability to improve his National Curriculum levels from Key Stage 2 to 3 had placed him in the 'underachieving' group. He would be described by some of his teachers as potentially disruptive, but when motivated would work extremely hard in class. He was placed in the lower sets and could be classed as a C/D borderline candidate. From informal conversations with Matthew, it was apparent that he did very little revision or homework at home and admitted that he will probably rely on what he has 'picked up' in class to get him through his GCSEs.

The pupil profiles have given a snapshot account of a handful of the underachieving group. These pupils were chosen because they are representative of the entire sample of underachievers. For some of the pupils described above, it is more obvious why they have been termed as 'underachieving'. For example, Clare and Matthew have both failed to lift their National Curriculum levels from Key Stage 2 to 3, while Paul, and to a lesser extent Robert, have difficulties with spelling which might make practical subjects more attractive. The placing of Julie and Luke is less clear and raises ethical issues about the need to continually push pupils to 'fulfil their potential'. Both these pupils achieved three Level 6s at Key Stage 3, well above the Government's targets for 14-year olds, and they have been placed in the higher sets where they will sit the highest papers and access the highest tiers of grades – and yet (on this model) they were labelled as 'underachieving'.

Glossary of terms and acronyms

CAT	Cognitive Ability Tests: standardized IQ-style tests, assessing verbal, non-verbal and spatial skills and used by a large number of schools in England and Wales
CSE	Certificate of Secondary Education
DfEE	Department for Education and Employment
DfES	Department for Education and Skills
EiC	Excellence in Cities
GCSE	General Certificate of Secondary Education: national examinations taken at the end of compulsory schooling, usually at age 16
Grades	Elements of the age-sequence structure of the American school system
Key Stages	Elements of the age-sequence structure of the English and Welsh National Curriculum. Comprises Key Stage 1 (ages 5–7, also known as Years 1 and 2), Key Stage 2 (ages 7–11, also known as Years 3–6), Key Stage 3 (ages 11–14, also known as Years 7–9), and Key Stage 4 (ages 14–16, also known as Years 10–11)
LEA	Local Education Authority
NCLB	No Child Left Behind: high-profile American federal legislation designed to raise standards in schools
OECD	Organisation for Economic Co-operation and Development
Ofsted	Office for Standards in Education: government agency responsible for inspecting publicly funded schools in England
PISA	Programme for International Student Achievement
PLASC	Pupil Annual School Census
TIMSS	Third International Maths and Science Study

References

Abedi, J. (2004), 'The No Child Left Behind Act and English Language learners: Assessment and accountability issues'. *Educational Researcher* 33(1), 4–14.

Abrams, F. (2000), 'Tall tales about long tail of failure'. *The Times Educational Supplement*, 1 December 2000.

Abrams, F. (2003), 'Quit agonising over exams'. *The Times Educational Supplement*, 5 September 2003.

ACCAC (1999), *The Comparative Performance of Boys and Girls at School in Wales*. Cardiff: The Welsh Office.

Adams, K. L. and Adams, D. E. (2003), *Urban Education: A Reference Handbook*. California: ABC-Clio Inc.

Angus, L. (1993), 'The sociology of school effectiveness'. *British Journal of Sociology of Education* 14(3), 333–45.

Annesley, F., Odhner F., Madoff E. and Chansky N. (1970), 'Identifying the first grade underachiever'. *Journal of Educational Research* 63(10), 459–62.

Anyon, J. (1997), *Ghetto Schooling: A Political Economy of Urban Educational Reform*. New York: Teachers College Press.

Arnold, R. (1997), *Raising Levels of Achievement in Boys*. Slough: NFER.

Arnot, M., David, M. and Weiner, G. (1996), *Educational Reforms and Gender Equality in Schools*, Manchester: EOC.

Arnot, M., Gray, J., James, M. and Rudduck, J. (1998), *Recent Research on Gender and Educational Performance*. London: HMSO.

Arnot, M., David, M. and Weiner, G. (1999), *Closing the Gender Gap: Postwar Education and Social Change*. Cambridge: Polity Press.

Arthur, B. (2004), 'Girls buck trend with poor results'. *The Times Educational Supplement*, 2 July 2004, www.tes.co.uk [accessed July 2004].

Baker, D. P. (1997), 'Good news, bad news, and international comparisons: comment on Bracey'. *Educational Researcher* 26(3), 16–17.

Baker, D. (2002), *Should We Be More Like Them? American High School Achievement in Cross-national Comparisons*. Brookings papers on education policy, Washington: Brookings Institution.

Barber, M. (1996), *The Learning Game – Arguments for an Education Revolution*. London: Cassell.

Barker, B. (1995), 'The gender factor: action at Stanground college'. *Management in Education* 9(3), 21–2.

Barnard, N. (1999), 'Asian students ahead in university challenge'. *The Times Educational Supplement*, 28 May 1999.

Bentley, T. (1998), *Learning Beyond the Classroom – Education for a Changing World*. London: Routledge.

Berliner, D. C. and Biddle, B. J. (1995), *The Manufactured Crisis: Myths, Fraud and the Attack on America's Public Schools*. Massachusetts: Perseus Books.

Black, P. (1998), *Testing: Friend or Foe? Theory and Practice of Assessment and Testing*. London: Falmer Press.

Black, P. (2000), 'Research and the development of educational assessment'. *Oxford Review of Education* 26 (3&4), 407–19.

Black, P., Harrison, C., Lee, C., Marshall, B. and Wiliam, D. (2003), *Assessment for Learning: Putting it into Practice*. Maidenhead: Open University Press.

Black, P. and Wiliam, D. (2001) *Inside the Black Box: Raising Standards Through Classroom Assessment*, Kings Assessment for Learning Group; Kings College London. http://www.kcl.ac.uk/depsta/education [accessed November 2003].

Black, P. and Wiliam, D. (2003) 'In praise of educational research: formative assessment'. *British Educational Research Journal* 29(5), 623–38.

Blair, T. (1996), Speech given at Ruskin College, Oxford, 16 December 1996. www.leeds.ac.uk/educol/documents/000000084.htm [accessed June 2004].

Blair, T. (2004), Speech given to the National Association of Headteachers in Cardiff, 3 May 2004. www.number10.gov.uk, [accessed 24 June 2004].

Blatchford, P. (2003), *The Class Size Debate: Is Small Better?*. Berkshire: Open University Press.

Blunkett, D. (2000), 'Boys must improve at same rate as girls'. DfES press notice, 20 August 2000. www.dfes.gov.uk/pns/DisplayPN.cgi?pn_id =2000_0368 [accessed August 2004].

Boe, E., May, H., Shin, S. and Boruch, R. (2002), *Student Task Persistence in the Third International Mathematics and Science Study: A Major Source of Achievement Differences at the National, Classroom and Student Levels*.

Philadelphia: Centre for Research and Evaluation in Social policy, University of Pennsylvania.

Brace, N., Kemp, R. and Snelgar, R. (2000), *SPSS for Psychologists – A Guide to Data Analysis using SPSS for Windows*. London: Macmillan Press Ltd.

Bracey, G. W. (1996), 'International comparisons and the condition of American education'. *Educational Researcher*, 25(1), 5–11.

Bracey, G. W. (1997), 'On comparing the incomparable: A response to Baker and Stedman'. *Educational Researcher*, 26(3), 19–26.

Bracey, G. W. (1998), 'Tinkering with TIMSS'. *Phi Delta Kappan*, September 1998. www.pdkintl.org/kappan/kbra9809.htm [accessed September 2003].

Bracey, G. W. (2003), 'Research: PIRLS before the press'. *Phi Delta Kappan*, 84(10), 795.

Brewer, D., Krop, C., Gill, B. P. and Reichardt, R. (1999), 'Estimating the cost of national class size reductions under different policy alternatives'. *Educational Evaluation and Policy Analysis*, 21(2), 179.

Brooksbank, D. (2001), 'The Welsh economy: A statistical profile'. *Contemporary Wales* 14, 164–92.

Brown, M. (1998), 'The tyranny of the international horse race', in *School Effectiveness for Whom? Challenges to the School Effectiveness and School Improvement Movements*, ed. Slee, R., Weiner, G. and Tomlinson, S. London: Falmer Press.

Budge, D. (1997), 'Stars of Asia acknowledged'. *Times Educational Supplement*, 27 June 1997.

Bylsma, P. J. (2004), 'Challenges and successes in Washington'. Paper presented at the American Educational Research Association Annual Meeting, San Diego, 12–16 April 2004.

Camara, W., Kimmel E., Scheuneman, J. and Sawtell, E. A. (2003), *Whose Grades Are Inflated?* New York: College Entrance Examination Board Research Report No. 2003–04.

Carr, M., Borkowsi, J. and Maxwell, S. (1991), 'Motivational components of underachievement'. *Developmental Psychology* 27(1), 108–18.

Cassidy, S. (2000), 'English test "too hard" for most 14-year-olds'. *Times Educational Supplement*, 28 January 2000.

Cassidy, S. (2000), 'Blunkett targets scourge of lad culture'. *Times Educational Supplement*, 25 August 2000.

Cattell, R. B. and Butcher H. J. (1968), *The Prediction of Achievement and Creativity*. New York: Bobbs-Merril.

Chaplain, R. P. (2000), 'Beyond exam results? Differences in the social and psychological perceptions of young males and females at school. *Educational Studies*, 26(2), 177–90.

Chester, M. D. (2004), 'Ohio's experience with AYP implementation, Fewer Schools than Expected'. Paper presented at the American Educational Research Association Annual Meeting, San Diego, 12–16 April 2004.

Chubb, J. E. and Loveless, T. (2003), 'Bridging the achievement gap', in *Bridging the Acheivement Gap*, eds Chubb, J. E. and Loveless, T. Washington: Brookings Institute.

Clark, B. (1988), *Growing Up Gifted*. Ohio: Merrill Publishing Co.

Coe, R. (2002), 'What is an effect size?'. *Building Research Capacity* 4, 6–8.

Coe, R. and Fitz-Gibbon, C. (1998), 'School Effectiveness Research: criticisms and recommendations'. *Oxford Review of Education* 24(4), 421–38.

Cohen, M. (1998), '"A habit of healthy idleness": boys' underachievement in historical perspective', in *Failing Boys? Issues in Gender and Achievement*, eds Epstein, D., Elwood, J., Hey, V. and Maw J. Buckingham: Open University Press.

Cohen, S. (1972), *Folk Devils and Moral Panics: The Creation of the Mods and Rockers*. London: MacGibbon and Kee.

Coleman, J., Campbell, E., Hobson C., McPartland, J., Mood, A., Weinfeld, F. and York, R. (1966), *Equality of Educational Opportunity*. Washington: US Government Printing Office.

Connell, R. W. (1994), 'Cool guys, swots and wimps: the interplay of masculinity and education'. *Oxford Review of Education* 15(3), 291–303.

Cox, C. B. and Dyson, A. E. (eds) (1969), *Fight for Education: A Black Paper*. London: Critical Quarterly Society.

Cummings, W. K. (1989), 'The American Perception of Japanese Education'. *Comparative Education* 25(3), 293–302.

Daugherty, R. (1995) *National Curriculum Assessment: A Review of Policy 1987–1994*. London: Falmer Press.

Daugherty, R. (2004), 'Assessment at Key Stages 2 and 3: a new approach in Wales'. *Teaching Wales*, 6, 7.

Davies, L. (1997), 'The rise of the school effectiveness movement', in *Perspectives on School Effectiveness and School Improvement*, eds White, J. and Barber, M. London: Institute of Education, University of London.

Dean, C. (1998), 'Failing boys, "public burden number one"'. *The Times Educational Supplement*, 27 November 1998. www.tes.co.uk [accessed September 2000].

DeCocker, G. (2002), 'What do National Standards really mean?', in *National Standards and School Reform in Japan and the US*, ed. DeCocker, G. New York: Teachers College Press.

Delamont, S. (1990) *Sex Roles and the School*. London: Routledge.

Delamont, S. (1999), 'Gender and the discourse of derision'. *Research Papers in Education* 14(1), 3–21.

DES (1985), *Education for All (The Swann report)*. London: HMSO.

DES (1987), *National Curriculum Task Group on Assessment and Testing Report*. London: HMSO.

DES (1988), *National Curriculum: Task Group on Assessment and Testing: A Report*. London: DES/Welsh Office.

DfEE (1996), *Youth Cohort Study: Trends in the Activities and Experiences of 16–18 Year Olds in England and Wales 1985–1994*. London: HMSO.

DfEE (1997), *Excellence in Schools*. London: HMSO.

DfEE (1999), *The Autumn Package*. www.standards.dfee.gov.uk/performance [accessed November 2001].

DfES (1995), *Statistics of Education: GCSE/GNVQ and GCE A/AS level Examination Results*. London: HMSO.

DfES (1996), *Statistics of Education: GCSE/GNVQ and GCE A/AS level Examination Results*. London: HMSO.

DfES (1997), *Statistics of Education: GCSE/GNVQ and GCE A/AS level Examination Results*. London: HMSO.

DfES (1998), *Statistics of Education: GCSE/GNVQ and GCE A/AS level Examination Results*. London: HMSO.

DfES (1998a), *Statistics of Education: Schools in England 1998*. http://www.dfes.gov.uk/rsgateway/DB/VOL/v000417/index.shtml [accessed August 2004].

DfES (1999), *Statistics of Education: GCSE/GNVQ and GCE A/AS level Examination Results*. London: HMSO.

DfES (2000), *Statistics of Education: GCSE/GNVQ and GCE A/AS level Examination Results*. London: HMSO.

DfES (2001), *Statistics of Education: GCSE/GNVQ and GCE A/AS level Examination Results*. London: HMSO.

DfES (2001a), *Schools Achieving Success*. London: HMSO.

DfES (2002), *Statistics of Education: GCSE/GNVQ and GCE A/AS level Examination Results*. London: HMSO.

DfES (2002a), 'Schools causing concern'. www.standards.dfes.gov.uk/sie/documents/scc_guidance.pdf [accessed July 2004].

DfES (2003), 'Aiming High: Raising the Achievement of Minority Ethnic Pupils'. London: DfES.

DfES (2003a), *Statistics of Education: GCSE/GNVQ and GCE A/AS level Examination Results*. London: HMSO.

DfES (2003b), *Youth Cohort Study: The Activities and Experiences of 16 Year Olds: England and Wales 2002*. www.dfes.gov.uk/statistics/DB/SFR [accessed February 2004].

DfES (2003c), 'Progress in International Reading Literacy Study (PIRLS)'. www.teachernet.gov.uk/pirls [accessed July 2004].

DfES (2003d), *Statistics of Education: Schools in England 2003*. http://www.dfes.gov.uk/rsgateway/DB/VOL/v000417/index.shtml [accessed August 2004].

DfES (2003e), *Statistics of Education: Permanent Exclusions from Maintained Schools in England*. Statistical Bulletin 08/03, London: HMSO.

DfES (2004), 'Five year strategy for children and learners: Putting people at the heart of public services'. London: HMSO.

DfES (2004b), *The Standards Site: What Are Specialist Schools?* www.standards.dfes.gov.uk/specialistschools [accessed June 2004].

DfES (2004a), *The Standards Site: Excellence in Cities Programme*. www.standards.dfes.gov.uk/sie [accessed June 2004].

DfES (2004c), *National Curriculum Assessment and GCSE/GNVQ Attainment by Pupil Characteristics, in England*. www.dfes.gov.uk/rsgateway/DB/SFR/ [accessed April 2004].

DfES (2004d), 'Chelsea completes FA Premiership line-up'. DfES Press Release, 24 May 2004. www.dfes.gov.uk/pns/DisplayPN.cgi?pn_id=2004_0112 [accessed June 2004].

DfES (2004e), 'Single sex teaching'. www.standards.dfes.gov.uk/genderandachievement/understanding/singlesex/ [accessed August 2004].

Department of Education (1999), *Education Statistics Quarterly*. US Department of Education. http://nces.ed.gov/quicktables/Detail.asp?key=396 [accessed May 2004].

Department of Education (2002), 'No Child Left Behind: Executive summary'. www.ed.gov/nclb/overview/intro/presidentplan/page_pg3.html [accessed June 2004].

Department of Education (2002a), *Education Statistics Quarterly*. US Department of Education, http://nces.ed.gov/Pubs2003/Hispanics [accessed May 2004].

Department of Education (2004), *Consolidated State Application Accountability Workbook: No Child Left Behind in New Jersey*. Washington DC: US Department of Education.

Dobbins, D. A. and Tafa, E. (1990), 'The "stability" of identification of underachieving readers over different measures of intelligence and reading'. *British Journal of Educational Psychology* 61, 155–63.

Dhody, F. (1999), 'Institutionally lazy and fashionable'. *The Times Educational Supplement*, 19 March 1999.

Drew, D. and Gray, J. (1990), 'The fifth-year examination achievements of black young people in England and Wales'. *Educational Research*, 32(2), 107–17.

Drew, D. and Demack, S. (1998), 'A league apart: statistics in the study of "race" and education', in *Researching Racism in Education: Politics, Theory and Practice*, eds Connolly, P. and Troyna, B. Buckingham: Open University Press.

Education Trust (2002) *The Funding Gap: Low-income and Minority Students Receive Fewer Dollars*. The Education Trust, August 2002. www2.edtrust.org/EdTrust/Product+Catalog/special+reports.htm# 2003 [accessed May 2004].

Edwards, T., Whitty, G. and Power, S. (1999), 'Moving back from comprehensive education?' in *Education Policy and Contemporary Politics*, ed. Demaine, J. London: Macmillan Press Ltd.

Ekstrom, R. B., Goertz, M. E., Pollack, J. M. and Rock, D. A. (1986), 'Who drops out of high school and why? Findings from a national study'. *Teachers College Record* 87(3), 356–73.

Elliott, J. (1996), 'School Effectiveness: research and its critics: alternative visions of schooling'. *Cambridge Journal of Education* 26(2), 199–224.

Elwood, J. and Gipps, C. (1999), *Review of Recent Research on the Achievement of Girls in Single Sex Schools*. London: London University Institute of Education.

EOC (1996), *The Gender Divide: Performance Differences between Boys and Girls at School*. London: HMSO.

Epstein, D., Elwood, J., Hey, V. and Maw J. (1998), 'Schoolboy fictions: feminism and "failing" boys', in *Failing Boys? Issues in Gender and Achievement*, eds Epstein, D., Elwood, J., Hey, V. and Maw J. Buckingham: Open University Press.

Epstein, D. (1998), 'Real boys don't work: "underachievement", masculinity and the harassment of "sissies"', in *Failing Boys? Issues in Gender and Achievement*, eds Epstein, D., Elwood, J., Hey, V. and Maw J. Buckingham: Open University Press.

ETAG (1998), *An Education and Training Plan for Wales*. Cardiff: Education and Training Action Group.

Evans, A. (2004), 'Coach is way forward'. *The Times Educational Supplement Cymru*, 2 July 2004, www.tes.co.uk [accessed August 2004].

Field, A. (2000), *Discovering Statistics Using SPSS for Windows*. London: Sage.

Finn, J. D. and Achilles, C. M. (1999), 'Tennessee's class size study: findings, implications, misconceptions'. *Educational Evaluation and Policy Analysis* 21(2).

Fitz-Gibbon, C. (2000), *Value Added for Those in Despair: Research Methods Matter*. Paper presented at the Annual Meeting of the

Education Society of the British Psychological Society, November 2000.

Flanagan, A. and Grissmer, D. (2003), 'The role of federal resources in closing the achievement gap', in *Bridging the Acheivement Gap*, eds Chubb, J. E., Loveless, T. Washington DC: Brookings Institute.

Fletcher, T. V. and Sabers, D. L. (1995), 'Interaction effects in cross-national studies of achievement'. *Comparative Education Review* 39(4), 455–67.

Forgione, P. (1998), *Achievement in the United States: Progress since 'A Nation at Risk?'*. http://nces.ed.gov [accessed June 2000].

Francis, B. (1999), 'Lads, lasses and (New) Labour: 14–16 year old students' responses to the "laddish behaviour and boys" underachievement debate'. *British Journal of Sociology of Education* 20(3), 355–71.

Francis, B. (2000), *Boys, Girls and Achievement: Addressing the Classroom Issues*, London: RoutledgeFalmer.

Frankel, E. (1960), 'A comparative study of achieving and underachieving high school boys of high intellectual ability'. *Journal of Educational Research* 53(5), 72–180.

Frosh, S., Phoenix, A. and Pattman, R. (2002), *Young Masculinities*. Hampshire: Palgrave.

Galley, M. (2004) 'Georgia reaches out to Japan for math-curriculum model'. *Education Week*, 17 March 2004.

Gibson, A. and Asthana, S. (1998), 'School performance, school effectiveness and the 1997 White Paper'. *Oxford Review of Education* 24(2), 195–210.

Gillborn, D. (1990), *'Race', Ethnicity and Education: Teaching and Learning in Multi-ethnic Schools*. London: Unwin Hyman.

Gillborn, D. and Gipps, C. (1996), *Recent Research on the Achievement of Ethnic Minority Pupils*. Ofsted, London: HMSO.

Gillborn, D. (1997), 'Young, black and failed by school: the market, education reform and black students'. *International Journal of Inclusive Education* 1(1), 65–87.

Gillborn, D. (1998), 'Racism, selection, poverty and parents: New Labour, old problems?'. *Journal of Educational Policy* 13(6), 717–35.

Gillborn, D. and Mirza, H.S. (2000), *Educational Inequality: Mapping Race, Class and Gender*. Ofsted, London: HMSO.

Gillborn, D. and Youdell, D. (2000), *Rationing Education – Policy, Practice, Reform and Equity*. Buckingham: Open University Press.

Gipps, C. and Murphy, P. (1994), *A Fair Test? Assessment, Achievement and Equality*. Buckingham: Open University Press.

Gold, M. J. (1965), *Education of the Intellectually Gifted*. Ohio: Charles E. Merril Inc.

Gorard, S., Taylor, C. and Fitz, J. (2003), *Schools, Markets and Choice Policies*. London: RoutledgeFalmer.

Gorard, S. and Smith, E. (2004), 'What is "Underachievement" at school?'. *School Leadership and Management* 24(2), 205–25.

Gorard, S. and Smith, E. (2004a), 'An international comparison of equity in national school systems'. *Comparative Education* 40(1), 15–28.

Gorard, S. (2001), 'International comparisons of school effectiveness: a second component of the "crisis account"?'. *Comparative Education* 37(3), 279–96.

Gorard, S. and Smith, E. (2004), *The Role of Feedback in Student Progress: A Small Scale Experiment*. Occasional paper 59, Cardiff University School of Social Sciences.

Gorard, S. (1999), 'Keeping a sense of proportion: the "politician's error" in analysing school outcomes'. *British Journal of Educational Studies*, 47(3), 235–46.

Gorard, S., Rees, G. and Salisbury, J. (1999), 'Reappraising the apparent underachievement of boys at school'. *Gender and Education* 11(4), 441–54.

Gorard, S. (2000), *Education and Social Justice*. Cardiff: University of Wales Press.

Gorard, S. (2001a), 'An alternative account of "boys' underachievement" at school'. *Welsh Journal of Education* 10(2), 4–14.

Gorard, S. (2002), *How Do We Overcome the Methodological Schism (or Can There Be a 'Compleat' Researcher)?* Occasional paper 24, Cardiff University School of Social Sciences.

Gore, T. and Smith, N. (2001), *Patterns of Educational Attainment in the British Coalfields*. DfES Research Report No. 314, London: HMSO.

Grissmer, D. (1999), 'Class size effects: assessing the evidence, its policy implications and future research agenda'. *Educational Evaluation and Policy Analysis* 21(2), 231.

Gurian, M. (2001), *Boys and Girls Learn Differently: Brain Based Differences*. San Francisco: Josey-Bass.

Halpin, T. (2001), 'Britain has the worst schools in Europe'. *Daily Mail*, 28 March 2001.

Hamilton, D. (1997), 'Peddling feel-good fictions', in *Perspectives on School Effectiveness and School Improvement*, eds White, J. and Barber, M. London: Institute of Education, University of London.

Haney, W. (2000), 'The myth of the Texas miracle in education'. *Education Policy Analysis Archives* 8(41). http://epaa.asu.edu/epaa/v8n41/ [accessed August 2004].

Hanushek, E.A. (1999), 'Some findings from an independent investigation of the Tennessee STAR experiment and from other investigations of class size effects'. *Educational Evaluation and Policy Analysis* 21(2), 143.

Haque, Z. (2000), 'The ethnic minority "Underachieving" group? Investigating the claims of "Underachievement" amongst Bangladeshi pupils in British secondary schools'. *Race Ethnicity and Education* 3(2), 145–68.

Harlen, W., Gipps, C., Broadfoot, P. and Nuttall, D. (1992), 'Assessment and the improvement of education'. *The Curriculum Journal* 3(3), 215–30.

Hayes, D. (2002), 'Wanted – more male primary teachers'. *The Times Educational Supplement*, 22 April 2002.

Heath, A. (2000), 'The political arithmetic tradition in the sociology of education'. *Oxford Review of Education* 26(3–4), 313–31.

Hedges, L. V. and Nowell, A. (1998) 'Black-white test score convergence since 1965', in eds Jencks, C. and Phillips, M., *The Black-White Test Score Gap*. Washington DC: Brookings Institute.

Henry, J. (2001), 'Missing the feminine influence'. *The Times Educational Supplement*, 1 June 2001, 16.

Herrnstein, R. J. and Murray, C. (1995), *The Bell Curve: Intelligence and Class Structure in American Life*. New York: Free Press.

Hitz, R. (1996), *Beware International Comparisons of Educational Achievement*. www.montana.edu/wwwpb/univ/hitz.htm/ [accessed June 2000].

HMSO (1998), *School Standards and Framework Act of 1998 Chapter 31*. www.legislation.hmso.gov.uk/acts/acts1998/19980031.htm [accessed August 2004].

Ho Sui-Chu, E. and Willms, J. D. (1996), 'Effects of parental involvement on eighth-grade achievement'. *Sociology of Education* 69, 126–41.

Hoff, D. J. (2001), 'A world class education eludes many in the US'. *Education Week*, 11 April 2001, 12.

Hochschild, J. (2003), 'Rethinking accountability politics', in *No Child Left Behind? The Politics and Practice of School Accountability*, eds Peterson, P., and West M. Washington DC: Brookings Institution.

Holden, C. (1993), 'Giving girls a chance: patterns of talk in co-operative group work'. *Gender and Education* 5(2), 179–91.

House of Commons (2002), 'Select Committee on Education and Skills: Minutes of evidence'. Memorandum submitted by D. Gillborn and S. Warren www.publications.parliament.uk/pa/cm200102/cmselect/cmeduski/1191–iv [accessed June 2004].

House of Commons (2003), *Secondary Education: Pupil Achievement*. Seventh Report of Session 2002–03, House of Commons Education and Skills Select Committee. London: HMSO.

Hughes, D. and Academy, A. (1992), 'Social class and educational disadvantage: are the schools to blame?', in *Class, Race and Gender in Schools – a New Agenda for Policy and Practice in Scottish Education*, eds Brown, S. and Riddell, S. Edinburgh: SCRE.

Husen, T. and Tujinman, A. C. (1994), 'Monitoring standards in education: why and how it came about', in *Monitoring Standards in Education: Papers in Honour of JP Keeves*, eds Tujinman, A.C. and Postlethwaite, T.N. Oxford: Elsevier Science Ltd.

Istance, D. and Rees, G. (1994), 'Education and training in Wales: problems and paradoxes revisited'. *Contemporary Wales* 7, 7–28.

Jackson, C. (1999), 'Underachieving boys? Some points for consideration'. *Curriculum* 20(2), 81–5.

Jackson, C. (2002), 'Can single-sex classes in co-educational schools enhance the learning experiences of girls and/or boys? An exploration of pupils' perceptions'. *British Educational Research Journal* 28(1), 37–48.

Jackson, D. (1998), 'Breaking out of the binary trap: boys' underachievement, schooling and gender relations', in *Failing Boys? Issues in Gender and Achievement*, eds Epstein, D., Elwood, J., Hey, V. and Maw J. Buckingham: Open University Press.

Japan Statistics Bureau (2002), *Japan in Statistics*. Ministry of Public Management, Home Affairs, Posts and Telecommunications. www.stat.go.jp/english/data/figures/index.htm [accessed May 2004].

Jencks, C. (1972), *Inequality: A Reassessment of the Effect of Family and Schooling in America*. New York: Basic Books.

Jencks, C. and Phillips, M. (1998), *The Black-White Test Score Gap*. Washington DC: Brookings Institute.

Johnson, M. (2002), '"Choice" has failed the poor'. *The Times Educational Supplement*, 22 November 2002.

Kane, T. J. and Staiger, D. O. (2003) 'Unintended consequences of racial subgroup rules', in *No Child Left Behind? The Politics and Practice of School Accountability*, eds Peterson, P. and West M. Washington DC: Brookings Institution.

Kellmer-Pringle, M. L. (1970), *Able Misfits*. London: Longman.

Kendall, L. and Schagen, I. (2004), *Pupils' Performance at Key Stages 3 and 4*. Paper 18/2003, Slough: NFER. www.nfer.ac.uk/research/eic.asp [accessed June 2004].

Keng, Z. and LeTendre, G. (1999), '"The dark side of . . ." Suicide, violence and drug use in Japanese schools', in *Competitor or Ally? Japan's Role in American Educational Debates*, ed. LeTendre, G. K. New York: Falmer Press.

Krueger, A. B. and Whitmore, D. M. (2003), 'Would smaller classes help close the black-white achievement gap?', in *Bridging the Achievement*

Gap, eds Chubb, J.E. and Loveless, T. Washington DC: Brookings Institute.

Kruse, A. (1992), '". . . we have learnt not just to sit back, twiddle our thumbs and let them take over". Single sex settings and the development of a pedagogy for boys in Danish schools'. *Gender and Education* 4(1/2), 81–100.

Lau, K. and Chan, D. W. (2001), 'Identification of underachievers in Hong Kong: do different methods select different underachievers?'. *Educational Studies* 27(2), 187–200.

Laureau, A. (1987), 'Social class differences in family-school relationships: the importance of cultural capital'. *Sociology of Education* 60, 73–85.

Lawrence, M., Demsey, S. and Goddard, S. (1997), 'Committed to the best results', *The Times Educational Supplement*, 11 July, p. 15.

Learner, S. (2001), 'Black boys inspired by gospel choir'. *The Times Educational Supplement*, 19 October 2001.

Lee J. (2002), 'Racial and ethnic achievement gap trends: reversing the progress toward equity?'. *Educational Researcher* 31(1), 3–12.

LeTendre, G. K. (1999), 'International achievement studies and myths of Japan', in *Competitor or Ally? Japan's Role in American Educational Debates*, ed. LeTendre, G. K. New York: Falmer Press.

LeTendre, G. K. (2002), 'Setting National Standards: educational reform, social change and political conflict', in *National Standards and School Reform in Japan and the US*, ed. Decocker, G. New York: Teachers College Press.

LeTendre, G. K. and Baker, D. (1999), 'International comparisons and education research policy', in *Competitor or Ally? Japan's Role in American Educational Debates*, ed. LeTendre, G. K. New York: Falmer Press.

Lewis, C. C. (1999), 'Resilient myths: Are our minds made up about Japanese education?', in *Competitor or Ally? Japan's Role in American Educational Debates*, ed. LeTendre, G. K. New York: Falmer Press.

Lieberman, M. (1993), *Public Education: An Autopsy*. Massachusetts: Harvard University Press.

Linn, R.L. (2003), 'Accountability: responsibility and reasonable expectations'. *Educational Researcher* 32(7), 3–13.

Linton, T. H. and Kester, D. (2003), 'Exploring the achievement gap between white and minority students in Texas: A comparison of the 1996 and 2000 NAEP and TAAS eighth grade mathematics test results'. *Education Policy Analysis Archives* 11(10). http://epaa.asu.edu/epaa/v11n10/ [accessed August 2004].

Lowenstein, L. F. (1982), 'An empirical study of the incidence, diagnosis, treatment and follow-up of academically underachieving children'. *School Psychology International* 3, 219–30.

Lynn, R. (1988), *Educational Achievement in Japan: Lessons for the West*. London: Macmillan Press.

Mac an Ghaill, M. (1988), *Young, Gifted and Black*. Buckingham: Open University Press.

Mac an Ghaill, M. (1989), 'Coming of age in 1980s England: re-conceptualising black students' schooling experience'. *British Journal of the Sociology of Education* 10(3), 273–86.

Mahony, P. (1998), 'Girls will be girls and boys will be first', in *Failing Boys? Issues in Gender and Achievement*, eds Epstein, D., Elwood, J., Hey, V. and Maw J. Buckingham: Open University Press.

Mann, C. (1998), 'The impact of working-class mothers on the educational success of their adolescent daughters at a time of social change'. *British Journal of Sociology of Education* 19(2), 211–26.

Mansell, W. and Cassidy, S. (2000) 'Gap between black and white expands'. *The Times Educational Supplement*, 27 October 2000.

Manzo, K. K. (2002), 'Japanese school children "cram" to boost achievement'. *Education Week*, 7 August 2002.

McCall, R. B., Evahn, C. and Kratzer, L. (1992), *High School Underachievers*. New York: Sage.

McNeil, L. M. (2000), 'Creating new inequalities: Contradictions of reform'. *Phi Delta Kappan* 81, 728–35.

Measor, L. (1999), 'Looking back at the boys: Reflections on issues of gender in classroom data', in *Researching School Experience – Ethnographic Studies of Teaching and Learning*, ed. Hammersley, M. London: Falmer Press.

Mellanby, J., Anderson, R., Campbell, B. and Westwood, E. (1996), 'Cognitive determinants of verbal underachievement at secondary school level'. *British Journal of Educational Psychology* 66, 483–500.

Meuret, D. (2002) 'School equity as a matter of justice', in *In Pursuit of Equity in Education*, eds Hutmacher, W., Cochrane D. and Bottani N. Dordrecht: Kluwer Academic Publishers.

Miliband, D. (2004), 'Using data to raise achievement'. Speech by David Miliband to The Education Network, 11 February 2004. www.dfes.gov.uk/speeches [accessed June 2004].

Millard, E. (1997), 'Differently literate: boys, girls and the schooling of literacy'. London: Falmer Press.

Millard, E. (1997a), 'Differently literate: gender identity and the construction of the developing reader'. *Gender and Education* 9(1), 31–48.

Mills, M., Martino, W. and Lingard, B. (2004), 'Attracting, recruiting and retaining male teachers: policy issues in the male teacher debate'. *British Journal of Sociology of Education* 25(3), 355–69.

Modood, T., Berthoud, R., Lakey, J., Nazroo, J., Smith, P., Virdee, S.

and Beishon, S. (1997), *Ethnic Minorities in Britain: Diversity and Disadvantage*. London: Policy Studies Institute.

Morris, M., Rutt, S. and Eggers, M. (2004), *Pupil Outcomes: The Impact of EiC*. Paper 24/2003, Slough: NFER. www.nfer.ac.uk/research/eic.asp [accessed June 2004].

Mortimore, P. (1991), 'The nature and findings of school effectiveness research in the primary sector', in *School Effectiveness Research: its Messages for School Improvement*, eds Riddell, S., and Brown, S. London: HMSO.

Mortimore, P. and Sammons, P. (1997), 'Endpiece: a welcome and a riposte to critics', in *Perspectives on School Effectiveness and School Improvement*, eds White, J. and Barber, M. London: Institute of Education, University of London.

Murphy, P. (1988), 'Gender and assessment'. *Curriculum* 9, 165–71.

Myhill, D. (1999), 'Boy zones and girl power: gender perceptions and preferences in English'. *Curriculum* 20(2), 86–99.

Nash, R. (2001), 'Class, "ability" and attainment: a problem for the sociology of education'. *British Journal of Sociology of Education* 22(2), 189–202.

National Commission on Excellence in Education (1983), *A Nation at Risk*. US Department of Education, Washington: US Printing Office.

NCES (2000), *NAEP 1999 Trends in Academic Progress: Three Decades of Student Performance*. National Centre for Educational Statistics 2000–469, Washington: US Department of Education.

NCES (2003), *The Nation's Report Card: Parents' Guide to NAEP*. National Centre for Educational Statistics 2003–480, Washington: US Department of Education.

NCES (2004), *National Assessment of Educational Progress: Reading Highlights 2003*. National Centre for Educational Statistics 2004–452, Washington: US Department of Education.

NFER (2001), 'The cognitive ability tests'. www.nfer-nelson.co.uk/cat [accessed May 2002].

NFER (2003), *Progress in International Reading Literacy Study (PIRLS)*. Slough: NFER.

Nelson, D.I. (2003), *What Explains Differences in International Performance? TIMSS Researchers Continue to Look for Answers*. Philadelphia: Centre for Research and Evaluation in Social Policy, University of Pennsylvania.

Newman, S., Wright, S. and Fields, H. (1990), 'Identification of a group of children with dyslexia by means of IQ-achievement discrepancies'. *British Journal of Educational Psychology* 61, 139–54.

NUT (2003), *Secondary Education: Pupil Achievement, Seventh Report of*

Session 2002–03. Written evidence presented to the House of Commons Education and Skills Committee, London: HMSO.

Nuthall, K. (2001), 'We are the biggest quitters in Europe'. *The Times Educational Supplement,* 1 June 2001. www.tes.co.uk [accessed December 2001].

Nuttall, D. (1979), 'The myth of comparability'. *Journal of the National Association of Inspectors and Advisers* 11, 16–18.

Nye, B., Hedges, L. V. and Konstantopoulos, S. (2002), 'Do low-achieving students benefit more from small classes? Evidence from the Tennessee class size experiment'. *Educational Evaluation and Policy Analysis* 24(3), 201–17.

OECD (2001), *Knowledge and Skills for Life: First Results from PISA 2000.* Paris: OECD.

Ofsted (1996), *Exclusions from Secondary School.* London: HMSO.

Ofsted (1999), *Raising the Attainment of Minority Ethnic Pupils – School and LEA Responses.* London: HMSO.

Ofsted (2003), 'Boys' achievement in secondary schools'. HMI–1659. London: Ofsted Publications.

Ofsted (2004), *Achievement of Bangladeshi Heritage Pupils.* HMI 513. www.ofsted.gov.uk [accessed June 2004].

Okan, K. and Tsuchiya, M. (1999), *Education in Contemporary Japan: Inequality and Diversity.* Cambridge: Cambridge University Press.

Orfield, G. (2000), 'Policy and equity: lessons of a third of a century of educational reforms in the United States', in *Unequal Schools, Unequal Chances: The Challenges to Equal Opportunity in the Americas,* ed. Reimers, F. Massachusetts: Harvard University Press.

Ouston, J. (1999), 'School effectiveness and improvement: Critique of a movement', in *Redefining Educational Management,* eds Bush, T., Bell, L., Bolam, R., Glatter, R. and Ribbins, P. London: Sage.

Paterson, L. (1992), 'Social class in Scottish education', in *Class, Race and Gender in Schools – A New Agenda for Policy and Practice in Scottish Education,* eds Brown, S. and Riddell, S. Edinburgh: SCRE.

Phillips, M. (1996), *All Must Have Prizes.* London: Little, Brown and Co.

Pickering, J. (1997), *Raising Boys' Achievement.* Stafford: Network Educational Press.

Pirie, M. (2001), 'How exams are fixed in favour of girls'. *Spectator,* 20 January 2001.

Platten, J. (1999), 'Raising boys' achievement'. *Curriculum* 20(2), 2–7.

Pong, S. (1998), 'The school compositional effect of single parenthood on tenth-grade achievement'. *Sociology of Education* 71, 23–43.

Popham, W. J. (2004), *America's 'Failing' Schools, How Parents and Teachers Can Cope with No Child Left Behind.* New York: RoutledgeFalmer.

Prais, S. J. (1991), 'Mathematical attainments: Comparisons of Japanese and English schooling', in *Judging Standards and Effectiveness in Education*, eds Moon, B., Isaac, J. and Powney, J. London: Hodder and Stoughton.

Prais, S. (2003), 'Cautions on OECD's recent educational survey (PISA)'. *Oxford Review of Education* 29(2), 139–63.

Project STAR (1990), *The State of Tennessee's Student/Teacher Achievement Ratio Project, Final Summary Report 1985–1990*. www.heros-inc.org/summary.pdf [accessed August 2004].

Project STAR (1999), *Project STAR: The Tennessee Student/Teacher Achievement Ratio Study, Background and 1999 Update*. www.heros-inc.org/star99.pdf [accessed August 2004].

Pyke, N. (1996), 'English lag behind in maths'. *The Times Educational Supplement*, 15 November 1996.

Rafferty, F. and Hackett, G. (1997), 'New Labour, new deal'. *The Times Educational Supplement*, 9 May 1997.

Raph, J. B., Goldberg, M. L. and Passow, A. H. (1966), *Bright Underachievers*. New York: Teachers College Press.

Raphael Reed, L. (1998), '"Zero tolerance": gender performance and school failure', in *Failing Boys? Issues in Gender and Achievement*, eds Epstein, D., Elwood, J., Hey, V. and Maw J. Buckingham: Open University Press.

Ravitch, D. (1995), *National Standards in American Education*. Washington: Brookings Institution.

Rea, J. and Weiner, G. (1998), 'Cultures of blame and redemption – when empowerment becomes control: practitioners' views of the effective schools movement', in *School Effectiveness for Whom? Challenges to the School Effectiveness and School Improvement Movements*, eds Slee, R., Weiner, G. and Tomlinson, S. London: Falmer Press.

Rees, G. and Delamont, S. (1999), 'Education in Wales', in *Wales Today*, eds Dunkerley, D. and Thompson, A. Cardiff: University of Wales Press.

Renold, E. (2001), '"Square-girls", femininity and the negotiation of academic success in the primary school'. *British Educational Research Journal* 27(5), 577–87.

Reynolds, D. (1997), 'East-West trade off'. *The Times Educational Supplement*, 27 June 1997.

Reynolds, D. and Farrell, S. (1996), *Worlds Apart? A Review of International Surveys of Achievement Involving England*. London: HMSO.

Reynolds, D. (1994), 'School effectiveness and quality in education', in *Improving Education: Promoting Quality in Schools*, eds Ribbins, P. and Burridge, E. London: Cassell.

Reynolds, D. and Murgatroyd, S. (1981), 'Schooled to fail?'. *The Times Educational Supplement*, 4 December 1981.

Riordan, C. (1990), *Girls and Boys in School – Together or Separate?* New York: Teachers College Press.

Robinson, P. and Smithers, A. (1999), 'Should the sexes be separated for secondary education – comparisons of single-sex and co-educational schools?'. *Research Papers in Education*, 14(1), 23–49.

Roesgaard, M. H. (1998), *Moving Mountains: Japanese Education Reform.* Aarhus: Aarhus University Press.

Rohlen, T. P. (2002), 'Wider contexts and future issues', in *National Standards and School Reform in Japan and the US*, ed. DeCocker, G. New York: Teachers College Press.

Rudalevige, A. (2003), 'No Child Left Behind: forging a congressional compromise', in *No Child Left Behind? The Politics and Practice of School Accountability*, eds Peterson, P. and West M. Washington: Brookings Institution.

Rumberger, R. W. (1983), 'Dropping-out of high school: the influence of race, sex and family background'. *American Educational Research Journal* 20, 199–213.

Rumberger, R. W. (1995), 'Dropping-out of middle school: a multilevel analysis of students and schools'. *American Educational Research Journal* 32(3), 583–625.

Salisbury, J. (1996), *Educational Reforms and Gender Equality in Welsh Schools.* Manchester: EOC.

Salisbury, J., Rees, G. and Gorard, S. (1999), 'Accounting for the differential attainment of boys and girls at school'. *School Leadership and Management* 19(4), 403–26.

Sammons, P. (1995), 'Gender, ethnic and socio-economic differences in attainment and progress: a longitudinal analysis of student achievement over 9 years'. *British Educational Research Journal* 21(4), 465–85.

Sammons, P., Hillman, J. and Mortimore, P. (1995), *Key Characteristics of Effective Schools – A Review of School Effectiveness Research.* London: Ofsted.

Sarah, E., Scott, M. and Spender, D. (1980), 'The education of feminists: the case for single sex schools', in *Learning to Lose: Sexism in Education*, eds Spender, D. and Sarah, E. London: The Women's Press Ltd.

Schmidt, W. H., McKnight, C. C., Cogan, L. S., Jakwerth, P. M. and Houang, R. T. (1999) *Facing the Consequences: Using TIMSS for a Closer Look at US Mathematics and Science Education.* Dordrecht: Kulwer Academic Publishers.

Schoolland, K. (1990), *Shogun's Ghost: The Dark Side of Japanese Education.* New York: Bergin and Garvey.

Schleicher, A. (1994), 'International standards for educational comparisons', in *Monitoring Standards in Education: Papers in Honour of JP*

Keeves, eds Tujinman, A. C. and Postlethwaite, T. N. Oxford: Elsevier Science Ltd.

Scourfied, J., Beynon, H., Evans, J. and Shah, W. (2002), *'Not a Black and White Issue' – The Experiences of Black And Minority Ethnic Children Living in the South Wales Valleys*. Cardiff: Barnardo's.

Sharma, Y. (2002), 'Short, sharp "schock" wakes Germany up'. *The Times Educational Supplement*, 27 September 2002.

Sharma, Y. (2002a), 'Rich nations fail to close achievement gap'. *The Times Educational Supplement*, 29 November 2002.

Shaw, M.C. (1966), 'Definition and identification of academic under-achievers', in *Educating the Gifted: A Book of Readings*, ed. French, J. L. New York: Holt, Rinehart and Winston Inc.

Shaw, M. (2003), 'Ways through laddish culture'. *The Times Educational Supplement*, 11 July 2003. www.tes.co.uk [accessed April 2004].

Shorrocks-Taylor, D. (1999), *National Testing: Past, Present and Future*. Leicester: The British Psychological Association.

Slater, J. (2001), 'Cultures in a class of their own'. *The Times Educational Supplement*, 14 December 2001. www.tes.co.uk [accessed December 2001].

Slee, R. and Weiner G. (1998), 'School effectiveness for whom?', in *School Effectiveness for Whom? Challenges to the School Effectiveness and School Improvement Movements*, eds Slee, R., Weiner, G., and Tomlinson, S. London: Falmer Press.

Smith, E. (1998), *An Analysis of Achievement Among Year 9 Pupils*. MA dissertation, Cardiff: University of Wales.

Smith, E. (2002), *Understanding Underachievement: An Investigation into the Differential Achievement of Secondary School Pupils*. PhD dissertation, Cardiff: University of Wales.

Smith, E. (2003), 'Understanding underachievement: an investigation into the differential achievement of secondary school pupils'. *British Journal of Sociology of Education*, 24(5).

Smith, E. (2005), 'Schooled to fail? Aspects of underachievement in Wales'. *Welsh Journal of Education*, forthcoming.

Smith, E., Ellis, D. and Freye, S. (2000), 'Underachievement in secondary schools: attitudes and gender difference among Year 9 pupils'. *Welsh Journal of Education* 9(1), 5–17.

Smith, E. and Gorard, S. (2002), *What Does PISA Tell us about Equity in Education Systems?* Occasional Paper 54. Cardiff: Cardiff University School of Social Sciences.

Smith, E. and Gorard, S. (2005), '"They don't give us our marks": the impact of formative assessment techniques in the classroom'. *Assessment in Education*, 12(1), 21–38.

Smithers, R. (2004), 'Number of schools in Special Measures rises'. *Guardian*, 7 February 2004.

Smithers, R. and Ward, A. (2004), 'Row over "no-fail" A-levels'. *Guardian*, 19 August 2004.

Social Exclusion Unit (1998), *Truancy and Social Exclusion*. London: HMSO.

Spendlove, D. (2000), 'A better look at boys'. *The Times Educational Supplement*, 8 September 2000.

Spielhofer, T., Benton, T. and Schagen, S. (2004), 'A study of the effects of schools size and single-sex education in English schools'. *Research Papers in Education* 19(2), 133–59.

Stanworth, M. (1983), *Gender and Schooling – A Study of Sexual Divisions in the Classroom*. Buckingham: Open University Press.

Stedman, L. C. (1997) 'International achievement differences: An assessment of a new perspective'. *Educational Researcher* 26(3), 4–15.

Stevenson, D. L. and Baker, D. P. (1987), 'The family–school relation and the child's school performance'. *Child Development* 58, 1348–57.

Stevenson, H. W. (1998), *A TIMSS Primer: Lessons and Implications for US Education*. www.edexcellence.net/library/timss.htm [accessed June 2000].

Stevenson, H. W. (2002), 'Individual differences and Japan's course of study', in *National Standards and School Reform in Japan and the US*, ed. DeCocker, G. New York: Teachers College Press.

Stobart, G. and Gipps C. (1997), *Assessment: A Teacher's Guide to the Issues*. London: Hodder and Stoughton.

Stokes, S. (2003), 'Sex and the joys of single life'. *The Times Educational Supplement*, 20 June 2003. www.tes.co.uk [accessed April 2004].

Strand, S. (2001), 'Exploring the use of reasoning tests in secondary schools: Letting the CAT out of the bag'. Paper presented to the Annual Conference of the British Educational Research Association, 13–15 September 2001, Leeds University.

Sukhnandan, L., Lee, B. and Kelleher, S. (2000), *An Investigation into Gender Differences in Achievement, Phase 2: School and Classroom Strategies*. Slough: NFER.

Swan, B. (1998), 'Teaching boys and girls in separate classes at Shenfield High School, Brentwood', in *Raising Boys' Achievement in Schools*, ed. Bleach, K. Stoke-on-Trent: Trentham Books.

Tate, J. and Clark, G. (2002), *No Child Left Behind: The Way Ahead*. Conservative Policy Unit, London: Conservative Party.

TeacherNet (2004), '*Class Size*'. www.teachernet.gov.uk/management/atoz/c/classsizes [accessed August 2004].

TEA (2003), 'Texas Education Agency: background to programme'. www.tea.state.tx.us [accessed August 2004].

TEA (2003a), 'Texas Education Agency: Statewide TAAS Results'. www.tea.state.tx.us/student.assessment/reporting/results/swresults/au gust/g8all_au.pd [accessed August 2004].

TEA (2003b), 'Texas Education Agency: student dropout rates'. www.tea.state.tx.us [accessed August 2004].

Tett, L. and Crowther, J. (1998), 'Families at a disadvantage: class, culture and literacies'. *British Educational Research Journal* 24(4), 449–60.

The Times Educational Supplement (1981), 'Schooled to fail? Setting the record straight for Wales'. Letters, 18 December 1981.

The Times Educational Supplement (1996), 'Reports of our dearth in maths are not exaggerated'. 22 November 1996.

The Times Educational Supplement (1997), 'Maths failure lingers after curriculum revolution'. 13 June 1997.

The Times Educational Supplement (2001), 'Black pupils narrow the GCSE gap'. 23 January 2001.

The Times Education Supplement (2002), 'Light behind the rhetoric'. 28 June 2002.

The Times Education Supplement (2004), 'Wales scraps school tests'. 13 July 2004. www.tes.co.uk [accessed July 2004].

Thorndike, R. L. (1963), *The Concepts of Over and Underachievement*. New York: Teachers College Press.

TIMSS (1996), 'Third International Maths and Science Study: highlights of results from TIMSS'. http://timss.bc.edu/timss1995i/TIMSSPDF/ P2HiLite.pdf [accessed August 2004].

Toenjes, L. A. and Dworkin, A. G. (2002), 'Are increasing test scores in Texas really a myth, or is Haney's myth a myth?'. *Education Policy Analysis Archives* 10(17). http://epaa.asu.edu/epaa/v10n17 [accessed August 2004].

Toenjes, L., Dworkin, A. G., Lorence, J. and Hill, A. N. (2003), 'High-stakes testing, accountability, and student achievement in Texas and Houston', in *Bridging the Achievement Gap*, eds Chubb, J. E. and Loveless, T. Washington: Brookings Institute.

Tolor, A. (1969), 'Incidence of underachievement at the high school level'. *Journal of Educational Research* 63 (2), 63–5.

Tomlinson, S. (1983), *Ethnic Minorities in British Schools: A Review of the Literature 1960–1982*. London: Heineman.

Torrance, H. and Pryor, J. (1998) *Investigating Formative Assessment: Teaching, Learning and Assessment in the Classroom*. Buckingham: Open University Press.

Tsuchida, I. and Lewis, C. C. (1999), 'A look at the other side of Japanese education – student responsibility and learning', in *Competitor or Ally? Japan's role in American Educational Debates*, ed. LeTendre, G. K. New York: Falmer Press.

Tsuneyoshi, R. (2000) *The Japanese Model of Schooling: Comparisons with the United States*. London: RoutledgeFalmer.

Turner, E., Riddell, S. and Brown, S. (1995), *Gender Equality in Scottish Schools*. Glasgow: EOC.

Tuss P., Zimmer J. and Ho H-Z. (1995), 'Causal attributions of under-achieving fourth-grade students in China, Japan and the United States'. *Journal of Cross-Cultural Psychology* 26(4), 408–25.

Wallace, W. (2000), 'Pa for the course'. *The Times Educational Supplement*, 17 November 2000.

Wallace, W. (2004), 'Mum and dad know best'. *The Times Educational Supplement*, 30 July 2004. www.tes.co.uk [accessed August 2004].

Warrington, M. and Younger, M. (1996), 'Goals, expectations and motivation: gender differences in achievement at GCSE'. *Curriculum* 17(2), 80–8.

Warrington, M. and Younger, M. (2003), ' "We decided to give it a twirl": single-sex teaching in English comprehensive schools'. *Gender and Education* 15(4), 339–50.

Weiner, G., Arnot, M. and David, M. (1997), 'Is the future female? Female success, male disadvantage and changing patterns in education', in *Education: Culture, Economy and Society*, eds Halsey, A. H., Lauder, H., Brown, P. and Stuart Wells A. Oxford: Oxford University Press.

West, A. and Pennell, H. (2002), 'How new is New Labour? The quasi-market and English schools: 1997 to 2001'. *British Journal of Educational Studies* 50(2), 206–24.

West, M. and Peterson P. (2003), 'The politics and practice of school accountability', in *No Child Left Behind? The Politics and Practice of School Accountability*, eds Peterson, P. and West M. Washington: Brookings Institution.

West, A., Noden, P. and Edge A. (1998), 'Parental involvement in education in and out of school'. *British Educational Research Journal* 24(3), 461–84.

White, K. R. (1982), 'The relation between socioeconomic status and academic achievement'. *Psychological Bulletin* 91(3), 461–81.

White, M. (1999), 'Introduction', in *Competitor or Ally? Japan's Role in American Educational Debates*, ed. LeTendre, G.K. New York: Falmer Press.

White, P. and Gorard, S. (1999), 'Ethnicity, attainment and progress: A cautionary note regarding percentages and percentage points'. *Research in Education* 62, 66–9.

White, P. and Smith E. (2005), 'What can PISA tell us about teacher shortages?'. *The European Journal of Education* 40(1).

Whitmore, J. R. (1980), *Giftedness, Conflict and Underachievement*. Boston: Allyn and Bacon.

Whittington, J. (1988), 'Large verbal – non-verbal ability differences and underachievement'. *British Journal of Educational Psychology* 58, 205–11.

Willms, J.D. (1986), 'Social class segregation and its relationship to pupils' examination results in Scotland'. *American Sociological Review* 51, 224–41.

Wiliam, D. and Black, P. (2002), 'Feedback is the best nourishment'. *The Times Educational Supplement, special supplement: 'Mind Measuring'*, 4 October 2002.

Winter, J. (2003), 'The changing prepositions of assessment practice: assessment *of, for* and *as* learning'. *British Educational Research Journal: Thematic Review* 29(5) 767.

WHO (2004). www.who.int/mental_health/prevention/suicide/coun try_reports.en [accessed July 2004].

Wossman, L. (2003), 'Central exit examinations and student achievement: International evidence', in *No Child Left Behind? The Politics and Practice of School Accountability*, eds Peterson, P. and West M. Washington: Brookings Institution.

Wrigley, T. (2003), 'Is "school effectiveness" anti-democratic?'. *British Journal of Educational Studies* 51(2), 89–112.

Yates, L. (1997), 'Gender equity and the boys debate: what sort of challenge is it?'. *British Journal of Sociology of Education* 18(3), 337–47.

Younger, M. and Warrington, M. (1996), 'Differential attainment of girls and boys at GCSE: some observations from the perspective of one school'. *British Journal of Sociology of Education* 17(3), 299–313.

Younger, M., Warrington, M. and Williams, J. (1999), 'The gender gap and classroom interactions: reality and rhetoric?'. *British Journal of Sociology of Education* 20(3), 325–41.

Younger, M., Warrington, M. and McLellan, R. (2002), 'The "Problem" of "underachieving boys": some responses from English secondary schools'. *School Leadership and Management* 22(4), 389–405.

Younger, M. and Warrington, M. (2002), 'Single-sex teaching in a co-educational comprehensive school in England: an evaluation based upon students' performance and classroom interactions'. *British Educational Research Journal* 2893, 351–73.

Younger, M. and Warrington, M. (2003), *Raising Boys' Achievement: Interim Report*. www.standards.dfes.gov.uk/genderandachievement/word/InterimReportAug03.doc?version=1 [accessed June 2004].

Yoneyama, S. (1999), *The Japanese High School: Silence and Resistance*. London: Routledge.

Index

Abedi, J. 50
Abrams, F. 11,37
Academy, A. 80
Achilles, C.M. 162–163
Aiming High 69–72, 75
Angus, L. 39
Annesley, F. 107
Anyon, J. 46, 54
Arnold, R. 64–5, 156
Arnot, M. 62–3, 68, 79, 84, 90
Arthur, B. 64
Asthana, S. 17, 39
attendance, in schools 118, 137–139
Argentina 13

Barber, M. 10, 14
Barker, B. 58, 66
Barnard, N. 91
Belize 13
Berliner, D.C. 25, 42–3, 55
Biddle, B.J. 25, 42–3, 55
Birmingham LEA 95–96
Black, P. 166–168
Black box, *see* formative assessment
Blair, T. 8, 13, 14
Blatchford, P. 161
Blunkett, D. 117, 156, 169
Boe, E. 34
Boys, *see* gender
Bracey, G.W. 22, 26, 30, 33–35, 46, 55
Brewer, D. 165
Brooksbank, D. 176
Brown, M. 32–5
Budge, D. 13
bullying 4, 53
Bush, G.W. 18–9, 36
Butcher, H.J. 108
Byers, S. 14, 62
Bylsma, P.J. 50

California 49–50, 162
Camara, W. 42
Carr, M. 107–8

Cassidy, S. 65, 169
Cattell, R.B. 108
charter schools 49, 54
Chester, M.D. 50
Chubb, J.E. 162
citizenship 61
Clark, B. 106
class sizes 156–157, 161–165
Clinton, B. 52
coalfields study 98
Coe, R. 16, 39, 163
cognitive ability tests (CAT) 113, 136–140,
    147–148, 177–8
Cohen, M. 63, 83
Cohen, S. 63
Coleman, J. 16
Connell, R.W. 64, 125
conservative government 14
coursework 63, 65
Cox, C.B. 83
Cummings, W.K. 52, 54
Cyprus 21
Czech Republic 52

Daily Mail 1, 13
Daily Express 13
Daily Telegraph 13
Davies, L. 39
Dean, C. 1, 61
DeCocker, G. 24–5, 54
Delamont, S. 66, 83, 89
Department of Education and Science (DES)
    1, 65, 68, 91, 165
DfES, *see* Department for Education and Skills
Department for Education and Employment
    (DfEE) 1, 16, 69
Department for Education and Skills (DfES)
    10, 13–5, 17, 34–5, 60, 64, 69, 75, 77,
    82, 90, 92, 96–7, 101, 145, 161, 165,
    169
Department of Education (US) 3, 21–2,
    47–50
Dobbins, D.A. 111

Dhody, F. 74
Drew, D. 91, 93, 102–3
Dyson, A.E. 83

economically disadvantaged students, academic
    achievement 3–5, 44, 60, 77–80, 97–104,
    112–114, 137–140, 159
Education Week 25
The Education Trust 47
Edwards, T. 15
Ekstrom, R.B. 79
Elliott, J. 17, 39
Elwood, D. 170
Epstein, D. 62
Equal Opportunities Commission 63
ethnic minority students, academic achievement
    18, 42–44, 50, 60, 68–76, 90–97, 101–104,
    145, 159–160
Excellence in Cities 4, 6, 15, 16, 17, 39–40, 57,
    94
exclusions 10, 72–73

faith-based schools 39
family background, and academic achievement
    37, 47, 78–79, 100–104
Finland 9
foundation schools 39
Field, A. 111, 179
free school meals 77–78, 118, 148
Finn, J.D. 162–3
FitzGibbon, C. 16, 39, 144, 155, 181
Flanagan, A. 43, 47, 164
Fletcher, T.V. 31
Forgione, P. 33
formative assessment 156, 165–168
Francis, B. 67, 123, 126, 130, 132, 137
Frankel, E. 106–7
Frosh, S. 126–7, 129–130, 133

Galley, M. 26
gender, and achievement gaps 60–68, 83–90,
    101–104, 112–114, 118–137, 148, 150
Georgia 26
Germany 9
Gibson, A. 17, 39
Gillborn, D. 68–9, 71–5, 91–5, 101
girls, see gender
Gipps, C. 71, 91, 95, 109, 116, 170
Goals 2000 initiative 52
Gold, M.J. 106, 109
Gorard, S. 12, 32, 37–9, 41, 65, 73, 83–6, 93,
    104, 144, 168
Gore, T. 98
Grissmer, D. 43, 47, 162, 164
Guardian, The 13
Gurian, M. 66

Halpin, T. 152
Hamilton, D. 39
Hanushek, E.A. 164
Harlen, W. 166
Harry Potter 13

Hayes, D. 66
Haney, W. 158, 160
Heath, A. 84,87, 103
Hedges, L.V. 43, 45
Henry, J. 64, 170
Herrnstein, R.J. 110
high stakes testing 3, 5, 18, 24, 28, 53, 57–58,
    152, 157
Hitz, R. 33
Hoff, D.J. 21
Hochschild, J. 42–3, 49
Holden, C. 66
House of Commons Education and Select
    Committee 16–16, 40, 76, 135, 142,
    172
Hughes, D. 80
Husen, T. 9

IQ *see* mental ability testing
international comparative tests 3, 9–10, 17,
    22–23, 28, 31–35, 57–59
international adult literacy survey 11
Istance, D. 10, 11

Japan 4, 21–29, 52–58
Jackson, C. 64, 169–171
Jencks, C. 16, 46, 79
Johnson, M. 11, 35, 38

Kane, T.J. 20, 49–50
Kellmer-Pringle, M.L. 107
Keng, Z. 27, 53
Kentucky 157
Kester, D. 158–160
Key Stage 2 62, 112–3, 118, 140
Key Stage 3 7, 16, 40, 62, 112–113, 119, 122,
    133–4, 136, 138, 140, 146–8
Korea 4, 11, 33, 52, 56
Krueger, A.B. 163–164
Kruse, A. 170

Labour government 13, 15
Lau, K. 107
Laureau, A. 80, 100
Learner, S. 1, 72
Lee J. 45
LeTendre, G.K. 10, 24–7, 30–1, 52–3
Lewis, C.C. 26, 52
Lieberman, M. 10
limited English proficiency 3, 18, 49–50
Linn, R.L. 51
Linton, T. H. 158–160
literacy, gender differences 65–66
Local Education Authorities 15, 17, 95–96, 156,
    168
long tail of underachievement 4, 11, 13, 17, 31,
    37, 69
Lord Mayor's banquet 11
Loveless, T. 162
low achievement 7
Lowenstein, L.F. 107
Lynn, R. 24

Mac an Ghaill, M. 64, 75
Macpherson report 74–5
Mahony, P. 64
Mail on Sunday 61
Major, J. 11–12
Mann, C. 79–80
Mansell, W. 96
Manzo, K.K. 25
McCall, R.B. 79, 101, 106–8, 145
McNeil, L.M. 160
Measor, L. 64, 66
Mellanby, J. 111
mental ability testing 106–111, 118, 143, 145
Meuret, D. 2–3
Miliband, D. 13, 171
Millard, E. 65–6
Mills, M. 66
Mirza, H. 71
Modood, T. 74
motivation, and academic achievement 137–139
Morris, M. 40
Morroco 13
Mortimore, P. 16
multi-level modeling 17, 180
Murphy, P. 65, 109
Myhill, D. 65

National Assessment of Educational Progress
    (NAEP) 20, 22, 41–42, 50, 51, 158–9
Nash, R. 111
National Commission on Excellence in
    Education (NCEE) 20–3
National Centre for Educational Statistics
    (NCES) 34, 43, 44, 49, 51
National Foundation for Educational Research
    (NFER) 12, 177
National Literacy Strategy 5, 13, 16, 17, 34
National Numeracy Strategy 5, 16, 17
National Union of Teachers 11
Nelson, D.I. 34, 58
New Jersey 51
New Labour 14, 57
New Mexico 50
Newman, S. 108
No Child Left Behind 3, 5, 18–19, 23, 31,
    46–51, 152, 157
    adequate yearly progress 48, 50–51
    minimum proficiency levels 19, 23, 48
    student subgroups 50
North Carolina 157
Nowell, A. 43, 45
Nuthall, K. 11
Nuttall, D. 32
Nye, B. 165

Office for Standards in Education (Ofsted) 12,
    14, 72–74, 90, 92, 96, 169
Ohio 50
OECD 12, 36, 66, 101
Okan, K. 27–8, 55–6
Orfield, G. 3, 18, 41, 46–7, 52
Ouston, J. 38

parental choice 15
parental involvement, in education 79–80, 118,
    137, 139
Paterson, L. 79
Peterson P. 18, 20, 22
Phillips, M. 10, 12
Pickering, J. 128
Pirie, M. 65
Platten, J. 66
policy borrowing 8–9, 23–26, 51, 53, 58
Pong, S. 101
Popham, W.J. 18, 49
Prais, S. 10, 32, 34
Programme for International Student Assessment
    (PISA) 3, 9, 11, 13, 21, 32–38, 57, 66, 152
Progress in International Literacy Survey
    (PIRLS) 11, 13, 21, 34
Pupil Level Annual School Census (PLASC) 70,
    77, 90, 92, 97–8
Pyke, N. 13

Qualifications and Curriculum Authority
    (QCA) 65, 156

reading achievement 35–38, 44
Reagan, R. 20
Rafferty, F. 14
Raph, J.B. 79, 107
Reed, L.R. 63–4
Ravitch, D. 19–22, 25
Rea, J. 39
Rees, G. 10, 11, 83
Renold, E. 64
Reynolds, D. 11–13, 152
Riordan C. 170
Robinson, P. 169–170
Roesgaard, M.H. 24, 28
Rohlen, T.P. 25–6, 54–5
Rumberger, R.W. 79, 100
Rudalevige, A 19

Salisbury, J. 62–3, 84, 89
Sammons, P. 16–7, 65
Sarah, E. 170
Schleicher, A. 9
Schmidt, W.H. 21–2, 33
school effectiveness research 16, 17, 38–39, 146,
    150
Schoolland, K. 26–7, 53
scholastic aptitude test (SAT) 20, 22, 41–43
Scourfield, J. 176
Segregation, of school systems 38, 47
sex, *see* gender
single sex teaching 64, 168–171
Singapore 21
Sharma, Y. 9–10
Shaw, M. 106, 169
Shorrocks-Taylor, D. 166
Slater, J. 9
Slee, R. 61
Smith, E. 32–3, 37–9, 41, 64, 67, 86, 126, 168,
    174, 180

Smithers, R. 15, 62
Smithers, A. 169–170
social exclusion unit 72
socioeconomic status, and academic achievement
    76–78, 82, 98–100, 115, 119–121,
    135–141, 151
South Africa 21
South Wales 112
special educational needs 3, 18
specialist schools 14, 15
Spendlove, D. 64–5
Spielhofer, T. 169
Sputnik 19, 31, 52, 106
Staiger, D.O. 20, 49–50
standards and effectiveness unit 14
Stedman, L.C. 21–2, 30
Stevenson, D.L. 80
Stevenson, H.W. 54
Stobart, G. 166
Stokes, S. 169
Strand, S. 177–8
suicide rates 4, 26–28, 53
Sukhnandan, L. 169–171
Swan, B. 169, 171
Swann report 68

Taiwan 11
target setting 4, 16
task group on assessment and testing (TGAT)
    65, 165–166
Tate, J. 10
TeacherNet 157
Tett, L. 80
Texas assessment of academic skills (TAAS)
    158–160
Texas education agency 158, 159, 161
Texas 19, 50, 157–161
third international mathematics and science
    study (TIMSS) 3, 11, 12, 21–22, 31–35,
    52, 84, 152
Thorndike, R.L. 105, 107–8, 114–5, 146
The Times Education Supplement 1, 12, 13, 25,
    38, 60, 61, 96, 168, 169
The Times 61
Toenjes, L.A. 158, 160
Tokyo University 24
Tolor, A. 106

Tomlinson, S. 74
traditional teaching methods 12, 13
Tsuchida, I. 27–8, 55–6
Tsuneyoshi, R. 27, 56
Turner, E. 63
Tuss P. 107
Tujinman, A.C. 9

United States 3–6, 8, 18, 19, 152
    academic achievement 20–23, 41–48, 58
        school dropout 160–161
    NCLB see NCLB
    Congress 19
    Republican administrations 19
    Testing see SAT and NAEP
Urban schools 47–48
USSR 19, 52

Vermont 49

Wallace, W. 1
Warrington, M. 65–7, 127, 132, 169–171
Washington state 50
Weiner, G. 1, 39, 62
Welsh Assembly Government 60
West, A. 15
West, M. 18, 20, 22
White, K.R. 79, 100
White, M. 54
White, P. 33, 73
Whitmore, J.R. 79, 106–7, 110
Whitmore, D.M. 163–164
Whittington, J. 111
Willms, J.D. 80, 100–1
Wiliam, D. 166–168
Woodhead, C. 61
World Health Organization 53
Wossman, L. 22
Wrigley, T. 16–7

Yates, L. 64
Youdell, D. 68, 74, 93, 95
Younger, M. 65–7, 127, 132, 169–171
Yoneyama, S. 26–7, 53, 57
Youth Cohort Study 71, 77, 92–94, 98, 100,
    102